PUBLIC ENTERPRISE IN MIXED ECONOMIES

SOME MACROECONOMIC ASPECTS

By Robert H. Floyd, Clive S. Gray, and R. P. Short

With an Introduction by Vito Tanzi

INTERNATIONAL MONETARY FUND • WASHINGTON, D.C. • 1984

The term "country," as used in this publication, does not in all cases refer to a territorial entity that is a state as understood by international law and practice; the term also covers some territorial entities that are not states but for which statistical data are maintained and provided internationally on a separate and independent basis.

International Standard Book Number
ISBN 0-939934-30-2 (softcover)
Price: US$12.00

FOREWORD

Publication of the present volume, with its three papers on macroeconomic aspects of public enterprise in mixed economies, marks an important stage in the Fund's interest in the public enterprise sector as affecting the macroeconomic stability of members with mixed economies.

In its periodic consultations with members and in negotiating country programs associated with the use of Fund resources, the Fund has often noted the presence of economic imbalances that arise in part from the implementation of government policies through the medium of public enterprises. Prominent among these are policies of controlling prices of public services, foodgrains, and other basic wage goods, which often prevent public enterprises from covering their costs, with corresponding fiscal and monetary repercussions. In part, these imbalances have related to the efficiency with which the producing units that make up the sector carry out the commercial role entrusted to them.

The Fund has taken interest in this aspect of the problem when the aggregate impact of inefficiency in the public enterprise sector as a whole or in a number of major producing units has resulted in budgetary deficits too large to be financed under conditions of monetary stability. In a number of countries the public enterprise deficit has been identified as a proximate cause of excessive credit creation, leading to monetary expansion, price inflation, and, ultimately, to balance of payments pressures.

With the publication of these papers, a largely untapped field—macroeconomic analysis of public enterprise in mixed economies—is being opened up for theoretical debate and statistical analysis. All three papers underline the contrast between the reliance that many governments place on public enterprise to promote growth and to achieve distributional and other objectives, and the paucity of the data that are gathered, collated, and analyzed as a basis for determining how far the objectives are being furthered and at what cost. The high priority that needs to be accorded such work in member countries cannot be doubted.

J. DE LAROSIÈRE
Managing Director
International Monetary Fund

September 1984

Contents

INTRODUCTION

The three papers in this volume reflect a view that analysis of the macroeconomic situation in countries with significant public enterprise sectors is enhanced by examining, among other things, the operations of the sector as a whole, or any industrial grouping therein, or even individual enterprises with sufficient weight to exercise a perceptible impact on macroeconomic parameters. Moreover, this interest obtains regardless of whether government imposition of noncommercial objectives on the sector or the latter's intrinsic efficiency in conducting commercial operations is regarded as the primary determinant of the outcome of those operations.

The ultimate implication of the papers is that, insofar as any facet of public enterprise operations is found detrimental to a country's macroeconomic stability, the formulation of remedies addressing the factors in question is properly the concern of national policymakers and others with responsibility for restoring stability. It is in this spirit that the first paper, by Robert H. Floyd, summarizes the main issues in the debate currently under way in many countries with regard to ways and means of ensuring that public enterprises promote the economic and social objectives set for them without undermining macroeconomic stability.

The second paper, by Clive S. Gray, establishes a conceptual framework for determining the macroeconomic impact of a country's public enterprise sector, or any portion of the sector that may be of interest in a specific context. Emphasis is placed on defining algebraic indicators of such impact. In the final paper, R. P. Short presents cross-country comparisons, for up to 90 countries, of those indicators that lend themselves to estimation on the basis of published statistics.

The remainder of this introduction addresses the following points: (1) defining the concept of public enterprise as used in the three papers; (2) illustrating, by way of a summary of Short's paper, the macroeconomic phenomena associated with public enterprise operations which have resulted in bringing the sector as such within the scope of Fund attention; (3) presenting highlights of the other two papers; and (4) drawing provisional conclusions with respect to priorities for future data collection and analysis.

Concept of Public Enterprise

As used in all three papers, "public enterprise" refers to an organization (1) whose primary function is the production and sale of goods and/or services, and (2) in which government or other government-controlled agencies have an ownership stake that is sufficient to ensure them control over the enterprise, regardless of how actively that control is exercised. Two of the papers cite a third criterion, that the enterprise have at least the nominal objective of substantially covering costs, but reject it on the ground that some governments persist, most often for the sake of preserving employment, in operating enterprises that have no prospects for breaking even, while their efficient counterparts elsewhere do indeed cover costs. Problems that arise in applying the definition for purposes of statistical analysis are discussed at length in Short's paper.

The discussion generally excludes government-owned banks, finance companies, insurance companies, and other financial institutions, on the ground that lumping the financial operations of these agencies with those of nonfinancial public enterprises would distort the analysis of macroeconomic issues associated with the latter. However, as indicated in Gray's paper, issues of efficiency in resource management arise with financial as well as nonfinancial public enterprises, and a bailout of a shaky state bank has similar fiscal and monetary implications to an equivalent subsidy to an inefficient steel mill.

Finally, restriction of the analysis to mixed economies excludes public enterprise in centrally planned economies from the scope of the volume. Short's data refer only to mixed economies. While portions of Floyd's and Gray's analyses would apply to centrally planned economies, special characteristics of those economic systems raise issues not considered in any of the papers.

Macroeconomic Parameters of Public Enterprise: A Summary of Short's Findings

The weight of the public enterprise sector in many mixed economies is illustrated by R. P. Short's finding that the sector accounted, in the mid-1970s, for an average (weighted by gross domestic product (GDP)) of 9.5 percent of GDP for close to 50 countries, not including the United States, and an average (weighted by investment) of 16.5 percent of gross fixed capital formation for over 70 countries, also excluding the United States. For developing countries alone the average share of GDP was 8.6 percent and of gross fixed capital formation, 25–27 percent.

Regardless of its weight in national output or investment, a public enterprise sector that is self-financing, or whose deficits, whether attributable to investment, inefficient operations, or pursuit of noncommercial objectives, are covered out of government resources or private savings under conditions of monetary stability, raises no issues of macroeconomic concern. However, questions of efficiency in resource allocation remain, and no country is spared what appears likely to be a permanent debate about how to ensure that its public enterprises operate more efficiently. Attainment of an acceptable level of efficiency in some cases might involve far-reaching institutional reforms, even compression of a sector that has mushroomed beyond adequate government control.

Such issues are perhaps of more direct concern to the World Bank than to the Fund. However, Short's data support the Managing Director's observation on the contribution of public enterprise deficits to balance of payments pressures in many Fund member countries.

For 25 developing countries for which data were available, Short estimates the average (weighted by GDP) overall public deficit, before reduction by government current transfers, at 5.5 percent of GDP during the mid-1970s. He further estimates that the overall deficit in developing countries increased by 2.5 percentage points of GDP between the late 1960s and mid-1970s.

Defining the "budgetary burden" of public enterprises as the residual of government transfers and loans, less loan service payments by the enterprises, Short estimates this burden to average 3.3 percent of GDP for 34 developing countries, compared with a 4.4 percent estimate for the central government's overall budget deficit in these countries. In other words, public enterprises accounted for three fourths of the central government deficit in the countries in question.

To the budgetary impact of public enterprise must thus be attributed a portion of the monetary instability that has arisen as governments have reverted to their central banks and/or credit markets to finance budget deficits. Above and beyond government borrowing, public enterprises also revert directly to the credit markets. In a minority of cases some enterprises are entitled to borrow directly from the central bank; in certain other cases commercial banks can rediscount public enterprise obligations with the monetary authority, with analogous impact. According to Short's computations, in 28 developing countries bank credit to public enterprises grew at 46 percent per annum in the mid-1970s (average rate weighted by GDP), compared with 27 percent for bank credit to other users. Public enterprises' share in outstanding bank credit virtually tripled, from 10 to 30 percent, over the 1970s. Econometric analysis suggests that expansion of credit to public enterprises translated one-for-one into additional units of total credit.

Short's paper does not extend the analysis into estimation of the impact of public enterprise deficits on monetary expansion, price levels, or international payments, since this cannot be handled via cross-country comparisons of the available data but rather requires closer analysis of individual country parameters. However, it is in such repercussions that the Fund's interest in public enterprise obviously culminates, and the conceptual framework for monetary analysis presented in the final segment of Gray's paper offers guidelines and formulas for appropriate computations.

Highlights of Floyd's Paper

Robert H. Floyd stresses five leading categories of issues that arise in reviewing the performance of the public enterprise sector as it functions in most mixed economies and in formulating solutions to the macroeconomic problems associated with public enterprise deficits.

1. *Issues of objectives*

Noncommercial objectives loom large in the establishment and operations of many public enterprises, but governments often fail to state them with sufficient clarity to guide managers concretely. Moreover, trade-offs between overlapping objectives are inadequately recognized, and the cost of achieving alternative objectives needs to be quantified as a basis for determining pricing policies and/or financial targets.

2. *Issues of control*

In many countries procedures for exercise of government control involve too much interference in operational matters that should remain the prerogative of management, and/or inadequate intervention at the policy level where adherence to government's objectives must be sought. More use should be made of financial targets as a control device.

3. *Issues of pricing*

Prices of public enterprise inputs and outputs traded in noncompetitive markets are frequently controlled by government at levels diverging from marginal opportunity cost, engendering financial losses and social costs that outweigh any transitory advantages from subsidizing particular groups of consumers and/or procedures. For pursuit of noncommercial objectives, explicit taxes and subsidies are generally preferable to price control, the use of which should be largely restricted to curbing abuse of market power.

4. *Issues of information*

Expansion and systematization of data collection on public enterprise operations by the ministry of finance or its proxy would yield a high return in most countries by way of providing elements for improved policy formulation at both the microeconomic and macroeconomic levels.

5. *Issues of financing*

The choice of optimal proportions of debt and equity capital in public enterprise financing is a much-discussed issue, but one of distinctly secondary importance to ensuring a level of return that covers the opportunity cost of all forms of capital. Another key issue is the privileged status of public enterprises as applicants for credit from public financial institutions and the credit market at large; in the short run this advantage tends to displace private borrowers, in the long run its inflationary impact is paramount. Also touched on are the question of government control of direct foreign borrowing by public enterprises and their entitlement to discretionary use of any foreign exchange earnings.

Highlights of Gray's Paper

Describing the intrinsic social efficiency of government in organizing scarce factors to produce goods and services for sale as the "quintessential policy issue" of public enterprise, Clive Gray's conceptual paper defines five logical stages in macroeconomic analysis of the public enterprise sector, starting with (1) aggregation of nominal (accounting) parameters and extending through (2) measurement of shares of public enterprise parameters attributable to government's imposition of noncommercial objectives compared with those reflecting commercial operations; (3) adjusting nominal prices for opportunity costs, especially but not solely the opportunity cost of capital, in order to correct for artificially low interest rates; (4) defining criterion values against which to measure public enterprise sector performance on a partial equilibrium basis—the principal such value being full coverage of opportunity cost, that is, zero deficits in an economic sense; and, finally, (5) comparison of adjusted public enterprise sector parameters with simulated outcomes of alternative modes of industrial organization within a general equilibrium framework. Gray suggests that country analysts, with encouragement and, potentially, technical assistance from international agencies such as the Fund, should be directing their attention to points 1–4, leaving the general equilibrium analysis to a later stage.

The bulk of the paper focuses on deriving algebraic indicators of the public enterprise sector's fiscal and monetary impact. On the fiscal side, some indicators compare the sector's performance with that of the private sector, while others measure its relative performance over time. One key fiscal indicator is the net balance of flows between government and the public enterprise sector, with special attention to the question of whether unrequited grants and implicit subsidies from government compensate the sector for financial losses incurred in its pursuit of noncommercial objectives. Classifying these objectives under economic stabilization, economic growth, income redistribution, localization/indigenization, and miscellaneous, Appendix I discusses ways of assessing the public enterprise sector's performance in achieving them vis-à-vis alternative approaches, notably via incentives to and regulation of the private sector.

Another key indicator is the public enterprise sector's aggregate return on capital stock, revalued to current replacement values, and comparison of that return with the social discount rate. Appendix II outlines a shortcut (Harberger's application of the perpetual inventory approach) to revaluation of the capital stock.

The concluding section on monetary indicators accents the public enterprise sector's appropriation of credit as a ratio to its share in output, and provides formulas for computing the impact of a given amount of credit creation to finance public enterprise deficits on money supply, price indices, and imports.

Conclusion

The intercountry statistical comparisons in which R. P. Short has pioneered indicate the order of magnitude of the macroeconomic problems arising from public enterprise operations and show these problems obtaining across a broad range of countries. From this point the focus must turn to in-depth analysis of individual countries, which should point the way to appropriate remedies, generally to be sought in the resolution of one or (usually) more of the issues identified by Robert H. Floyd, by assessing the extent to which financial imbalances of the public enterprise sector result from inefficient operation, excessive investment, and/or imposition of other noncommercial objectives on enterprises. Application of the guidelines in Clive S. Gray's paper is commended to staff members of national and international agencies charged with such assessment.

Helpful comments on the papers in this volume were received from a number of staff members in the Fund's Fiscal Affairs Department, in particular from Alan A. Tait, Deputy Director; A. Premchand, Advisor; Ved P. Gandhi, Division Chief; Peter S. Heller, Division Chief; and Pedro Radó, Senior Economist. Comments were also received from Ana María Jul, Assistant Division Chief, and José Fajgenbaum, Economist, in the Western Hemisphere Department of the Fund.

Rasheed O. Khalid, Deputy Director, Fiscal Affairs Department, and Ernst-Albrecht Conrad, Division Chief, reviewed the papers for publication.

The book was edited and prepared for publication by Rosanne Heller. The staff of the Graphics Section of the Fund helped in a number of ways: Kenneth Hutcherson oversaw the production and typesetting process, and Hördur Karlsson and Carlos Cornelio designed the cover. The production process in the Fiscal Affairs Department was coordinated by Moira M. Lavery, and the typing and coding were done by Lyndsey B. Livingstone, M. Regina Llana, Nita Merchant, and Sonia A. Piccinini.

The opinions expressed in the papers are those of the authors and do not necessarily represent the views of either the Fund or other staff members.

VITO TANZI
Director
Fiscal Affairs Department
International Monetary Fund

Some Topical Issues Concerning Public Enterprises

ROBERT H. FLOYD*

The growing importance of public enterprises in many developed and developing countries has led to increased concern with their operations and to increased focus on numerous issues arising from their activities.[1] The purpose of this paper is to review certain issues that arise from the operations of public enterprises with particular emphasis on their relevance to macroeconomic and financial policymaking. Almost any one of these issues might in itself be the topic of a more detailed study, which suggests that their treatment in this paper is likely to be somewhat cursory.

Financial variables are of paramount interest when the policy objectives are aimed primarily at influencing financial imbalances. In such cases, direct concern would focus on short-run indicators of the financial performance of public enterprises and their impact on financial markets rather than, for example, the levels of employment. However, real economic variables should not be ignored. Indeed,

*Mr. Floyd is a Senior Economist in the Middle Eastern Department of the International Monetary Fund.

[1] For the purposes of this paper, a public enterprise may be defined as any government-owned or controlled unit that produces and sells industrial, commercial, or financial goods and services to the public. Although a more rigid definition seems both elusive and undesirable in view of the variety of legal and organizational forms encountered in various countries, in order to distinguish public enterprises more clearly from governmental and quasi–governmental bodies, such as school districts and charitable organizations, it is perhaps useful to require that the revenues of public enterprises should be more or less related to their output and that at least some day-to-day operational autonomy should be in the hands of the managers of the enterprise rather than the ministerial authorities.

1

public enterprises often incur unsustainable financial imbalances (or deficits) in the course of attempting to influence real variables through the pursuit of noncommercial objectives. Especially in these cases policymakers should be obliged to compare the benefits and the costs and to assess the impact on the real variables in question of alternative measures aimed also at curbing the financial deficits in the short run. Furthermore, with the extension of the time horizon, real economic variables become of even greater interest. Indeed, when the policymakers' objective is to reduce widespread cost and price distortions and structural maladjustments in production and trade, it is inevitable that the impact of public enterprises' operations on real economic variables must be taken into account. Nevertheless, for financial policymakers paramount interest will center on the financial facet of these activities of public enterprises and on the broader impact of their operations on financial markets.

The focus on macroeconomic variables begs the question as to why and when an individual public enterprise or group of public enterprises would be of macroeconomic significance. In general, public enterprises that are operated profitably, efficiently, and in conformity with commonly accepted commercial principles would not constitute a drain on financial resources or lead to monetary expansion. Indeed, their impact would not be significantly different from privately owned enterprises carrying out similar functions. Even though in some cases these public enterprises may provide sources of quick government revenues, profitability is usually limited to a normal return to capital if operations are efficient and hence do not involve monopoly abuses. Consequently, such public enterprises are less likely to be of interest to policymakers than are public enterprises that are not operated profitably, efficiently, or in accordance with generally accepted commercial principles. The latter group is likely to constitute an ongoing drain on financial markets that may lead to inflationary credit expansion. Alternatively, it may generate less profit than efficiently operated firms. Furthermore, such operations may lead to inefficient mobilization and allocation of scarce resources or an undesirable pattern of income distribution.

The focus on the macroeconomic impact of public enterprises leads to another observation. If public enterprises' operations are of a relatively small scale and are unimportant in the overall economy, they are unlikely to have significant impact in financial markets. This suggests that there are two distinct situations in which the financial activities of public enterprises are of potential macroeconomic impact. First, even one or a few enterprises may have a macroeconomic impact if the enterprises' financial activities are sufficiently large relative to the economy. Petroleum enterprises, other natural resource extraction companies, and agricultural marketing companies are frequent examples of such public enterprises. Second, the situation can arise when the government's policies vis-à-vis public enterprises in general, even though each one is small, are such as to alter the aggregate financial performance of all public enterprises sufficiently to have a macroeconomic impact. For example, output prices of public enterprises may be constrained in a probably futile effort to constrain inflationary pressures arising from other causes, such as excessive monetary expansion. This situation could arise even when there are relatively few or no large public enterprises capable individually of having a macroeconomic impact.

In the first situation any of a variety of causes may lead to the macroeconomic impact and some of these causes may be outside the government's control. For example, depressed world commodity prices often have seriously adverse implications for important public enterprises' financial performances. In such cases the scope for remedial action by the government to minimize the macroeconomic impact may be limited to certain cases, as for example, the domestic operations of agricultural marketing boards, where government-imposed pricing policies constrain the boards' flexibility to adjust to external price movements. Often such pricing policies are pursued with economy-wide income redistribution objectives and may be politically difficult to reverse despite their potential macroeconomic implications. Managerial inefficiency and too large a scale of operation relative to the size of domestic demand are also frequent causes of financial losses by important enterprises. Managerial inefficiencies may be corrected by various microeconomic actions, such as changing management.

In the second situation, the government's policies themselves give rise to the macroeconomic impact without any particular exogenous influences, and reversal of those policies may be assumed to reverse the macroeconomic impact. Numerous policies may lead to such results but most often they are policies designed to influence the prices of inputs and outputs, the selection of material and labor inputs, and the composition of outputs to be produced.

I. PUBLIC ENTERPRISE ISSUES—AN OVERVIEW

In analyzing the issues arising with public enterprises and various aspects of their operations, it will occasionally be useful to view them within the conceptual framework of the financial and economic variables that may be affected. These may be grouped into three categories: (1) the direct impact of public enterprises on bank credit and the balance of payments (the "credit impact" and the "balance of payments impact"); (2) the direct impact of public enterprises on the budget through explicit financial transactions between the government and public enterprises (the "budget or fiscal impact"); and (3) the longer-run "structural impact" of public enterprises' operations on resource allocation and income distribution often reflected in implicit subsidies or taxes. Categories (1) and (2) will have (at least theoretically) quantifiable impacts on financial markets. Category (3) is equally important but would be more difficult to quantify. All three categories can reflect the results of the use of public enterprises as instruments of discretionary policy actions or inaction.[2] Many public enterprise actions may have an indirect impact in these areas as well, and, where possible, they should also be identified and quantified.

The list of issues relating to public enterprise activities is virtually without limit. The remainder of this section will only introduce the more important issues; more detailed discussions of these issues are left for subsequent sections. In addition to the analytical framework, it is useful to categorize these issues into some common areas. Admittedly, the lines of demarcation between various issues and categories of issues are not always distinct, and, in some cases, one issue may be very closely related to other issues. Nevertheless, there would seem to be about five convenient categories into which most issues may be classified.

In many countries *issues of objectives* of public enterprises are of considerable operational importance. For example, it may be useful to recognize that public enterprises may have either macroeconomic or microeconomic objectives or both. Similarly, there may be both financial and nonfinancial objectives, and commercial and noncommercial objectives. To a large degree the issues of objectives involve relationships between political policymakers and public enterprise managers. Many of the difficulties that are likely to arise with public enterprises may be the result of ill specified and often conflicting

---

[2] Issues may also be viewed in the context of the time frame in which they may be relevant. Issues could be categorized by whether they have long-term or ongoing importance, or are relevant mainly in the medium run or the short run. Issues of continuing interest focus primarily on the institutional arrangements for determining and implementing government policy and on data indicating the direct impact of the public enterprise sector on domestic and external financial markets. Furthermore, in the longer run, not only the level of financial variables but also their structure and the appropriateness of the government's general policies toward public enterprises with regard to allocative and distributional objectives (and in some cases even a few significant individual enterprises' practices, e.g., energy pricing) should be taken into account. It is in this context that the various supply-side effects of public enterprises become most important. Issues of short-term relevance would include primarily those related to the impact of public enterprise operations on stabilization. These could include the direct use of public enterprises for noncommercial objectives such as price stabilization, employment, and a more favorable balance of international payments.

objectives that government or public enterprise officials assign to public enterprises. Perhaps more than other categories, issues of objectives are likely to have an impact on the broadest array of economic variables mentioned previously.

Related to issues of objectives are *issues of* the *method* and *extent of control*, that is, the control over public enterprises' activities that is exercised by the government. The methods by which control is exercised can be of great importance. For example, efforts to control by giving general policy guidance aimed at all public enterprises may have significantly different effects on the efficiency of operations and hence on profitability than efforts to control the quantities or prices of productive inputs and outputs through specific directives to managers. In general, these issues are likely to be institutional and consequently are more relevant to longer-term variables, such as resource allocation and income distribution. Issues on the extent of control would include both the actual and potential control that is exercised by the government, or even the absence of control. Invariably, these would include consideration of what is to be controlled. Should the government attempt to control real variables, such as the level of employment, the sources of supply of inputs (e.g., from another public enterprise), and the level of output? Or should the government focus its control efforts on financial targets, such as the rate of return, the level of profits, the planning and financing of investment, the distribution of profits, and the enterprise's capital structure? Clearly, these issues are likely to be relevant to almost any time frame and could have an impact on almost any economic variable.

Perhaps more than all others, *issues of pricing* arise with regard to public enterprises. For a variety of reasons output prices often do not reflect the full costs of inputs employed with the result that consumption of the output is subsidized. The cost of the subsidy may be financed by a government transfer to the producing public enterprise, reduced profits and reserves for the public enterprise, increased resort to credit by the public enterprise, or some combination of these. In either case potential resources for the public sector are forgone. Less objectionable to most financial policymakers (and almost certainly less common) are public enterprises that generate unusually large profits for the public sector and are in some senses a "taxing" authority. However, the pricing issues involved are far more complex than simply generating accounting profits. For example, is it possible to ascertain whether output or input prices are at appropriate levels, and, if so, how does one do so? Are there acceptable justifications for prices that result in losses or profits? What macroeconomic objectives might be accomplished by public enterprise pricing policies? Indeed, what should be the objectives of public enterprise pricing policy and what would be the implications of different objectives for financial flows? Obviously, pricing issues are more likely than most to have a direct impact on financial variables, such as bank credit or budget transfers and receipts, and are likely to do so in the short term.

The importance of *informational issues* is perhaps best illustrated by the acute lack of information on public enterprises' operations and their financial impact in many countries. A major issue is the question of what information is relevant to or necessary for various types of financial and macroeconomic analysis. For example, is information on public enterprise employment practices and wage bills needed to analyze the credit impact or the balance of payments impact? Are data on particular prices useful, or is it adequate to know only the extent of credit to public enterprises? What information is relevant to assess the balance of payments, fiscal, and structural impacts of public enterprises' operations? These issues per se are not likely to have any significant direct impact on economic variables. However, through the availability of better information and its use by policy-makers, significant improvement in public enterprise policies may be obtained that could have positive effects on various economic variables.

The final set of issues to be discussed relate to the various *sources of finance*. The review focuses on how the sources and types of finance may vary according to the activity actually being financed and on the implications the various sources and types of credit for public enterprises may have for credit creation, monetary expansion, and (both directly and indirectly) the balance of payments and foreign exchange availability.

II. ISSUES OF OBJECTIVES

Certainly among the most important aspects of public enterprises' activities are the objectives they pursue. It has been said that "the special character of public enterprise is simply that its management is normally less subject to pressures to seek profits, and more attentive to the other objectives expressed by the agencies with which it must deal. . . .To benefit from public enterprise, it is above all important to create channels for careful definition of the economic and social objectives it is meant to serve."[3] A major cause of problems with public enterprises' operations is the absence of clearly defined, consistent,

---

[3] John B. Sheahan, "Experience with Public Enterprise in France and Italy," in William G. Shepherd and Associates, ed., *Public Enterprise: Economic Analysis of Theory and Practice* (Lexington: D.C. Heath and Company, 1976), p. 176.

and precisely communicated objectives for the managers of enterprises. This void is likely to dampen severely managerial incentives with a resulting adverse impact on the efficient internal operations of the enterprise, and it may also result in other actions by managers of public enterprises which are contrary to national interests.

An important related issue is the question of who should determine objectives. Only the government has the perspective to assess national interests and their relation to the operations of public enterprises. Consequently, insofar as a public enterprise's operations relate to national interests, the government should determine the objectives assigned to various public enterprises. Can any a priori judgment be made as to which agencies of the government might be appropriately involved in the determination of objectives? Some countries have established ministries that supervise all public enterprises. However, these ministries have often tended to become spokespeople for the public enterprises rather than instruments for government control over the enterprises. Indeed, a broad array of ministries would need to be represented in the formulation of government objectives. Since the operations of public enterprises almost always involve financial implications, it would seem prudent to include the finance ministry. Also the central bank should be represented as public enterprises often have substantial credit requirements and often absorb or generate large amounts of foreign exchange. Since scarce economic resources are devoted to public enterprises, the planning ministry should be included in the formulation of objectives, especially those related to investment plans. Moreover, each public enterprise is usually under the auspices of at least one technical ministry, which should also be included in the determination of at least technical objectives. The presence of representatives from other agencies may also be desirable for determining objectives of particular public enterprises, but in general it is probably best to minimize the involvement of agencies not directly concerned with or affected by a public enterprise's operations. Whether the organizational arrangements to achieve this representation should be left ad hoc or be institutionalized cannot be determined a priori. Indeed, the best arrangements may vary from country to country, but it seems reasonable that in most cases they would center in the finance ministry.

In contrast to officials of the government, managers of public enterprises should not be entrusted with assessing the national interests with respect to their firms. Apart from lack of relevant knowledge, they might also be influenced by personal or other motives narrower than the national interests. However, managers of public enterprises should be consulted about their role in carrying out assigned objectives related to national interests in order to ensure that the objective is realistic and that a particular firm is an appropriate instrument for achieving it. Furthermore, the government should avoid defining objectives relating to internal managerial or operational aspects of public enterprises that have no strategic national implications. In these matters managers should be left free to exercise their special talents to best advantage.[4] It should be noted that allowing a public enterprise to operate on a fully commercial basis may be the government's primary and perhaps sole objective. Furthermore, in some cases this would not necessarily be a bad second-best policy in view of the difficulty in specifying alternative objectives and the possible staff requirements needed to administer them.

Three overriding questions concerning objectives would seem to be of importance to the analysis of public enterprises' macroeconomic impact. First, in the case of multiple objectives, are they mutually consistent? Second, does the public enterprise have techniques available to achieve the various objectives? Third, and most important, what is the estimated financial impact? With regard to the first two questions, since many enterprises are likely to be given multiple objectives, care should be taken to ensure that the objectives are mutually consistent or at least that when there are to be trade-offs some indication of priority among them is given. Furthermore, it will be important to ensure that sufficient and appropriate instruments are available to public enterprises to accomplish their objectives. For example, long-run growth is not likely to be consistent with short-term price stability if the latter is achieved by holding public enterprise prices fixed.

In general, the pursuit of most objectives, whether they be commercial or noncommercial, financial or nonfinancial, is likely to have an impact on a public enterprise's financial performance that may or may not be quantifiable. Where possible, the quantification of the financial implications of nonfinancial objectives and the taking into account of their costs is crucial to the establishment of realistic overall ex ante, financial objectives or targets for public enterprises. Establishing financial objectives has several advantages. In addition to providing a guideline for ex post evaluation, financial objectives provide public enterprise managers with both guidance and incentives to improve internal efficiency. Furthermore, since a public enterprise's potential profitability, its internally generated investable funds, and its credit requirements are all, in part, a function of the financial

---

[4] For a discussion of the importance of specifying objectives see Leroy P. Jones, *Public Enterprise and Economic Development: The Korean Case* (Seoul: Korea Development Institute, 1975), pp. 140–52.

implications of noncommercial objectives, their quantification will also have the advantage of providing an initial indication of their financial impact. In some cases the effects may be sufficiently large to be taken into account in financial and macroeconomic policies.[5]

The manner in which financial objectives are defined can have significant economic implications. On the whole, economists have tended to favor specification of pricing policies rather than setting financial targets, such as rates of return or profit levels.[6] First, it is argued that financial targets may obstruct allocative efficiency since allocatively efficient pricing and investment policies imply a particular surplus or deficit for a public enterprise that may differ from that set by the government. Second, investment decisions may be distorted if target and market rates of return differ. Third, financial targets may be used as a justification to charge prices in excess of allocatively efficient marginal cost prices. Finally, internal efficiency may not be enhanced if the financial targets are not enforced.

All these objections are oriented essentially to microeconomics. They are all founded in a concern for determining prices in accordance with long-run marginal costs in order to achieve efficient resource allocation and input mix. However, there are counterarguments based on both micro- and macroeconomic considerations. First, the preference for pricing rules over financial targets ignores the government's revenue needs, and financial targets can serve as a form of indirect taxation. Second, the use of lump-sum financial targets rather than rates of return could reduce the chance that investment decisions would be distorted.[7] Third, financial targets may well increase X-efficiency by more than any induced loss of allocative efficiency.[8] Finally, it is certainly true that, in practice, marginal cost pricing is

---

[5] The importance of determining financial objectives and assessing financial performance of individual public enterprises is discussed in Glenn P. Jenkins, "An Operational Approach to the Performance of Public Sector Enterprises," Harvard Institute for International Development, Development Discussion Paper No. 47 (November 1978).

[6] For a more detailed discussion see David Heald, "The Economic and Financial Control of U.K. Nationalised Industries," *Economic Journal* (June 1980), pp. 243–65.

[7] In India, lump-sum targets are used for projected losses, but rates of return are used for projected profits. See *Performance Aims and Financial Targets of Central Government Public Enterprises 1982–83 and 1983–84*, Government of India, Bureau of Public Enterprises, Ministry of Finance (New Delhi, April 1982).

[8] X-efficiency refers essentially to the quality of managerial decisions and actions. The internal operations of public enterprises would be X-efficient if it were not possible to increase profits through reductions of inefficient managerial practices, such as employment of excess labor or payment of wages in excess of levels prevailing in the private sector. Such practices are thought to be common, especially in public enterprises in many developing countries.

seldom practiced by public enterprises and such prices are difficult to identify in practice.[9]

In summary, the primary issues of objectives would appear to include the need to recognize, define, communicate, and evaluate any noncommercial objectives of public enterprises that are of legitimate national interest. These objectives should be feasible and, if not consistent, at least the relevant trade-offs among multiple objectives recognized and their financial impact should be at least crudely quantified. This information can then be used as an input to the quantification of financial objectives for the operations of public enterprises. While in theory there may be some preference for expressing financial objectives as pricing policies, in practice, financial targets may be just as desirable.

III. ISSUES OF CONTROL

Should the government exercise controls over public enterprises? Who should exercise any controls, what types or methods of control should be employed, and what aspects of public enterprises' operations should be controlled? All of these questions need to be addressed when considering control of public enterprises. Although there are few clear answers to any of these questions, many issues of control are closely related to some of the preceding discussion of objectives.

Perhaps the most obvious control issue arises from the serious problems of managerial incentives in public enterprises. It is commonly perceived that poor management resulting from inadequate incentives is largely responsible for much of the inefficiency in public enterprise operations. In turn, the absence of managerial incentives is often attributed to overly rigid controls that constrain the ability of managers to exercise their creative talents and to adapt the enterprise's operations to changes in market conditions. This suggests that government controls over the internal management of public enterprises should be minimized in order to avoid unduly interfering with managerial decision making. It also suggests that controls should not normally be imposed on such production decision variables as the appropriate combination of factor inputs, the prices paid for those inputs, and the timing of production.

However, this does not imply that no controls should be imposed

---

[9] It could be argued that managers would prefer financial targets so long as traditional managerial variables, for example, input and output prices and output levels, are left to management's discretion. In contrast, if they are fixed externally, managers are likely to prefer pricing targets to possibly unachievable financial targets.

over public enterprises. Indeed, so long as public resources are committed to these enterprises there is every reason to expect that public enterprises should be at least monitored, and perhaps given some operational guidelines, to ensure the public interest is served. Furthermore, it must be acknowledged that even internal objectives and controls can have significant effects on pricing, dividend practices, and profitability of public enterprises, and, that in some cases the government might need to ensure that these are not inconsistent with macroeconomic policy considerations. Thus, there will be some inevitable conflict between the need for accountability for the public interest and the need for managerial flexibility and innovation within the public enterprise.[10]

At least some degree of government control may be needed to serve a variety of purposes and objectives other than coordination of macroeconomic and financial policies. Controls may be needed over investment project plans to ensure they are consistent with national priorities. Controls may be used to coordinate the activities of more than one public enterprise when there are important linkages between these enterprises. Often controls are imposed that may be intended to serve a regulatory function, such as curbing monopoly powers of public enterprises, although public enterprise control should not be regarded as a substitute for antitrust regulation of private enterprise. Finally, in order to be effective, controls may require a feedback of information that may be used as inputs to the determination and evaluation of other government policies, in particular, monetary and fiscal policies.

The actual agency of the government that should be empowered to control public enterprises would depend on a variety of factors and would be related to the agencies involved in determining objectives. For example, many technical aspects of enterprises' operations may not have financial implications. However, in most cases they are likely to have substantial financial implications, particularly in the case of decisions about investment projects. For example, if the port authority were a public enterprise, any technical decision to expand port capacity would clearly have major financial implications. Consequently, in many such cases, both a technical ministry, such as the transport ministry, and the finance ministry would be involved in the enterprise's investment decision. Since such ministries have tended to represent their own interests rather than those of the public enterprise

---

[10] For a discussion of some aspects of these problems, see William G. Shepherd, "Objectives, Types, and Accountability" in William G. Shepherd and Associates, ed., *Public Enterprise: Economic Analysis of Theory and Practice* (Lexington: D.C. Heath and Company, 1976), pp. 33–47; and C.D. Foster, *Politics, Finance and the Role of Economics: An Essay on the Control of Public Enterprise* (London: Allen and Unwin, 1971).

and since they often view each public enterprise or problem in isolation, separate public enterprise ministries have been established in
some countries to represent the concerns of public enterprises. However, as noted previously, these ministries have often tended to ignore
the broader interests of the government.

The broader public interest therefore would seem to be best served
by an alternative administrative organization to act as a funnel for
control. There is no uniquely preferred arrangement, and the best
solution will almost certainly vary with the individual country's institutional arrangements. One interesting arrangement has recently been
tried in Papua New Guinea. For any enterprise over which the Government wishes to establish some measure of control, an ad hoc planning committee is appointed, comprised of representatives of the
Department of Finance, any concerned technical ministry, the National Planning Office, and the enterprise itself. The ad hoc committee
is charged with defining clearly the Government's objectives for the
enterprise (with the eventual aim of quantifying their financial implications and budgetary impact) and serving as an ongoing conduit
by and through which associated controls can be implemented.

Among the most sophisticated institutional arrangements and control techniques are those that have been employed in France.[11] Although no effort is made here to describe all these arrangements, two
general changes that were intended to be implemented after 1967
and to facilitate placing responsibility for efficient management solely
on the enterprise are of particular interest.[12] First, the Government
was to identify clearly and to reimburse fully the costs of any noncommercial activities that it imposed on the enterprise. As a result
there has been considerable progress in defining and costing the burden of social obligations and shifting them onto the Ministry of Economy and Finance.[13] The efforts to make more explicit the areas in

---

[11] For a complete description of French control arrangements see National Economic
Development Office, *A Study of UK Nationalised Industries, Background Paper No. 2,
Relationships of Government and Public Enterprises in France, West Germany and Sweden*
(1976).

[12] In 1967, a working group prepared a study (the Nora Report) of the control
apparatus which has had considerable influence over French control efforts for several
years. The Nora Report essentially advocated clear definitions of, and distinctions
between, the responsibilities of the public enterprise, its technical or sponsoring ministry, and the Ministry of Economy and Finance.

[13] National Economic Development Office, op. cit. It should be noted, however, that
others have questioned the extent of progress. Cassese states that, "In France, the Nora
Report proposed reversing 'the burden of proof,' requiring the government financially
to motivate and compensate the public enterprises. However, in France, as in Italy,
the compensation mechanism has been purely theoretical."See Sabino Cassese, "Public
Control and Corporate Efficiency," in *State-Owned Enterprise in the Western Economies*,
ed., by Raymond Vernon and Yair Aharoni (New York, 1981), p. 155.

which normal commercial considerations are supplemented by additional considerations of social policy and their attendant costs or revenue losses are sometimes referred to as the concept of "transparency."[14]

The second major change was the attempt to increase the autonomy and efficiency of management and to ensure concurrently compliance with government objectives through the negotiation of *contrats de programme*.[15] These planning contracts were essentially agreements between the Government and individual enterprises. They were designed to provide management at least some flexibility with regard to pricing of outputs and inputs, input and output mixes, the distribution of operating profits, and some assurance of financing for approved longer-term investment programs. For the Government, the agreements were intended to ensure that major government objectives would be pursued and that there would be some means of assessing management's performance following the granting of greater autonomy.[16]

Another method of control that has sometimes been advocated is to let public enterprises compete with other public enterprises. In practice, there have been few instances of competition with only other public enterprises. More generally it might be argued that public enterprises may be controlled by letting them compete with any other enterprises, either public or private. Although this might be expected to be effective, a few studies of this situation indicate that there is still X-inefficiency in public enterprises operating in competition with other enterprises.[17] However, there are also at least some notable examples of publicly owned enterprises that have proven themselves to be ef-

---

[14] For further discussion see Sweden, Department of Industry, *State Business; Public Enterprise Experience in the EEC*, prepared by Metra Oxford Consulting (Oxford, 1978), pp. 168–70.

[15] The *contrats de programme* were also aimed at measuring managerial efficiency through inclusion of a comprehensive indicator of performance referred to as the *productivité globâle des facteurs*.

[16] Such contracts were negotiated with the railways and the electrical industry in 1969. By 1977 all of these agreements had lapsed. However, four new agreements were signed in 1979, and in 1981 the Government announced its intention of expanding the use of contracts. Many difficulties were encountered with these contracts, but most essentially reflected difficulty by both the Government and the enterprises in defining, quantifying, and abiding by long-term commitments to provisions relating to the various objectives of each party. For example, enterprise managers would find it difficult to agree to estimates of a wage bill projection in the absence of agreement from often powerful labor unions. Apparently, the Government also had similar problems since it retained the right to alter price and investment decisions as necessary to regulate the economy. Recently, the Government of Senegal has begun to use contracts with some of its public enterprises, referring to them as *contrats-plan*.

[17] See Richard Pryke, "The Comparative Performance of Public and Private Enterprise," *Fiscal Studies*, Vol. 3 (July 1982), pp. 68–81; also Richard Pryke, *The Nationalised Industries: Policies and Performance Since 1968* (Oxford: Martin Robinson, 1981).

ficient competitors in industries, for example, the automobile industry, dominated by private enterprises.

Leaving aside other questions of the techniques and organization of controls, focus now on the aspects of public enterprises' organizations and operations which should be subject to government controls. The controls available to governments may take a variety of forms. Formal controls may include statutory controls that are specified in legislation, but these are often too broad in scope to be of day-to-day use. For example, formal controls may include the power to appoint the chief executive and board members of enterprises. However, in practice this control may be limited by the fact that the tenures of public enterprise managers are often longer than those of government officials. Consequently, managers may become somewhat indispensable.[18] Legislation often bestows on governments, and in some cases particular ministers, the power to issue policy directives to public enterprises, especially those that are legally organized as statutory authorities. Less common is legislation authorizing governments to issue directives to publicly owned companies organized under general company legislation. In these cases the government usually operates through its representatives on the Board of Directors rather than issuing directives directly to the enterprise. Informal controls through the exercise of various pressures and moral suasion applied by government officials to public enterprise managers may, in fact, be the most effective means to influence the operations and policies of enterprises. However, informal controls have the inherent disadvantage that they may be ad hoc in nature, uncoordinated, and perhaps contradictory.

Budgetary controls are sometimes exercised over the revenues and expenditures of public enterprises. These may take many forms, including approval of budgets, or specific expenditures, or investment projects, and authority to regulate the prices charged by the enterprise. A major problem with many budgetary controls is their adverse impact on managerial incentives. For example, requirements for prior approval of specific expenditures could restrict management's ability to react to changing market conditions. Consequently, governments have applied more general and less restrictive controls aimed at various economic variables.

More general controls could aim, for example, to achieve a certain level of profits or rate of return, or to chart the course of public enterprises' investment by requiring that outlays for investment projects of public enterprises be subject to the same planning process as those of the government, or to restrict the access of enterprises to

---

[18] See William G. Shepherd and Associates, op. cit., p. 44.

short-term bank credit. Such controls may be closely related to the objectives that take the form of targets and ceilings against which the actual performance of the enterprise is to be subsequently assessed. For example, an overall profitability objective could be used in conjunction with investment plans of public enterprises to determine other financial subtargets, such as their overall borrowing requirements. If projections of other sources of net credit and investment expenditures were available, an estimate of public enterprise borrowing from the banking system (i.e., credit impact) or the government (i.e., at least part of the fiscal impact) could be prepared. These same subtargets can be used as control variables. For example, by such a procedure one could establish cash limits on public enterprises' financing requirements from all sources other than internally generated funds such as loans, equity injections, and grants. Such a system of cash limits was introduced in the United Kingdom in 1978 in order to strengthen expenditure controls.[19] The use of controls on external financing requirements could, when aggregated for all relevant public enterprises, be a useful input into financial stabilization programs for both the short and long terms.

While there may be a case for establishing profit objectives and credit objectives and controls for public enterprises, there would seem to be no similar reason to establish either objectives or controls for the balance of payments impact or for the use or generation of foreign exchange by an individual public enterprise. If limits were placed on foreign exchange usage, they might inhibit a public enterprise from competing with other users of foreign exchange in the marketplace. Indeed, such an objective might be taken as an allocation rather than a ceiling. Finally, even if foreign exchange were abundant, such an objective might result in imports of a similar amount even though market forces might have normally resulted in a different composition of foreign and domestic material inputs.

These observations suggest some tentative conclusions concerning government controls over public enterprise activities. They should be minimized in order to reduce their adverse impact on managerial incentives. They should relate to clearly identifiable objectives and should be as general in nature as possible. They should aim at achieving certain measurable financial objectives that reflect the estimated

---

[19] Cash limits have been criticized as encouraging the use of self-finance, possibly with the result that unjustifiable investments might be undertaken when self-financing is available and economically justifiable investments forgone when self-financing is not available. However, there is no a priori reason to assume that improper investment decisions necessarily follow appropriate financial decisions. Indeed, the two should be essentially independent with each public enterprise's investment plans being made in comparison with macroeconomic constraints and with the competing demands for investment funds from other public enterprises.

financial impact of pursuing noncommercial objectives. Finally, ceilings are best suited for variables whose expansion is undesirable, and targets for those whose expansion is desirable. These considerations may be applied to one variable—prices—whose control is often advocated.

IV. ISSUES OF PRICING

The prices that public enterprises charge for their outputs and pay for their inputs have given rise to numerous issues, but this discussion will focus on only four that seem particularly germane to the economic variables discussed previously. First, how should prices be determined and should they be set to generate a profit? Second, how should public enterprise prices be determined when monopoly elements are present, and under what circumstances, if any, should public enterprise prices be regulated? Third, are adjustments to public enterprises' prices an appropriate or an effective technique to tax or to subsidize public enterprise outputs and inputs? Finally, what external constraints limit the flexibility of public enterprises' pricing actions?

Public enterprise pricing policies and the techniques employed to determine their prices have been the subject of considerable discussion over the years. Much of the discussion has been within a microeconomic context and has focused on the measurement of marginal opportunity costs.[20] The attention to marginal cost reflects the ever present objective of ensuring efficient use of the economic resources when determining the prices of the goods and services produced by public enterprises. The achievement of allocative efficiency requires that the prices paid by consumers for the output of goods and services by public enterprises should cover, at the margin, the opportunity costs to society of resources used as inputs to production, basically the land, labor, and capital employed either directly by the public enterprise or indirectly in the production of materials, fuels, and services used by the public enterprise in the production process.

However, in practice there are a number of problems in the application of the marginal cost principles. The primary problem concerns the identification and measurement of marginal costs. Marginal costs are difficult to identify because the marginal product and the inputs used in its production are difficult to identify, especially within

---

[20] Any use of resources by public enterprises involves a cost in terms of forgone opportunities for potential alternative private and public uses of these resources; these costs are often referred to as social opportunity costs. The opportunity cost of any resource input is defined to be its value in its next best alternative use.

the current technological framework and with the possibility of a number of by-products. Another problem may arise with the valuation of inputs. In competitive markets, the market prices paid by the public enterprise for labor, materials, etc., represent their opportunity costs. However, due to the exercise of monopoly power by sellers of inputs or of monopsony power by the enterprise in the purchases of inputs, in some cases (e.g., water in hydroelectric projects) opportunity costs of inputs may be remote from market valuation. Also, marginal costs are dependent on the level of technology, the peak utilization of the capacity, and the time and life of production equipment, and are therefore variable over time.

As a result of the difficulties in quantifying marginal opportunity costs, more practical pricing procedures have been sought. One approach is to adopt a trial and error pricing process aimed at setting prices in the short run, to equal the greater of (1) the running or operating costs of the plant capacity being partly used, or (2) the price required to restrict demand to that plant's capacity.[21] It would also be prudent in most cases to avoid excessive price adjustments in the short run as these may reflect only highly temporary fluctuations in demand.

Perhaps the most common method of determining prices in practice is to use some form of average accounting costs plus some markup for a profit margin. However, accounting costs are not necessarily related to social opportunity costs of resources. Accounting costs usually depict historical costs and reflect at least to some extent technological and financial history rather than current and potential usage of resources. In particular, depreciation charges based on historical costs are not likely to reflect opportunity costs during inflationary periods. Depreciation practices may also be arbitrary, may vary among industries, and may not accurately reflect either the length of an asset's useful life or the pattern over time of its use. To address the problem of historical costs versus current costs, it has been suggested that replacement cost depreciation should be adopted in the place of historical costs. However, marginal cost pricing is based on the value in current use of existing assets and not on their hypothetical replacement in the future, and consequently replacement and marginal costs may differ. Nevertheless, periodic asset revaluations and adjustments in depreciation allowances will ordinarily bring accounting costs closer to opportunity costs and thus assist in establishing prices based on the latter.

Another difficulty is that average costs cannot always be used as a

---

[21] Ralph Turvey, *Economic Analysis and Public Enterprises* (Totowa, New Jersey, 1971), p. 74.

proxy for marginal costs. In a world with fixed technology, marginal and average costs in the long and short runs are equal when the scale of plant is optimum, that is, when long-run and short-run costs are simultaneously minimized. However, under conditions of rapidly changing technology, marginal and average costs are not likely to coincide in either the long or the short run. Consequently, average cost pricing may not lead to optimum resource allocation.[22]

Given the difficulty of measuring marginal opportunity costs and the fact that most of the alternatives to marginal cost pricing lead to inefficient resource allocation, an acceptable approach might be to set prices that would result over the medium or long term in a rate of return to capital commensurate with the returns obtainable in alternative uses as adjusted in accordance with the concept of transparency. Although not perfect, such a practice would, at least with respect to capital inputs, capture the essence of the marginal opportunity cost pricing principle.[23] Since the government's capital invested in a public enterprise is itself a resource input, if marginal cost pricing were followed it can be expected, in general, that the capital employed in the enterprise would earn a return equal to its opportunity cost just as any other input to the production process.[24]

This approach requires that neither monopoly nor monopsony power enables a firm to charge output prices (or pay input prices) that do not reflect opportunity costs, with the result that profitable operations are not allocatively efficient. Pricing in the case of monopoly is par-

---

[22] A more exhaustive catalog of difficulties that are encountered when attempting to apply marginal cost pricing in practice can be found in A.M. Henderson, "Prices and Profits in State Enterprise," *The Review of Economic Studies* (1948–49), Vol. XVI (1) No. 39, pp. 13–24.

[23] Henderson, in proposing a similar pricing technique, described the task of choosing an alternative to marginal cost pricing as ". . . an ungrateful task, for there is no possibility of being right, it is merely a matter of producing an acceptable compromise which shall not be too grossly wrong." See Henderson, op. cit., pp. 20–21.

[24] For overall profitability the measurement that is relevant for economic purposes would not distinguish between various legal forms that investment capital might take. All capital should be expected to earn its opportunity cost, and consequently, as an initial approximation the relevant measure of income includes all forms of return to capital, in particular both profits (either distributed or retained) and interest payments for long-term borrowings. Similarly, the relevant measurement of capital includes all long-term assets, including all equity (including retained earnings) and long-term borrowings. Profits should be defined after deduction of replacement cost depreciation allowances but before income tax payments. Capital should be measured after asset and liability revaluation where necessary to compensate for inflation and after deducting cumulative depreciation allowances. A more substantive discussion of relevant measurements of payments to various forms of capital can be found in the second paper in this volume, "Toward a Conceptual Framework for Macroeconomic Evaluation of Public Enterprise Performance in Mixed Economies," by Clive Gray.

ticularly difficult because a profit can usually be generated even though the public enterprise is not being efficiently operated. Excessive costs or noncapital factor payments can be passed on to consumers in higher output prices without any reduction in profits. Indeed, the presence of monopolistic elements provides one of the clearest justifications for government regulation of public enterprise prices, and perhaps one of the most common examples would be publicly owned utilities.

The regulation of a public enterprise's prices may also be justified even in the absence of the exercise of monopolistic power by the public enterprise. Often, social opportunity costs of production may differ from private costs as reflected by the market prices paid for resource inputs. For example, social costs of production may exceed private costs if a producing enterprise's waste material pollutes the environment. Efficient resource allocation requires that all social opportunity costs, including the cost of the externality, be reflected in the output's price. If they are not, sales and profits may exceed allocatively efficient levels.

Other exogenous noncommercial government objectives, such as social objectives relating to the distribution of income, may lead to regulation (both formal and informal) of public enterprises' pricing decisions. It is not uncommon for the prices charged for goods and services purchased or produced by public enterprises to differ from opportunity costs of resources and materials because of efforts to subsidize the use of an input or consumption of the enterprise's output. For example, the government may prefer to reduce the price of basic goods or services (e.g., rice or health services) rather than to provide tied grants for its consumption to the poorer sections of the community. The transparency concept requires, in order to avoid generating subsidies of unknown (and perhaps undesired) magnitudes when prices are deliberately altered for distributional or allocative considerations, that the extent to which revenues or costs are affected should be at least crudely quantified and evaluated. When financial losses are incurred, an explicit subsidy to the public enterprise may be required in the government's budget.

Governments have also pursued stabilization objectives through public enterprises' pricing policies. Very little research has been done in studying the results of these attempts. However, the direct impact of public enterprises' pricing decisions on overall price levels is likely to be limited and, in any case, is dependent on the size and strategic role of the enterprise. Furthermore, efforts to maintain prices at specified levels could result in reduced government revenues or increased government expenditures, leading in turn to higher government borrowing with attendant inflationary risks. It is therefore possible that the regulation of public enterprise prices as a tool of macroeconomic policy would be strongly counterproductive.[25]

While price adjustments may be needed to adjust for monopoly elements or for differences between social and private costs or may be desired for distributional purposes, it is not necessary that direct price regulation be employed. Even though the inclusion of a tax element in public enterprises' prices has been practiced for generations, it has been shown that under most circumstances there may be substantial differences between a public enterprise price increase and an equal tax increase, and that for many purposes an explicit tax may be preferred. In particular, from the viewpoint of raising revenues for the government's budget, a tax is likely to be more reliable and more predictable than a price increase and is likely to raise equal revenues with fewer distortions.[26] Also, a tax would probably be the preferred method of levying a charge aimed at reflecting social costs not included in the financial costs of production, because the use of a price increase might have the undesired result that some of the proceeds would accrue to non-capital factors and material inputs, some of which may already be paid more than the value of their marginal product. Finally, tax increases are more likely than price increases to be uniform across firms and consequently might introduce fewer distortions into the pricing system. Similarly, when they can be administered, direct budget subsidy payments to the desired recipient groups are more desirable than price reductions as a method of subsidizing a particular segment of the population.

However, for some purposes other than monopoly restraint pricing action may still be preferred, primarily when public sector revenues, rather than only government revenues, are of concern. For example, if the public enterprise were operating at a loss, a price increase would probably increase the receipts of the enterprise whereas a tax might reduce its receipts and profits further. If the government had been financing the enterprise's deficit by budgetary subsidies, a price increase might result in reduced government expenditures and smaller

---

[25] Chu and Feltenstein have estimated that in Argentina government transfers to cover public enterprise losses were proportionately ten times as inflationary as the financing of private enterprises' losses through commercial bank borrowings primarily because it is assumed that only in the former case are the losses translated into high-powered money through central bank financing of the government deficit. See Ke-Young Chu and Andrew Feltenstein, "Relative Price Distortions and Inflation: The Case of Argentina, 1963–76," International Monetary Fund, *Staff Papers*, Vol. 25 (September 1978), pp. 452–93. Another aspect of stabilization policy is the tendency in some countries to use public enterprises as an employer of last resort of unnecessary or unqualified labor. Such policies would have an adverse impact on public enterprises' finances and would lead to inefficient production of goods and services.

[26] Robert H. Floyd, "Equivalence of Product Tax Changes and Public Enterprise Price Changes," International Monetary Fund, *Staff Papers*, Vol. 28 (June 1981), pp. 338–74.

budgetary and public sector deficits. Furthermore, only a price increase could reduce the level of implicit subsidies that do not require the transfer of financial resources from the government to the enterprise.

Turning to external limitations on public enterprise pricing flexibility, it is obvious that domestic or international market competition would effectively constrain public enterprises to keep prices in rough alignment with competitors. In these cases the scope for achieving social and stabilization objectives solely through public enterprises' pricing practices would be limited, but efficient resource allocation will probably be enhanced. In such cases, tariff and domestic tax policies would be the preferable instrument to alter the prices of goods in order to effect social and stabilization objectives.

The resource or material input and output prices that would reflect marginal cost pricing, other government policies, and the constraints resulting from various market conditions are shown in Table 1.[27] The matrix depicts the feasible relationships between the marginal opportunity costs (MOC) of resource or material inputs and outputs and the output prices charged (OP) and the input prices paid (IP) by public enterprises. When enterprises compete in the market for inputs, the marginal opportunity costs of inputs, including capital in any form, may be represented by its free market price (MPI), or its value in alternative uses. Adjustments to opportunity cost prices may be viewed as separate and quantifiable elements of input and output prices. These include allocative adjustments for the differences between social and private costs (SC) and benefits (SB) and implicit or explicit distributional subsidies to, or taxes on, inputs and outputs (DSI, DTI, DSO, DTO).

When public enterprises compete with other purchasers in markets for resource and material inputs and must therefore pay at least the going market prices, the only way in which the government could influence a public enterprise's decision with regard to the hiring and mix of these inputs would be to impose a tax or charge on its payments for the input or to subsidize its use by the enterprise. However, since the public enterprise is a price taker, the incidence of the tax or subsidy will be on the profits of the public enterprise. When the markets for inputs are competitive, the only other feasible variations from the market price are a subsidy applying either to all enterprises or to only publicly owned enterprises and a tax applying to all resource inputs.

---

[27] A matrix similar to that depicted in Table 1 was developed by Malcolm Gillis and Charles E. McLure, Jr., in "Standards of Conduct for Public Enterprises," in Richard Musgrave, *Fiscal Reform in Bolivia: Final Report of the Bolivian Mission on Tax Reform* (Cambridge: Harvard University, 1981), pp. 546–49. It has been altered as necessary to conform to the purposes of this paper.

Table 1. Public Enterprises: Output and Input Prices

| Monopoly (Cartel) Seller | Competitive Seller |
| Competitive Buyer | Competitive Buyer |

Export-oriented output	
$OP = CP$	$OP = WP$
$IP = MPI + SC - SB - DSI + DTI$	$IP = MPI + SC - SB - DSI + DTI$
Domestically oriented output	
$OP = MOC + SC - SB - DSO + DTO$	$OP = MPO$
$IP = MPI + SC - SB - DSI + DTI$	$IP = MPI + SC - SB - DSI + DIT$

CP:	Cartel price;
DSI (DSO):	Distributional subsidy to an input (output);
DTI (DTO):	Distributional tax on an input (output);
MPI:	Free market price of input;
MPO:	Market price of output;
IP:	Input price paid by public enterprise;
MOC:	Marginal opportunity cost;
OP:	Output price charged by public enterprise;
SB:	Social benefit subsidy to correct allocative market imperfections;
SC:	Social cost tax to correct allocative market imperfections;
WP:	World price.

In the absence of such taxes or subsidies, the price paid by the enterprise will equal the input's marginal opportunity cost (i.e., $IP = MPI$).[28]

Similar constraints affect the determination of the prices of outputs by public enterprises. A public enterprise whose output markets were export oriented would not be able to impose a social or distributional charge in addition to the competitive world price or the world cartel price since buyers would not be willing to pay these charges and would switch to other sources of supply. Furthermore, there is no obvious reason why an exporting country would want its enterprises to attempt to subsidize foreign buyers either because of distributional or social externality considerations. Therefore, neither subsidy nor tax elements are likely to enter into output pricing considerations when the markets are predominantly foreign, and the output price would equal the world competitive or cartel price.

If a public enterprise's output is oriented mainly toward domestic markets, and if the public enterprise faces either foreign or domestic

---

[28] The input pricing relationships in Table 1 do not reflect situations in which the public enterprise does not employ opportunity cost pricing. Suppose that a public enterprise chooses to pay workers a higher wage than they could earn in alternative private employment. In such a case the relationship would be $IP = MPI + SI$ where SI is a subsidy to workers. With mobile factors that are not fully employed it is possible that the enterprises may pay less than the market price ($IP < MPI$) because the latter exceeds the factor's opportunity cost ($MPI > MOC$).

competition, in the absence of protective tariffs many of the same considerations apply. Although a public enterprise could presumably implement a subsidy by charging a lower price than its competitors, this would not be a particularly effective subsidization technique since the subsidy would accrue only to the customers of the public enterprise and would result in a lower return to the enterprise. Furthermore, in the absence of a rationing mechanism, such subsidies would be open-ended and could lead to high levels of subsidization without any guarantee that the public enterprises' customers are the members of society that the government wishes to subsidize. Finally, in the absence of a budgetary grant such a subsidy would result in a reduction in profits and would represent a departure from marginal cost pricing for at least one input, namely, equity capital.

If outputs are sold primarily in domestic markets, and if the enterprise is a monopoly, social and distributional charges or subsidies can be implemented by varying output prices from opportunity cost levels. However, if the financial effects of these variations are not explicitly budgeted, they would directly affect the profitability of the enterprise in a perverse manner. For example, it would make little sense for a social charge levied on an undesirable or luxury product of an enterprise to result in higher profits to the enterprise. Consequently, even when tax and subsidy policies can be effected through the price mechanism alone, there is still a strong case for taking them explicitly into the budgetary and tax process.

In summary, the discussion indicates that in the absence of specific reasons to the contrary, public enterprises should expect to operate profitably and should price their outputs and purchases accordingly. Direct government regulation of prices would seem appropriate in only limited circumstances, primarily when monopoly elements are present or when existing prices are inappropriate. In general, explicit taxes and subsidies are the preferred instruments for achieving allocative, distributional, and stabilization objectives. Finally, external constraints will in many circumstances limit the effectiveness of using public enterprise prices to achieve noncommercial objectives. However, these practices are rarely observed which suggests that either public enterprises themselves have not achieved efficient internal operations, or that governments may not be pursuing rational tax, subsidy, or pricing policies with regard to public enterprises, or both.

V. ISSUES OF INFORMATION

One of the most striking aspects of public enterprises is the general lack of information about them. Governments often do not have balance sheets, operating statements, or other current data on their operations. Even when some data are available, they are often not comparable among various public enterprises. Little information is available outside individual countries. For example, in the *Government Finance Statistics Yearbook, 1981* there are no data for any country on transfers from government to public enterprises, and useful data on transfers from public enterprises are limited to about 30 countries.[29] *International Financial Statistics* publishes data on credit to public enterprises for only about ten countries. The general lack of information greatly restricts the ability of the government to exercise effective control over individual enterprises and especially to analyze their collective impact on macroeconomic aggregates.

There is no clear explanation for the lack of information. However, two possibilities arise. First, the growth of the public enterprise sector and the proliferation in the number of public enterprises has often occurred in an ad hoc manner such that the desirability of information on their operations may not have been initially evident. Consequently, few efforts would have been made to develop information sources. Second, in many cases private enterprises were transformed into public enterprises when governments bought controlling interests from shareholders of existing joint stock companies. In cases of public enterprises organized as joint stock companies, there may be legal barriers to the provision of information. Furthermore, the government's links to the actual management of such enterprises may be somewhat ill defined. Often the only link is the government representatives on the Board of Directors of such companies. Typically these representatives themselves may not even be aware of the needs of the government for various statistical information.

There have been no surveys to date reviewing the routinely available information on public enterprises and their operations in a broad range of countries.[30] There have been a few country-specific studies that have assembled some available data, but these have been entirely ad hoc and follow no consistent pattern. This almost total lack of generally available data has doubtlessly hampered efforts to undertake research in almost any aspect of public enterprises' economic impact. This is probably particularly true when data on more than one public enterprise would be required.

The data requirements of governments and other users interested

---

[29] International Monetary Fund, *Government Finance Statistics Yearbook*, Vol. V, 1981 (Washington, D.C., 1982).

[30] The difficulties encountered in assembling and using data on public enterprises have been noted in the paper in this volume by R.P. Short, "The Role of Public Enterprises: An International Statistical Comparison."

in the analysis of the economic impact of public enterprises would seem to fall into essentially two basic categories. To the extent that specific objectives are assigned to certain enterprises and to the extent that the government wishes to exercise control over some or all activities of particular enterprises, data of a microeconomic nature would be required. This suggests that the data required might be rather more detailed than merely broad aggregates. However, for purposes of macroeconomic analysis, such micro-oriented data from individual enterprises would be of interest only if it had a significant macroeconomic impact. This suggests that, in such cases, microeconomic data would be of interest only for a few large enterprises. For example, an agricultural marketing board might provide large subsidies to agricultural producers, food marketing enterprises might provide large subsidies to consumers, and oil or other natural resource companies' operations may involve the collection of a natural resource rent. Any of these may have significant effects on the macroeconomic aggregates, and data users may have an interest in more micro-oriented data than might ordinarily be expected in order to analyze microeconomic variables with macroeconomic impacts.

More generally, for macroeconomic analysis, interest would focus on data that would be useful as inputs to formulating and evaluating macroeconomic policies. The statistics of interest would not necessarily deal with the operations of any one particular enterprise, and their preparation would entail compilation of bits of data from virtually all public enterprises. Such information would include various aggregates such as the generation and usage of foreign exchange by the public enterprise sector, the projected and actual net financial flows between the government and the public enterprise sector, bank credit to the sector, and various other aggregates relevant to macroeconomic policymaking and evaluation. If such indicators were available, they would permit some assessment of the overall impact of the various government policies vis-à-vis the public enterprise sector, such as constraints on output pricing adjustments. Clearly, the compilation of such data would be a task well beyond mere ad hoc occasional efforts, and the unavailability and importance of such statistics suggest a need to establish an information reporting system that would facilitate the collection and compilation of data on an ongoing basis in many countries.

An information system would aid the authorities in formulating and evaluating economic and financial policies by regularizing the flow of information to the analytical staffs responsible for studying economic conditions and advising policymakers. Any information reporting system would need three main elements: (1) the sources from which data may be obtained for processing; (2) an agency with responsibility for processing the data into aggregates relevant to macro-policymaking purposes; and (3) the recipient users of the data. In addition to the fairly standard data, such as the level of profits or losses and the various rates of return to various capital and equity portions, other statistics that would be useful as inputs to formulating and evaluating macroeconomic policies should be generated routinely by the system along with possible interpretations of their implications. The generation of such data should result in substantially enhanced use of available information by enabling policymakers to shift from their present focus on the microeconomic measurements relating to the internal efficiency of particular enterprises and to focus in addition on the macroeconomic impact, including efficient mobilization and utilization of resources for development.

In summary, for various reasons little information is available on the activities of public enterprises in most countries. This merely compounds the other difficulties governments encounter in their efforts to analyze and control public enterprises. It is important, therefore, that information systems be developed in countries to generate routine and timely data for use in evaluating both the micro- and macroeconomic impact of public enterprise operations.

VI. ISSUES OF FINANCING

Perhaps no other issues surrounding public enterprises are of more direct relevance to macroeconomic and financial analysis than are those concerning the finances of public enterprises. The range of financing issues is broad, and it is useful to divide them into essentially three groups for purposes of this paper. First, there are issues that relate primarily to the initial financing of an enterprise or to the subsequent financing of major projects or investments of the ongoing operations of enterprises. Second, some issues are of interest primarily because they may have implications for credit creation, monetary expansion, and indirectly for the balance of payments. Third, some issues are of interest because they may have direct implications for the balance of payments.

The question of how an enterprise is initially financed revolves mainly around whether equity or debt financing is employed. In the broadest sense capital from all sources and in any form is essentially homogeneous and pricing policies should be established to yield a return equal to its opportunity cost. Any differences between the returns to different forms of capital should reflect identifiable causes. For example, the financial return to equity capital might include compensation to the shareholders for their greater exposure to risk or their ownership rights to resource rents that would not be reflected in the return-to-loan capital. Nevertheless, public enterprises may, and often do, prefer equity capital because they look upon it as entailing little or no cost.[31] However, there are more practical differences between debt and equity capital that may influence the choice between the two. In particular, there is a legal obligation in the case of debt to pay the interest due (although this is often not rigorously enforced) which in turn requires the generation of a positive cash flow from the enterprise's operations. This suggests that for public enterprises in construction or in gestation and for some unprofitable enterprises, in particular those in decreasing cost industries, there may be a preference for equity financing from the point of view of cash flow requirements. However, the preference should not be interpreted as justifying lower prices for the eventual output than would result from appropriate costing of all capital.

There may also be some preference by public enterprise managers for equity capital in cases of enterprises whose operations are unprofitable as a result of deliberate government policy to subsidize outputs or inputs. By avoiding the necessity of generating cash for interest payments, the enterprise can more easily finance any subsidy. However, there are caveats to this conclusion. Unwanted and perhaps even unknown subsidies may also develop and be masked by financing practices that permit low or negative profits. Indeed, these practices may provide welcome excuses to the managers of inefficient enterprises to cover their own shortcomings. Consequently, when such practices are employed, it is especially important for the government to evaluate fully the desirability and extent of every subsidy and its costs in terms of forgone profits or interest payments so that the level of subsidy is not de facto left to the enterprises' managers or to the whims of the market.

There are other arguments over the debt-to-equity ratio that are generally spurious. First, there is no uneven economic burden on an enterprise with a relatively high debt-to-equity ratio due to high interest expenses. This misconception results from failure to consider both interest payments and dividends as payments to capital. This also suggests that variations in the dividend rates of different public enterprises resulting solely from variations in the debt-equity ratio are not necessarily meaningful comparisons. Finally, in the case of private enterprises it is sometimes useful to manage the debt-equity ratio in order to preserve the control of certain equity shareholders.

---

[31] See the observations concerning the attitudes of public enterprise managers discussed in Raymond Vernon and Yair Aharoni, *State-Owned Enterprise in the Western Economies* (New York: 1981), p. 16.

However, with public enterprises, both equity and loan capital are usually provided by the government or by other government-controlled enterprises, such as public financial enterprises. In such cases, preservation of equity shareholder control has little significance.

Closely related to debt versus equity issues is the question of the appropriate distribution of profits, if any, to the government in its role as stockholder. Assuming that public enterprises' profits should be subject to the same taxes as those of private enterprises, and given the previous discussions with regard to pricing, and investment planning, an appropriate dividend policy, as well as some inappropriate ones, is clear.[32] The amount of dividend will be the result of pricing policies that reflect opportunity costs and other government objectives, approved investment expenditures of the enterprises, and their needs for working cash balances. Thus, an appropriate and consistent dividend policy will *not* imply that a fixed proportion or absolute amount of profits should be transferred to the government from every profitable public enterprise. Indeed, dividends may not even be necessary in certain circumstances. Profits and depreciation allowances may be left with an enterprise if it has investment projects approved by the government on which these funds can be disbursed in the reasonably foreseeable future. However, if the profits of an enterprise (plus the cash equivalent of depreciation allowances) are more than the expenditures expected on approved projects in the reasonably near future, then the excess profits would be an initial approximation to a reasonable dividend. Nevertheless, in order to enhance incentives to efficient managerial practices, consideration should be given to allowing firms to retain some profits within the overall framework of national priorities. However, there are two strong exceptions to these remarks. To the extent that public enterprise profits represent natural resource rents or monopoly profits, it is reasonable to expect that this should be transferred fully to the government.

Turn now to the second category of financial issues—those that are of interest because they have implications for credit creation, monetary expansion, and, indirectly, the balance of payments. To the extent that public enterprises employ bank credit for normal commercial operations, their credit demands may have as much merit as those of private enterprises. The substantive questions of merit revolve around whether public enterprises have any easier access to credit than do private enterprises and whether credit facilities are made available for noncommercial purposes. It is almost axiomatic that for numerous reasons public enterprises probably do have somewhat easier access

[32] Robert H. Floyd, "Some Aspects of Income Taxation of Public Enterprises," International Monetary Fund, *Staff Papers*, Vol. 25 (June 1978), pp. 310–42.

to credit than do private enterprises. Even when the government does not explicitly guarantee a public enterprise's debt, banks almost certainly regard a public enterprise's borrowings as having at least the implicit guarantee of the government. Much the same point could probably be made with regard to suppliers' credits. Furthermore, there are frequent examples of bank financing being provided to cover the operating losses of public enterprises which result from the pursuit of noncommercial objectives. And, furthermore, in many countries the financial institutions themselves are public enterprises that are consequently likely to be particularly sympathetic to the credit requests of other public enterprises. In some cases, this de facto credit rationing in favor of public enterprises may distort the allocation of national savings such that public enterprises are able to obtain credit for uses with lower social returns than alternative private sector activities.

Two essential questions appear to summarize the issues with regard to credit granted to public enterprises in excess of its requirements for normal commercial operations. First, is any excess a reflection of the pursuit of deliberate, government-endorsed noncommercial objectives or is it a reflection of inefficiency in the enterprise? Second, what are the implications of the excess for credit creation and availability and how does it differ according to whether the credit is provided to the enterprise or to the government? The first questions require an effort to identify and to qualify the financial impact of the government's noncommercial objectives, and to access residually the inefficiency of its commercial operations. The second questions will in a large measure depend on how the central bank acts to accommodate the borrowing of public enterprises and what credit instruments may be rediscounted. Such policies would vary from country to country and from time to time, but in general one might expect that debt of public enterprises is less likely to be rediscountable (and, hence, less likely to be monetized) than the direct debt instruments of the government. This suggests that, at least in the short run, credit demands of public enterprises in excess of their normal operating requirement are more likely to result in crowding out private sector borrowers and in increases in the costs to private borrowers than in expansion of total credit.

In the longer run, the result is less clear but seems more likely to be reversed. It is unlikely that financial institutions would be willing or able to carry in their asset portfolios constantly increasing and/or unrepayable debts of public enterprises. The viability of the financial institution requires that these debts be repaid. However, the debtor enterprises would be able to repay only with the assistance of the government which in turn will increase its use of bank credit through either deposit drawdowns or direct borrowing. In the latter case the conversion from credit to the enterprises to credit to the government involves potential monetary expansion if a rediscountable debt instrument is issued.

The final category of issues related to financing includes issues that are of direct relevance to the balance of payments. Essentially two distinct issues appear relevant. First, there is the potential impact on the balance of payments of public enterprises' borrowing from either domestic or foreign sources and their access to development financing. Second there are the foreign exchange resources that might be potentially available from a public enterprise's exploitation of some form of monopoly power or rents, usually natural resource rents.

Public enterprises can and often do borrow substantially in international capital markets. According to partial data compiled by the International Bank for Reconstruction and Development (IBRD), gross borrowings in international markets by public enterprises totaled $25.0 billion in 1978.[33] However, even these data are not comprehensive; they include only borrowings in the form of foreign bonds, Euro-currency credits, and bank lending. Loans from international agencies, governments (including on-lending), and suppliers' credits are not included. Nevertheless, these data are believed to represent about 70 percent of gross foreign borrowings of public enterprises.

Two types of problems may be encountered in regard to foreign borrowing. First, these borrowings have been increasing, and while by and large they are intended to finance expansions of new projects, there may be cases where the proceeds are used for current purposes. The implications of such borrowing are clear in that the latter type tends to be inflationary. Second, the controls on these would appear to be inadequate in some cases. For example, in Portugal, public enterprises do not need the approval of the Ministry of Finance and can borrow after informing the central bank. Variations of this are to be found in other countries. In Ivory Coast, although regulations require consultation it would appear that the relevant authorities (the *Caisse Autonome d'Amortissement*) have not been very effective in preventing borrowing from external sources without its approval. It would also appear that requirements for prior approvals have in some cases given rise to perverse effects. For example, in Mexico, state enterprises placed orders with foreign suppliers (by resorting to suppliers' credits) rather than with domestic suppliers in part because less time was required. It is therefore essential that budgetary and other mechanisms be strengthened to permit an overall coordination and at the same time prevent unintended adverse consequences.

---

[33] IBRD, *Borrowing in International Capital Markets*, May 1980 (Washington, D.C., 1980).

The second set of issues relating directly to the balance of payments pertain to public enterprises that generate foreign exchange through foreign sales. However, the normal commercial results are of less interest than situations in which the exporting public enterprise generates substantial amounts of foreign exchange through exercise of some form of monopoly power or the exploitation of natural resource rents or both. The most obvious examples are, of course, the various oil exporting and other natural resource producing and exporting companies, many of which are fully or partially government owned. The issue in such cases is the appropriate distribution of foreign exchange among the enterprise, the government, and any private sector shareholders. While private sector owners certainly have a claim to a proportional share of all profits, there is no obvious reason that they should have an a priori claim to any earned foreign exchange. Of course, the exporting enterprise itself might be given some preferential allocation of foreign exchange if it were believed necessary to ensure that its operations could be continued. However, this does not imply that it or any other exporting enterprise should be permitted to retain foreign currency balances in excess of normal commercial requirements. Consequently, one could ordinarily expect that essentially all foreign exchange proceeds would be converted into local currency through official channels.

To summarize, as long as all forms of capital yield their opportunity cost, the choice between debt and equity financing is of secondary importance. Bank credit to public enterprises is of concern primarily insofar as it exceeds normal commercial requirements. In the short run such credit is more likely to crowd out other potential borrowers, but in the long run it seems more likely to be inflationary. Furthermore, public enterprises are often large borrowers in international markets, and more effective controls on these borrowings seem desirable. Finally, whenever a public enterprise generates foreign exchange earnings, balances in excess of normal commercial requirements should be converted into local currency through normal channels.

VII. SUMMARY AND CONCLUSIONS

Until recently public enterprises have generally been viewed as individual entities that had no particular role as a stabilization policy instrument in unplanned economies. In reality, this view had little merit since public enterprises' pricing and employment policies were frequently manipulated by policymakers, although usually with more concern for political tenure than for macroeconomic stabilization. With the growth of the public enterprise sector in many developing countries, there has been an increasing awareness that public enterprises collectively can, and often do, affect the economy as a whole either as a result of government policies vis-à-vis the sector or because a few enterprises are relatively so important in the economy. This has given rise to questions concerning the appropriate policies for governments to follow with regard to the public enterprise sector and has raised the question as to what issues are of relevance to macroeconomic policymakers?

This paper has reviewed a variety of issues concerning public enterprises and their financial and macroeconomic impacts. No effort has been made to resolve those issues which remain the subject of controversy. However, where a general consensus has been reached, at least in theory, on an issue (e.g., marginal cost pricing), the results of that consensus have been presented. No effort has been made to this point to assess the relative importance of any of the issues reviewed. However, it would seem useful to conclude the paper with at least the personal assessment of the author as to the relative importance of these issues.

Progress is probably most advanced in the area of pricing issues. At least in theory the appropriate procedures are clear. Indeed, there is even a growing expertise in the quantification of allocative and distributive adjustments. Nevertheless, probably the single most important outstanding issue of pricing, and an issue that should receive more attention in the future, is that of what techniques should be applied in practice over a broad spectrum of public enterprises in order to approximate the marginal cost pricing objectives. Closely connected with these would be techniques to quantify the financial costs of the government's noncommercial objectives. Insofar as the latter may facilitate use of lump-sum limits on costs, the problems of the unit price subsidy (or tax) element may be reduced.

Probably the issues of highest priority for future work are those concerned with channels of control and information flows. Governments are increasingly being forced to accept the need to impose more financial discipline on their enterprises if for no other reason than to avoid undesirable results in financial markets and on macroeconomic variables. It is clear that existing systems have not coped well with these needs and it is also clear that governments generally have little understanding of either the policies they wish to pursue or the information they require to evaluate them, or the macroeconomic variables that will be affected by these policies. Until these rather basic, if somewhat institutional, matters are resolved, advances in more technical issues are unlikely to yield any significant improvement in the macroeconomic impact of public enterprise operations.

REFERENCES

Cassese, Sabino, "Public Control and Corporate Efficiency," in *State-Owned Enterprise in the Western Economies*, ed. by Raymond Vernon and Yair Aharoni (New York: St. Martin's Press, 1981).

Chu, Ke-Young and Andrew Feltenstein, "Relative Price Distortions and Inflation: The Case of Argentina, 1963–76," *Staff Papers*, International Monetary Fund (Washington), Vol. 25 (September 1978), pp. 452–93.

Floyd, Robert H., "Equivalence of Product Tax Changes and Public Enterprise Price Changes," *Staff Papers*, International Monetary Fund (Washington), Vol. 28 (June 1981), pp. 338–74.

———, "Some Aspects of Income Taxation of Public Enterprises," *Staff Papers*, International Monetary Fund (Washington), Vol. 25 (June 1978), pp. 310–42.

Foster, C. D., *Politics, Finance, and the Role of Economics: An Essay on the Control of Public Enterprise* (London: Allen and Unwin, 1971).

Gillis, Malcolm and Charles E. McLure, Jr., "Standards of Conduct for Public Enterprises," in Richard Musgrave, *Fiscal Reform in Bolivia: Final Report of the Bolivian Mission on Tax Reform* (Cambridge: Harvard University, 1981), pp. 546–49.

Heald, David, "The Economic and Financial Control of U.K. Nationalised Industries," *Economic Journal* (London) (June 1980), pp. 243–65.

Henderson, A. M., "Prices and Profits in State Enterprise," *The Review of Economic Studies* (1948–49), Vol. XVI (1), No. 39 (Clevedon, Avon, United Kingdom), pp. 13–24.

India, Government of, Bureau of Public Enterprises, Ministry of Finance, *Performance Aims and Financial Targets of Central Government Public Enterprises 1982–83* (New Delhi: April 1982).

International Bank for Reconstruction and Development, *Borrowing in International Capital Markets*, May 1980 (Washington: IBRD, 1980).

International Monetary Fund, *Government Finance Statistics Yearbook*, Vol. V, 1981 (Washington: IMF, 1982).

Jenkins, Glenn P., "An Operational Approach to the Performance of Public Sector Enterprises," Harvard Institute for International Development, Development Discussion Paper No. 47 (November 1978).

Jones, Leroy P., *Public Enterprise and Economic Development: The Korean Case* (Seoul: Korea Development Institute, 1975).

National Economic Development Office, *A Study of U.K. Nationalised Industries, Background Paper No. 2, Relationships of Government and Public Enterprises in France, West Germany, and Sweden* (London: National Economic Development Office, 1976).

Pryke, Richard, "The Comparative Performance of Public and Private Enterprise," *Fiscal Studies*, Vol. 3 (Oxford: July 1982), pp. 68–81.

———, *The Nationalised Industries: Policies and Performance Since 1968* (Oxford: Martin Robinson, 1981).

Sheahan, John B., "Experience with Public Enterprise in France and Italy" in *Public Enterprise: Economic Analysis of Theory and Practice*, ed. by William G. Shepherd and Associates (Lexington: D.C. Heath and Company, 1976).

Shepherd, William G., "Objectives, Types, and Accountability" in *Public Enterprise: Economic Analysis of Theory and Practice*, ed. by William G. Shepherd and Associates (Lexington: D.C. Heath and Company, 1976).

Sweden, Government of, Department of Industry, *State Business*; *Public Enterprise Experience in the EEC*, prepared by Metra Oxford Consulting (Oxford: 1978).

Turvey, Ralph, *Economic Analysis and Public Enterprises* (Totowa, New Jersey: 1971).

Vernon, Raymond and Yair Aharoni, *State-Owned Enterprise in the Western Economies* (New York: St. Martin's Press, 1981).

Toward a Conceptual Framework for Macroeconomic Evaluation of Public Enterprise Performance in Mixed Economies

CLIVE S. GRAY*

Considering that operating deficits of public enterprises are a major contributor to fiscal imbalance and excessive credit creation in many countries, especially but not only developing nations, it would seem that the macroeconomic impact of the public enterprise sector has hitherto received less attention than it deserves. The primary objectives of the present paper are to stimulate increased focus on this issue and to propose a conceptual framework within which analysis of individual country situations might proceed. The framework stops short of examining alternative remedies that might be proposed by local or outside analysts in response to a given situation of imbalance.

The quintessential policy issue surrounding the role and size of the public enterprise sector in any country is considered in the paper to be the intrinsic social efficiency of government in organizing scarce factors of production to produce goods and services for sale. A separate, and perhaps slightly secondary issue of policy, is the public enterprise sector's efficiency as a vehicle for accomplishing noncommercial objectives of government. The paper argues that assessment of sectoral efficiency in production presupposes careful netting out of costs and revenue losses attributable to pursuit of noncommercial

*Mr. Gray is a Fellow of the Harvard Institute for International Development and consultant to the Fiscal Affairs Department of the International Monetary Fund.

35

objectives. These are classified into five categories—economic stabilization, economic growth, income redistribution, localization/indigenization, and miscellaneous. Issues of how to assess the public enterprise sector's efficiency in pursuing the objectives, and whether public enterprise is the only or even the most efficient vehicle for doing so, are considered in an initial appendix.

By providing a macroeconomic picture of the comparative efficiency, and consequences of any comparative inefficiency, of the public enterprise sector, information on its fiscal and monetary impact will form an important and relatively new input into policy discussions within many governments concerning sectoral reform. It will open up a wider range of reform options than is suggested in the bulk of the current literature on public enterprise, stressing as it does micro approaches to improvement of management efficiency and application of social benefit-cost calculus to appraisal of public enterprise investments. At one extreme, some governments may wish to consider compressing the sector by discontinuing or divesting themselves of a certain portion of it, especially in branches of production apart from public utilities and others traditionally regarded as "natural monopolies."However, it is essential that external analysts and advisors preserve ideological neutrality concerning the intrinsic merits and drawbacks of state ownership of the means of production as opposed to alternative modes of industrial organization, and the present paper adopts such a stance.

Ideally one would assess the public enterprise sector's macroeconomic impact by comparing observed national income, and fiscal and monetary parameters with those obtaining under a baseline alternative simulated within a general equilibrium framework. However, because of the computational effort involved, such an approach will rarely be feasible; moreover, specification of baseline alternatives cannot avoid value judgments, and is thus a questionable exercise for outsiders. More feasible, and at the same time more acceptable to policymakers, will be a partial equilibrium approach in which observed parameters are compared with criterion values.

The paper argues that the most useful criterion values are those taking as their point of departure zero or "normal" profitability of the public enterprise sector, that is, costs of all factors being covered, including capital, after observed values are adjusted for monopoly profits, border prices of tradables, and costs and revenue losses (net of subsidies) associated with pursuit of noncommercial objectives. This is because the principal burdens imposed by the public enterprise sector at a macroeconomic level in many countries arise from subsidies and credit it receives from government, and credit from the financial sector, in order to compensate for operating losses.

The principal components of the public enterprise sector's national income, fiscal and monetary parameters are listed and described in Section V. Fiscal parameters include accounting magnitudes—notably taxes, interest, and capital payments from the public enterprise sector to government, unrequited transfers and capital payments from government to the sector—as well as implicit transfers to, and implicit subsidies from government, the latter comprising tax subsidies and a pervasive subsidization of capital. On the monetary side one looks initially at gross use of credit, then goes behind this to measure sectoral impact on money supply, the level of inflation, interest rate structure, and the balance of payments, always paying particular attention to credit creation in compensation for enterprise deficits.

I. POLICY BACKGROUND

Of such gravity are the shortcomings that have been brought to light by recent performance evaluations of public enterprises in mixed economies, especially developing countries but not limited to them, that one would have expected a significant proportion of the burgeoning literature in this field to add it all up and assess the impact of the public enterprise sector on various countries' fiscal and monetary situations in the short run as well as economic growth and fulfillment of other sociopolitical objectives over the medium and long term. Among the parameters that one would want to see measured and evaluated are the shares of the public enterprise sector in nominal and adjusted financial flows from and to the central government, including implicit taxes and subsidies; the proportion of central government deficits accounted for directly and indirectly by public enterprises; the impact of public enterprise operating deficits on credit creation, money supply, inflation, and interest rates; and ultimately, the number of percentage points of growth gained (or sacrificed) as compared with some baseline pattern of industrial organization.

Even if one established, within a reasonable confidence interval, that a country's budget deficit and money supply would have been X_1 and X_2 billion currency units less in year t, its inflation rate y percent less in the same year, and its gross domestic product (GDP) growth rate over the past five years z percentage points higher under the baseline regime, it could nevertheless be concluded that these represent costs of achieving certain noncommercial objectives. Public enterprises are, after all, supposed to serve social as well as economic objectives, and a certain increment in inflation or the sacrifice of some GDP growth may be regarded as a necessary, even modest, price to be paid for certain social benefits.

On the other hand, since the launching of the great debate on trade-offs between GDP growth and social justice, the evidence generated in many slow-growing and fast-growing economies has suggested that social benefits gained by sacrificing efficiency are often largely offset by social as well as economic losses. Hence, in some countries, one finds a number of policymakers questioning the effectiveness of public enterprises in achieving social and development goals. They look to their staff or outside consultants to measure the resultant social and economic losses and investigate alternative strategies for the future.

The current academic research is concentrating on the methodology of performance evaluation of individual enterprises, the behavior of public enterprise managers, the impact of government policies on the enterprises, and the search for ways and means of making them serve their commercial and noncommercial objectives more efficiently. Analysis of macroeconomic performance would constitute a logical extension of the research, which could then go on to examine the full spectrum of reform possibilities.

II. USEFULNESS OF A CONCEPTUAL FRAMEWORK

The present paper aspires to initiate the process of designing a conceptual framework by means of which government decision makers, and local as well as outside economists advising them, might evaluate the macroeconomic impact or performance of a country's public enterprise sector by comparing the actual picture with putative outcomes of baseline alternatives. Such comparisons should indicate the magnitude of the problem and provide a basis for determining the policies to be pursued as well as the volume of resources to be enlisted in resolving it. In some cases, only incremental reforms may be suggested, in others, more extreme measures may be indicated.

While strict neutrality on the relative merits of state and private ownership of the means of production should be observed, a full range of policy alternatives on how to reduce a large budget deficit arising from operations of public enterprises in mixed economies should be considered. A reform program might confine itself to changes in management procedures in selected enterprises; it might entail new sector-wide policies in such areas as government control over managerial initiative, pricing of inputs and outputs, minimum financial returns to be required on new public enterprise investments, and for servicing of outstanding government loans; and, at the extreme, it might embrace the premise that no intermediate measures would convey as much social benefit as outright divestiture of certain state holdings.

A necessary disclaimer at the outset is that the present paper does not address the question of remedies for any given shortcomings that may be identified in a country's public enterprise scenario; rather, it confines itself to indicators and criteria for determining whether remedies need to be sought. What specific remedies to prescribe is an issue that must be faced by the authorities of the country in question, along with any advisers they may choose to consult. Optimal remedies will take into account economic and political factors peculiar to each country's situation. At the same time, in almost every case, consideration of potential remedies short of divestiture will necessitate resolving one or more of the five categories of issues—determination of objectives, control procedures, pricing, generation of information, and financing—outlined by Robert H. Floyd in the preceding paper in this volume.

Once the conceptual framework has been agreed, consideration must be given to ways and means of measuring the indicated parameters. This involves assessing the data base country by country and determining what resources must be applied, whether purely local or including technical assistance, to expand it. As with other categories of data, country statistics differ widely in their coverage of public enterprises. At one extreme, some governments tabulate operating account and balance sheet data for all public enterprises individually and on a consolidated basis, broken down by sectors and/or categories of enterprises. At the opposite extreme, some act as though government's stake in the sector imposed no more responsibility for centralized financial reporting than the national statistics office bears vis-à-vis the private sector. In such cases, one may have to consider oneself fortunate to locate such bits and pieces of centralized data (apart from annual reports of the individual enterprises, with the delays to which those are often subject) as central and/or commercial bank claims on public enterprises; transfers to and from government that are identified in the budget—dividends, certain types of tax payments, and debt service in one direction and operating subsidies and capital infusions in the other; and possibly accounts of major public utilities that are sometimes found in national statistical publications.

Just as a series of adjustments are made in raw government finance data in order to compute economically relevant coefficients and indicators with respect to the interaction between government and the economy, so also the public enterprise data will have to be adjusted to give meaningful macroeconomic indicators. Some of these adjustments will not be cut and dried but will require the exercise of judgment, and will be subject to wide margins of error and uncertainty. Such adjustments involve, for example, the estimation of implicit taxes and subsidies associated with alternative pricing policies, the use of border prices to adjust operating accounts, and the attribution of costs to actions in pursuit of social objectives.

In principle every government that maintains public enterprises should be collecting and analyzing such data for itself, eventually sharing it with its international creditors for their own review and interpretation. To encourage this, the creditors should press upon governments the usefulness of the parameters described below as guides to policy, urge them to allocate adequate resources to their measurement, and, where appropriate, arrange technical assistance to support the effort. However, until such initiatives have borne fruit, outside users will have to improvise with incomplete data, seeking as always to equate the marginal returns to time invested in satisfying their wide range of data needs.

The significance of the findings that can be obtained already by analysis of incomplete nominal parameters relating to public enterprise is illustrated in R.P. Short's concluding paper in this volume. In an analysis comparing data from close to 90 countries there can be no question of adjusting financial profits and losses for implicit taxes and subsidies, or assessing the financial burden of pursuing noncommercial objectives. Nor is it possible to estimate the impact of public enterprise deficits on price levels and external payments. However, in sketching the magnitude of the sector's deficit, comparing it with overall government deficits, assessing the budgetary burden of public enterprise, and showing how increases in bank credit to the sector have translated one-for-one into increases in total credit outstanding, Short has pioneered in establishing highly suggestive indicators of the magnitude of the macroeconomic problem. His work should serve as an inspiration to national planners to deepen the analysis of their countries' data and identify the proximate causes of macroeconomic imbalances in public enterprise performance as a prerequisite for the design of appropriate remedies.

III. DEFINITION AND COVERAGE OF PUBLIC ENTERPRISE SECTOR

The present paper, along with its two companions in this volume, focuses on the macroeconomic performance of the public enterprise sector in mixed economies—that is, economies where nonstate-owned units account for a significant proportion of output by enterprises with more than, say, 5, 10, or 20 employees (whatever standard is used in a given country to define medium-scale producers). Two key characteristics of a mixed economy with reference to the subject of the volume are that (1) the performance of private and, if relevant, other nonstate-owned enterprises provides a basis of comparison with public enterprise performance, and (2) for the production of any given set of goods and services in medium-sized and larger units, it is open to the state to consider one or more forms of industrial organization other than public enterprise, without contravening the underlying national ideology.

Many of the parameters proposed for measurement and evaluation are no less relevant to analysis of public enterprise performance in centrally planned economies. However, the economic environment in such countries, featuring the dominant role of noncommercial objectives, close integration of public enterprise and state finances, and lack of alternatives for comparison with the performance of state-owned units, changes the parameters of evaluation sufficiently to require modifications in the analytical framework.

Mixed economies can be classified in turn among developing and industrial countries. Developing countries have received the preponderant share of attention in the recent literature on public enterprise, and inasmuch as it is fiscal and monetary imbalances in these countries that currently absorb the major share of the International Monetary Fund's (IMF) resources, inevitably the contribution of the public enterprise sector to those imbalances is currently of greater interest to the IMF than is any analogous phenomenon with respect to the industrial nations. Nevertheless, the analytical framework of the paper applies to both sets of countries, as does R.P. Short's statistical analysis. Factors that apply preponderantly to developing rather than industrial countries will be so identified in the text.

The literature generally recognizes three conditions as characterizing a public enterprise: (1) government control over the entity, de facto or potential, which need not be synonymous with majority ownership; (2) production of goods and services for sale as the entity's primary function; and (3) existence of a policy that revenues should cover at least a substantial proportion of costs.[1]

For its part, the IMF's *Manual on Government Finance Statistics* divides the public enterprise sector into two components: (a) public financial institutions and (b) nonfinancial public enterprises.[2] With respect to category (a), financial institutions are defined as "enterprises primarily engaged in either acceptance of demand, time, or savings deposits,

---

[1] Compare, for example, Malcolm Gillis, "The Role of State Enterprises in Economic Development," *Social Research*, Vol. 47 (Summer 1980), pp. 248–89.

[2] International Monetary Fund, *A Manual on Government Finance Statistics* (Draft) (Washington, D.C., 1974). (Hereinafter referred to as the *Manual.*)

or in both incurring liabilities and acquiring financial assets in the market";[3] if "owned and/or controlled by the government" they are further described as public financial institutions.[4]

Category (b) is defined as "government-owned and/or -controlled units which sell industrial or commercial goods and services to the public on a large scale."[5] Comparing (b) with the three conditions cited above, the phrase "on a large scale" conveys somewhat imprecisely the previous notion (2) that selling goods and services is the entity's primary function. However, the *Manual* definition would accord public enterprise status to an entity operating under a permanent mandate to furnish its goods and services at less than a "substantial" proportion of cost.

Numerous instances can be cited of enterprises that operate profitably as either public or private entities in some countries while similar enterprises cover as little as half or even less of their financial costs in other countries, yet to avoid the political costs of large-scale displacement of labor the governments in the latter cases maintain the entities in full knowledge that appreciable cost recovery at any future time is a pipe dream.[6] It would be inappropriate to exclude such enterprises from the framework of the present paper, which accordingly applies only conditions (1) and (2), namely, (1) government control, and (2) trading as the primary function.

Clearly one must look separately at public financial institutions in contexts that have little to do with the basic policy issues surrounding public enterprise. On the other hand, for some purposes, it is useful to look at both categories of enterprises together. What will be referred to in this paper as the "quintessential" issue of public enterprise—that is, the efficiency of the state in achieving social objectives as entrepreneur and manager of revenue-generating activities—is very much present in government ownership and operation of commercial banks, insurance companies, and certain types of development finance institutions.

Accordingly, with regard to those fiscal indicators not encompassing credit operations of public financial institutions, this paper deals with a public enterprise sector that encompasses both nonfinancial units and a subset of public financial institutions including commercial and cooperative banks, commercial bank finance companies, insurance companies, stockbrokers, and other credit institutions that service a

---

[3] *Manual*, p. 32.

[4] Ibid., p. 35.

[5] Ibid., p. 29.

[6] Such is the case, for example, with aging heavy industries such as steel and shipbuilding in some industrial countries.

diversified clientele. Virtually the only public financial institutions totally excluded from coverage are the central bank and development finance companies whose sole function is to act as conduits for public credit, foreign or domestic, to a relatively small number of large-scale borrowers, public or private.[7]

For a discussion of additional issues that arise in applying the definition of public enterprise in concrete situations, and specifically in determining what proportion of shareholding by government qualifies an enterprise as public, the reader is referred to Section I of the following paper by R.P. Short.

IV. LOGICAL STAGES IN MACROECONOMIC EVALUATION OF PUBLIC ENTERPRISE PERFORMANCE

It is useful to define five successive stages in the process of arriving at a comprehensive assessment of the macroeconomic performance of the public enterprise sector: (1) measurement of nominal parameters characterizing the sector; (2) decomposition of the nominal parameters by attribution to commercial and noncommercial objectives; (3) adjustment of the nominal parameters for implicit taxes and subsidies; (4) comparison of adjusted parameters with criterion values (partial equilibrium approach); and (5) comparison of adjusted parameters with putative or simulated outcomes of baseline alternatives (general equilibrium approach).

Measurement of Nominal Parameters Characterizing the Public Enterprise Sector

The first step in analyzing, for example, the fiscal impact of the public enterprise sector is to measure and record the various nominal financial flows in either direction between the sector and the government. Simple addition yields totals for gross flows in each direction and subtotals for related components, while simple subtraction then gives an aggregate net flow as well as net figures for the various components. The various measures can be divided by other parameters to obtain indicators such as the ratio of gross fiscal transfer to government to value added or capital invested. Findings that Country A's aggregate net flow in year t amounted to X million currency units

---

[7] Commercial banks and other financial institutions meeting the definition used in this paper may also act as conduits for such credit, but it is by no means their sole, or even primary, function.

from government to the public enterprise sector, and that transfers from the sector to government comprised a gross return of y percent on the replacement value of public investment,[8] represent initial crude measures of the sector's fiscal impact.

Similarly, in analyzing monetary impact, one begins by computing the sector's net use of credit (loans outstanding to public enterprises less their deposits with financial institutions). Or in studying its impact on social objectives, one looks at whatever indices can be compiled with respect to sectoral employment; purchase of goods and services within a region, including the payroll; local share ownership; etc.

Decomposition of Nominal Parameters by Attribution to Commercial and Noncommercial Objectives

Execution of this second stage in the analysis is indispensable for drawing eventual policy conclusions. The essential task is one of estimating the portion, if any, of each component of public enterprise operating accounts which is attributable to the enterprises' following government directives in pursuit of noncommercial goals. The residual portion of each parameter is then regarded as corresponding to the enterprises' pursuit of commercial objectives, and it is these magnitudes that enter into indicators of the sector's intrinsic social efficiency.

The policy implications of this differentiation may be illustrated as follows: suppose it is established that the public enterprise sector in Country A over the past year contributed X (amount) to the government budget deficit and Y to credit expansion (X being included in, and normally less than Y); the portions of X and Y attributable to noncommercial and commercial objectives are estimated at X_1 and Y_1, and X_2 and Y_2, respectively. Suppose it is further estimated that the public enterprise sector must contribute amounts B and C to reduction of the budget deficit and credit expansion, respectively, in a given future period, for which the sector's contributions to the budget deficit and credit expansion are projected at X^* and Y^* in the absence of corrective measures, X_1^* and Y_1^* being accounted for by pursuit of noncommercial goals and X_2^* and Y_2^* by pursuit of commercial goals.

The policy issue then becomes one of deciding what proportions of B and C to achieve via one or more of three different routes: (1) improving the management of public enterprises; (2) reorganizing

---

[8] Calculating and applying the replacement value of capital assets involves a departure from nominal magnitudes; however, it falls short of adjusting the latter for social opportunity cost, which is allocated to stage 3 below.

the sector to enhance the role of commercial incentives (divestiture being only one of several possible approaches in this respect); and/or (3) modifying directives to public enterprises with respect to pursuit of noncommercial objectives.

It goes without saying that a comprehensive assessment of sectoral impact must encompass indicators of public enterprise performance in achieving the noncommercial objectives set for it as well as in achieving a satisfactory financial return on invested capital after making due allowance for costs and losses incurred in meeting those objectives. Appendix I discusses the noncommercial objectives and describes briefly some indicators that one might seek to measure in this connection.

The following list summarizes and categorizes government's noncommercial objectives in establishing and maintaining public enterprises, as discussed in Appendix I.

a. *Economic stabilization*

(1) Control of inflation;

(2) Food security; and

(3) Dampening economic downturns, with special reference to surges in unemployment.

b. *Economic growth*

(1) Expanding absolute levels of investment, output, exports, income, and employment; and

(2) Accelerating industrialization.

c. *Income redistribution*

(1) Promotion of small-scale producers through credit;

(2) Other approaches to vertical redistribution of income; and

(3) Geographical redistribution (promoting regional equity).

d. *Localization/indigenization*

(1) Supply sources;

(2) Asset ownership and control;

(3) Jobs; and

(4) National policymaking.

e. *Miscellaneous objectives*

Keeping in mind the distinction between commercial and noncommercial objectives helps one to deal with an ambiguity that arises in

referring to the "macroeconomic impact of the public enterprise sector." To many a casual listener this phrase would suggest the incremental impact on fiscal and monetary parameters of organizing a
certain set of economic activities around public enterprises as opposed
to placing them under private ownership and control. But insofar as
the evaluator is merely recording nominal parameters that characterize the entities making up the public enterprise sector, one is including effects, the proximate causes of which are government policies
vis-à-vis noncommercial objectives that could in many cases be applied
nearly as effectively, or perhaps even more effectively, to private
firms. In such cases, then, it is more precise to distinguish two different
macroeconomic impacts: (1) the impact of government policy in pursuit of noncommercial objectives X, Y, and Z as implemented through
the public enterprise sector; and (2) the impact of public enterprise
commercial operations as a reflection of the sector's intrinsic efficiency
in generating value added through manipulation of productive factors.[9]

Adjustment of Nominal Parameters for Implicit Taxes and Subsidies

In this stage the analysis takes account of the fact that market or
controlled prices frequently overstate or understate social opportunity
costs, the latter being inflated by implicit taxes or deflated by implicit
subsidies before coming to light as nominal or accounting magnitudes.
An analysis aspiring to measure the impact of the public enterprise
sector in real terms must thus adjust the observed values for these
implicit transfers.

For example, the discussion below in "The Fiscal Impact of the
Public Enterprise Sector" examines in some detail the argument that
the public enterprise sector in mixed economies rarely covers the full
social opportunity cost of the public capital invested in it. In an opportunity cost sense, real operating outlays are thus higher than nominal costs, and the discrepancy between accounting and real operating
profit is covered by an implicit government subsidy.

Likewise, a public utility or other natural monopoly that is allowed
to charge prices above levels that would cover the full social opportunity costs of production of an entity operating at an efficiency level
considered reasonable by the appropriate authorities is collecting an

---

[9] Methodological considerations associated with netting out the financial impact of
pursuit of noncommercial objectives by public enterprises are discussed in Section V
in the subsection, "The Fiscal Impact of the Public Enterprise Sector."

implicit tax from consumers. If the entity's actual costs correspond to the aforementioned "reasonably" efficient level, then the government's pricing policy is allowing it a return in excess of capital opportunity cost; and if the excess return is being transferred to government (via dividends, excess profits tax, or some other mechanism), then the implicit tax proceeds are accruing to government. Conversely, if the entity is absorbing the proceeds, either as retained profit or by operating inefficiently and incurring unreasonable costs, then the implicit tax is accompanied by an implicit subsidy to the enterprise.

Adjustment procedures are explored in greater detail below in "The Fiscal Impact of the Public Enterprise Sector."

Comparison of Adjusted Parameters with Criterion Values (Partial Equilibrium Approach)

In this next-to-last stage, one takes the leap into normative analysis, comparing adjusted public enterprise sector parameters with criterion values as a basis for judging whether the former are "adequate," or conversely as a basis for identifying measures that should be taken to "improve" them. The comparison makes sense only after the parameters have been decomposed and adjusted as per the two preceding subsections. With respect to the attribution between commercial and noncommercial objectives, analysts adhering to the present paper's emphasis on the intrinsic social efficiency of public enterprise as a producer of goods and services will focus on comparisons featuring the parameter values attributable to public enterprise commercial operations. The criterion values may be historical values for the public enterprise sector itself; they may be measures of analogous parameters for a set of private firms; they may be based on international comparative data; or they may represent merely theoretical norms.

For example, one may ask whether the public enterprise sector's commercial operations, reflected in parameter values from which the impact of supplemental costs and/or revenue losses attributable to pursuit of noncommercial objectives has been netted out, are generating more or less before-tax profit now, per unit of value added or capital stock valued at replacement cost, than they did five years ago; or how these ratios compare with analogous ones for private firms.

The single most prevalent criterion value for assessing the commercial performance of public enterprise in a partial equilibrium framework is zero profitability, with adjusted revenues covering the social opportunity costs of all inputs and productive factors including capital. (Such a position is sometimes described as one of "normal" profitability, with "supernormal" profits absent.) Capital comprises, of course, not only the stock of fixed capital valued at replacement cost but also inventories and other working capital, whose importance normally exceeds that of fixed capital in the case of enterprises engaged primarily in marketing.[10]

Consistency requires that if capital is to be valued at its social opportunity cost, then so also must labor. For those subscribing to the doctrine of a near-zero social opportunity cost of unskilled labor in economies or localities afflicted by severe unemployment or underemployment this opens up the possibility of discounting a sizable portion of public enterprise wage bills. On the other hand, analysts concerned about fiscal and monetary stability will justifiably incline to approaches that stress the disutility of effort and/or the benefits obtainable via potential alternative uses of resources devoted to enhancing the consumption of public enterprise employees. According to these approaches, endorsed by the present paper, downward adjustment of public enterprise wage and salary bills to account for divergence of social opportunity cost from market rates should not exceed a small fraction reflecting generation of tax payments via the workers' consumption expenditure.

Use of the zero profitability criterion value reflects an implicit comparison with a private-sector, free-market standard, on the presumption of neoclassical theory that private firms operating under conditions of pure competition exactly cover their opportunity costs, with subnormal profits leading to exit of firms and supernormal profits attracting new entrants. Similarly, according to theory, firms of apparent high profitability that persist in that state are in fact merely compensating for risks, covering the opportunity cost of extraordinary entrepreneurial skills, or earning scarcity rents attributable to factors such as favorable location.

The preoccupation with public enterprise operating deficits in many analyses dealing with problems of the sector reflects a tacit, if not explicit, acceptance of the zero profitability norm. (On the other hand, given pressures of time and the absence of information, most studies rarely distinguish the components of public enterprise parameters attributable to pursuit of commercial and noncommercial objectives.)

Apart from looking at commercial performance, one may also compare the efficacy of the public enterprise sector with standard indices, however determined, as a vehicle for government pursuit of the noncommercial objectives listed above under "Decomposition of Nominal

---

[10] The opposite adjustment applies with respect to the value of construction in progress and investment still in the start-up phase, which should be excluded from capital stock for purposes of applying this criterion.

Parameters by Attribution to Commercial and Noncommercial Objectives."

Comparison of Adjusted Parameters with Putative/ Simulated Outcomes of Baseline Alternatives (General Equilibrium Approach)

Normative evaluation of the public enterprise sector's macro-economic impact culminates in this stage, where the attempt is made to estimate the net impact of sector operations on key economic and social parameters as compared with the operations of an assumed baseline industrial organization. Here is where such ultimate questions are posed as: how much more (or less) is the government budget deficit, given the public enterprise sector as it operates today, than it would have been had the baseline situation prevailed? How much have public enterprise operations contributed to money supply, inflation, and the cost of borrowing, as compared with levels that would have prevailed in the baseline situation? How much more (or less) employment is there; how much greater (or smaller) is the Gini coefficient of income inequality than it would have been; and how much more (or less) disposable income is generated in disadvantaged regions?

To the extent these questions can be answered, the analyst will have succeeded in measuring both types of macroeconomic impact identified on page 46. That is, he or she will know how effective the public enterprise sector is, compared with the assumed baseline industrial organization, as society's agent in implementing noncommercial objectives; and an index of the comparative efficiency of its commercial operations will have been obtained.

The key problem with conducting this kind of analysis, of course, is the heroic assumptions one must make about the baseline situation. What kind of government policy does one assume? In lieu of establishing public enterprises outside the standard core of power, water supply, posts and telecommunications, the railroad, national airline, etc., should one assume that government would have adopted an entirely passive approach to industrial development? To what extent (or under what circumstances that must be further assumed) would the market have stepped in and created economic activity to fill the putative vacuum left by governmental abstention? What would have been the fiscal and monetary consequences of the alternative private sector expansion (or nonexpansion)?

There can be no unambiguous answers to these questions; rather, the analyst must model one or more baseline alternatives, making the assumptions explicit, and compare the actual outcome, given the public enterprise sector as it functioned in the real world, with the outcome predicted on the basis of those assumptions. It is highly desirable that economists in governments making substantial use of public enterprise should conduct such exercises. Given the complexity and, in most countries, novelty of the approach, this is an area in which staff economists in international development institutions could provide strategic help. Yet so value-laden are the assumptions underlying the various alternative models that one imagines only with difficulty an IMF or World Bank staff report undertaking to lay out a comprehensive baseline alternative with which the performance of Country A's public enterprise sector should be compared and the sector's net impact on fiscal, monetary, and social aggregates assessed.

* * * * * * * * * * *

Following the methodological discussion in this section, the remainder of this paper focuses on specific indicators of the public enterprise sector's macroeconomic impact. The organization of the remaining segments reflects in part the logical progression of the five stages above and in part a focus emphasizing fiscal and monetary stabilization over economic growth and the efficiency of public investment.

V. EVALUATING ECONOMIC AGGREGATES OF THE PUBLIC ENTERPRISE SECTOR

The three subsections of this section will examine as many different categories of economic aggregates:

1. Summary accounts of the public enterprise sector;

2. Indicators of fiscal impact; and

3. Indicators of monetary impact.

Summary Accounts of the Public Enterprise Sector

This subsection considers the estimation of the public enterprise sector's shares in national product, investment, savings, and capital stock, along with various measures of its resource balance vis-à-vis the rest of the economy.

Aggregation of standard accounting magnitudes across the sector as a whole, differentiated by industrial groupings, or, if useful for policymaking, a few large enterprises, constitutes the first step in constructing these macroeconomic indicators. Details of the format will vary among countries with different accounting systems, but the basic elements entering into the computation of the national income accounts should be present. The most severe obstacles to preparation of accounting aggregates arise because (1) in many countries public enterprises have varying financial years, and (2) the uniform standards and formats (if any) prescribed for public enterprise accounting have rarely been refined to a sufficient level of detail to remove variations in procedure.

Table 1 illustrates a consolidated public enterprise account for the West African nation of Mali, a country falling well within the United Nations "least developed" category whose government is nonetheless, as regards production of this type of data, a long jump ahead of many featuring per capita incomes several times as high.[11]

The aggregates of primary interest from the viewpoint of the national income accounts may be grouped under three headings, as is done in Table 2, defining the public enterprise sector's shares in national product, investment, and saving, respectively. Also of interest, particularly for purposes of cross-country comparison, as per the following paper by R.P. Short, are the ratios of the respective public enterprise parameters to GDP.

The aggregates lend themselves to various manipulations with a view to assessing the resource balance between the public enterprise sector and the rest of the economy. Beginning with the national income parameters, the ratio of public enterprise savings (gross) to investment measures the share of capital expenditure that is internally financed; subtracted from unity it gives the share of public enterprise investment financed by the rest of the economy and the outside world.

A first approximation to overall resource balance is given by the sector's gross expenditure, current (excluding depreciation) plus capital, less sales; since the subtraction nets out intrasectoral transactions these do not have to be estimated. Looking at the resource balance from varying points of view, one might want to examine a variant where the deficit is reduced by adding nongovernment capital transfers to sales, on the ground that capital resources which the public enterprise sector attracts competitively from the private sector represent less of a "burden" on the rest of the economy. In some cases a further reduction by expanding revenues to include current government transfers could be justified on the supposition that these

---

[11] The format of the financial statements is modeled after Table 2 in a May 15, 1980, office memorandum to staff of the Fund's Fiscal Affairs Department by then Department head Richard Goode, entitled "Nonfinancial Public Enterprises." Modifications in that format and the source of the Mali data are described in notes to the table.

Table 1. Consolidated Financial Statements, Public Enterprise Sector, Mali, 1976

(In millions of Mali francs)

A. Profit and Loss Statement

1. Value of production
   a. Turnover — 97,704
   b. *less:* Indirect taxes — −10,247
   c. *plus:* Subsidies — 0
   d. *equals:* Operating Income (if any) — =87,457
   e. *plus:* Change in stock of finished goods/work in progress — +1,032
   f. *equals:* Value of production — =88,489
2. Operating expenditure
   a. Use of purchased goods and services — 73,070
   b. Wages and salaries — 7,144
   c. Depreciation and other provisions — 4,662
   d. Subtotal — 84,876
3. Operating surplus [1(f) − 2(d)] — 3,613
4. Interest — 3,229
5. Operating surplus less interest before tax (3-4) — 384
6. Direct taxes — 2,948
7. Operating surplus less interest after tax (5-6) — −2,564

B. Sources and Applications of Funds Statement

1. Sources of funds
   a. Depreciation and other provisions — 4,662
   b. Net profit after tax (if any) — [see 2(a)i]
   c. New government equity contributions — 3,029
   d. Borrowing (net of repayments)
      (i) Long- and medium-term — 3,203
      (ii) Short-term — 15,526
      (iii) Subtotal — 18,729
2. Applications of funds
   a. Current
      (i) Net loss after tax (if any) — 4,136
      (ii) Miscellaneous current applications — 2,437
      (iii) Subtotal — 6,573
   b. Long-term
      (i) Fixed investment — 7,475

C. Balance Sheet (December 31, 1976)

1. Liabilities
   a. Net worth (paid-up equity) — 21,882
   b. Borrowings and other liabilities
      (i) Long-term — 19,682
      (ii) Short-term — 75,405
      (iii) Subtotal — 95,087
2. Assets
   a. Gross fixed assets — 63,335
   b. *less:* Accumulated depreciation — −24,389
   c. *equals:* Net fixed assets — 38,946
   d. Other long-term assets — 12,247
   e. Current assets
      (i) Inventories — 36,326
      (ii) Receivables, loans, advances — 24,345
      (iii) Other current assets — 5,105
      (iv) Subtotal — 65,776
3. Total net assets = liabilities — 116,969

8. Nonoperating income and expenditure		
a. Nonoperating income	1,349	
b. Nonoperating expenditure	2,921	
c. Net nonoperating income (a-b)	-1,572	
9. Net profit after tax [7 + 8(c)]	-4,136	
(ii) Other long-term		
(iii) Subtotal	1,759	9,234
c. Short-term		
(i) Change in inventories	-2,135	
(ii) Change in receivables, loans and advances	+11,714	
(iii) Change in other current assets	+1,034	
(iv) Subtotal		10,613
3. Total sources = applications		26,420

D. Operational indicators

1. Net worth/total net assets = 21,882/116,969 = 18.7 percent
2. Inventories/operating income = 36,326/87,457 = 41.5 percent
3. Operating surplus less interest before tax/operating income = 384/87,457 = 0.4 percent
4. Debt/equity = 95,087/21,882 = 4.34
5. Return (operating surplus) on total net assets = 3,613/116,969 = 3.1 percent

Source: Republic of Mali, Ministère de Tutelle des Sociétés et Entreprises d'Etat, Analyse de la Situation Financière du Secteur d'Etat au 31 Décembre 1976, Bamako, October 1977, Tables 5, 11, and 14.

The format of these financial statements is modeled on that of Richard Goode, "Nonfinancial Public Enterprises," Appendix I, Table 2, "Financial Analysis of Operations of NPEs," IMF Fiscal Affairs Department, May 15, 1980 (unpublished). Major departures from Goode's format are: (1) introduction of turnover and indirect taxes as determinants of operating income; (2) relabeling of item A(2)a, "use of purchased goods and services;" (3) placement of nonoperating income and expenditure following computation of after-tax operating profit; and (4) introduction of sources and applications of funds statement.

The source of the Malian data does not provide a basis for distinguishing depreciation and other provisions, nor for interpreting item 2(a)ii, miscellaneous current applications ("contributions diverses"), which presumably contains any dividend payments or redemption of government equity. Clarification of these items would be desirable for subsequent economic interpretation of the accounts (cf. Table 2).

Table 2. Computation, Based on Enterprises' Financial Statements, of the Public Enterprise Sector's Share in National Product, Investment, and Saving

Table 1 Terminology	Equivalent According to United Nations[1]
A. *Public enterprise sector's share in national product*	
Wages and salaries	Compensation of employees (including employer contributions to social security pensions, insurance, etc.)
Operating surplus	Operating surplus
Depreciation	Consumption of fixed capital
plus: Indirect taxes *less:* Subsidies	Indirect taxes, net of subsidies
Total (= value added)	Total = GDP at purchasers' values[2] *less* consumption of fixed capital = Net domestic product (NDP) at purchasers' values[2] or: *less* indirect taxes, net = GDP at factor incomes[3] or: *less* consumption of fixed capital *and* indirect taxes, net = NDP at factor incomes[3]
B. *Public enterprise sector's share in investment*	
Fixed investment	Fixed capital formation
Change in inventories	Increase in stocks Total = gross capital formation *less* consumption of fixed capital = net capital formation
C. *Public enterprise sector's share in saving*	
Depreciation	Consumption of fixed capital
Operating surplus less interest after tax (less dividends, if any)	Retained income Total = gross saving[4]

[1] United Nations, Statistical Office, *A System of National Accounts* (New York, 1968).
[2] Conventionally referred to as GDP at market prices.
[3] Conventionally referred to as GDP at factor cost.
[4] The United Nations publication reserves the term "saving" for retained income. This study favors the concept of "gross saving" inclusive of depreciation to maintain the validity of the national income accounting identity: investment − saving = imports − exports, wherever investment is treated on a gross basis, as is customary in developing economies.

compensate for services the public enterprise sector provides in pursuing government's noncommercial objectives.

Also of interest is the public enterprise sector's current balance; to arrive at this one might begin with an operating balance, given by sales revenue less expenditure on noncapital goods and services, then add receipts of current transfers to the revenue side and interest, dividend and direct tax payments to the expenditure side. Variants including and excluding depreciation may be calculated to distinguish between the sector's real and financial balance.[12]

Two major adjustments are required to convert public enterprise sector aggregates obtained from financial accounts into magnitudes that reflect social opportunity cost. First, the application of depreciation rates determined for tax purposes to historical investment cost is a poor guide to the annual charge that should be made against output to express the cost of maintaining existing productive capacity. Even a revalued capital stock reflecting current replacement cost is an imprecise measure of productive capacity under conditions of rapid technological change. Still, given even the lowest inflation rates prevalent today, it constitutes an economically more significant base for computing depreciation than does historical cost; and construction of any alternative would be subject to debate and uncertainty. Altering tax-based depreciation rates to accord with asset lives that reflect current rates of obsolescence compensates for part of the imprecision associated with any cost-based estimates of capital stock.

Upward adjustment of depreciation/consumption of fixed capital does not affect the computation of value added/GDP or gross saving, since it is offset one-for-one by reduction of another component of value added and saving, namely, before-tax profit/operating surplus (or by increased losses); however, it widens the gap between gross and net measures of output and investment.

The second major adjustment required is to recompute before-tax profit/operating surplus by revaluing at border prices plus indirect taxes all tradable goods and services sold and purchased by the public enterprise sector. When applied in the computation of manufacturing sector GDP in countries that are establishing high-cost import-substituting industries behind high protective barriers, this adjustment has the effect of reducing the sector's share of GDP by several percentage points. In not a few industries, it converts a respectable value-added figure, derived from the financial accounts, into a negative sum (i.e., the industry earns or saves less foreign exchange than it consumes via current inputs and utilization of investment goods and services). In many countries, the adjustment will likewise create negative value added in some public enterprises and significantly reduce the sector's share of total GDP.

Of no less interest than the public enterprise sector's share in annual investment flows is the value of its capital stock. This is essential for

---

[12] Each variant of resource balance described in these two paragraphs is computed on an internationally comparative basis by R.P. Short in the following paper.

determining, inter alia, the implicit capital subsidy as part of the public enterprise sector's fiscal impact. (See the discussion in the "Fiscal Impact of the Public Enterprise Sector," below.)

Computation of capital stock is perhaps the most complex of the statistical exercises involved in tabulating aggregates of the public enterprise sector. But in light of the critical role of this parameter in public enterprise performance evaluation, it is appropriate for international agencies to try to sensitize governments to its significance, and urge that local staff resources be devoted to measuring it and keeping the measure up-to-date. A primary component of updating is, of course, annual revaluation to compensate for inflation.

One of the major problems in estimating capital stock is how to take inflation into account in computing depreciation. Appendix II outlines a procedure for this based on the perpetual inventory method, which enables one to build up the capital stock estimate from constant-price investment series (using prices of the year whose annual flows are being analyzed), additional parameters being the asset lives of major capital goods categories and the growth rates of capital stock and value added over an initial period when the two rates can be assumed to be approximately equal.

The constant-price investment series should in turn be adjusted for divergences of nominal prices of capital assets from social opportunity cost. Perhaps the most prevalent cause of downward divergence is overvaluation of the exchange rate, sometimes involving maintenance of a multitiered rate structure giving preference to capital goods imports, especially those of public agencies.

A divergence in the opposite direction arises where investment is financed by foreign capital inflow that is tied to a particular activity, such that its opportunity cost is the reverse flow of service payments rather than benefits arising from an alternative use should the activity in question not be carried out. This divergence is also discussed in Appendix II, along with a suggested approach to correcting for it.

In conclusion, once the national income and capital stock aggregates for the public enterprise sector or subsets of it have been computed in absolute terms, it is a simple matter to calculate them as proportions of GDP or (with respect to savings and investment) as proportions of the national or subsectoral totals of the variables in question. These coefficients begin to have policy significance—for example, the statement that Country A's public enterprise sector accounted for 60 percent of gross capital formation in 1982, in the context of other evidence about the economy, may suggest either that Country A's investment and growth would have been very much less without the leading role played by the sector or, conversely, that the sector appears to be crowding out private investment. Even greater policy significance attaches to findings that internally generated resources (depreciation and retained earnings) of the sector in question covered, say, 20 percent of its investment expenditure, meaning that 80 percent had to be provided by government and the private sector; that the sector's aggregate deficit vis-à-vis the rest of the economy amounted to 5 percent of GDP; or that it ran a current surplus equivalent to 2 percent of GDP.

Fiscal Impact of the Public Enterprise Sector

Under this heading, the paper takes as its point of departure financial flows between government and the public enterprise sector, excluding from the analysis only payments at fair market value—or, in the absence of competition, social opportunity cost of production— for goods and services rendered. For purposes of subsectoral analysis, flows within the public enterprise sector are also taken into account, although these cancel each other out when the sector as a whole is examined in relation to government. The following categories of flows are listed, classified as accounting magnitudes or implicit transfers, and then examined individually:

Flows from the public enterprise sector to government

Taxes and royalties.

Increase of arrears in government payment for goods and services.

Payments of return on investment:
   a. Interest; and
   b. Dividends.

Redemption of capital:
   a. Amortization of government loans; and
   b. Redemption of equity.

Lending to government by nonfinancial public enterprises.

Expenses and revenue losses arising from pursuit of noncommercial objectives.

Discrepancy between fair market value—in the absence of competition, social opportunity cost of production—and actual prices paid by government.

Flows from government to the public enterprise sector

Purchase of equity.

Debt transactions:
   a. Lending by government;

  b. Increase in arrears of tax payments to government; and
  c. Repayment of government borrowings from public enterprise
      sector.

Interest on government borrowings.

Unrequited transfers to the public enterprise sector.

Tax subsidies:
  a. Implicit tax revenue retained by public enterprises; and
  b. Conventional tax subsidies.

Capital subsidy.

Flows within the public enterprise sector

  Purchase of equity.

  Debt transactions.

  Payments of return on investment.

  Cross-subsidies, notably provision of goods and services below fair
      market value or, in the absence of competition, social opportunity
      cost.

Fair market value of payments for goods and services may be defined as the mean price prevailing in arm's length transactions of
comparable scale during the relevant period; to the extent that government purchasers are exempt from payment of sales and excise
taxes and the like, it should be measured net of these. Payments at
other than fair market value involve implicit subsidies in one direction
or the other that must be taken into account in drawing up the fiscal
balance. Without competition to define fair market value, the presence
of subsidies would be signaled by prices diverging from the social
opportunity cost of production of the goods and services in question.
Estimation of either fair market value or social opportunity cost within
an acceptable margin of uncertainty may, of course, involve substantial
effort.

An ultimate measure of fiscal impact is the net balance of all relevant
flows. The most obvious criterion value for assessing sectoral performance in this connection is zero—that is, if there is a net flow
from the public enterprise sector to government, one may say the
sector's fiscal impact is positive; a net flow in the opposite direction
signifies a negative impact; and if flows in both directions cancel out,
one may say the impact is neutral.

In general, however, this naive approach has limited policy significance. For example, the flow of investment capital from government
to the public enterprise sector in a given year will be heavily influenced
by the public investment program being implemented at that time,

the optimal composition of which has little to do with the factors that influence the reverse flows of taxes and returns on previous investment. Moreover, the flow of capital from government is sensitive to the preferences of capital sources for lending directly to public enterprises as opposed to two-stage lending through government.

Accordingly, this paper classifies the flows into various categories and manipulates them to obtain indicators that can be compared with appropriate criterion values. Flows from the public enterprise sector to government are listed in the subsection below, those from government to the public enterprise sector on page 68. The first part of each of these subsections lists flows that comprise accounting magnitudes available in financial reports, while the flows described in the second part, corresponding to the second and third stages of analysis outlined in Section IV above, consist of implicit values requiring estimation.

The subsection "Financial Flows Within the Public Enterprise Sector," deals briefly with flows between public enterprises, particularly cross-subsidies. A final subsection, the "Fiscal Impact of the Public Enterprise Sector: Conclusion," summarizes the components of the fiscal balance, both accounting magnitudes and implicit values, in tabular form.

An assumption underlying the presentation is that computation of any indicator bearing on the commercial efficiency of public enterprise, and in particular any indicator on which public enterprise performance is to be compared with that of the private sector, has adjusted all relevant parameters for costs and revenue losses attributable to pursuit of noncommercial objectives.

Financial Flows from the Public Enterprise Sector to Government

Accounting Magnitudes

Taxes and royalties. This heading deals with the following indicators (throughout this section, the superscript P refers to the public enterprise sector, the superscript F to the private sector, and the subscript t to a year):

$TAX_{i,t}$ = total government receipts from tax/tax category i in year t;

$TAX_{i,t}^{P}$ and $TAX_{i,t}^{F}$ = payments by the public enterprise and private sectors, respectively, of tax/tax category i in year t (category 1 representing direct taxes);

$\dot{p}$ = rate of price inflation from year $t-1$ to year t;

PRF_t^P and PRF_t^F = accounting profits of the two sectors in year t; and

VAL_t^P and VAL_t^F = value added in the two sectors in year t.

The indicators are:[13]

$\dfrac{TAX_{i,t}^P}{TAX_{i,t}}$ = public enterprise sector's proportional share in total government receipts from tax/tax category i in year t.

$\dfrac{TAX_{i,t}^P}{TAX_{i,t}} - \dfrac{TAX_{i,t-1}^P}{TAX_{i,t-1}}$ = change in that share from year $t-1$ to year t.

$\dfrac{TAX_{i,t}^P - TAX_{i,t-1}^P}{TAX_{i,t-1}^P}$ = proportional change in nominal tax payments of public enterprise sector.

$\dfrac{TAX_{i,t}^P/(1 + \dot{p}) - TAX_{i,t-1}^P}{TAX_{i,t-1}^P}$ = real proportional change in sectoral tax payments.

$\dfrac{TAX_{1,t}^P}{PRF_t^P} \Big/ \dfrac{TAX_{1,t}^F}{PRF_t^F}$ = proportional comparison of ratio of direct tax payments in year t to accounting profit as between public enterprise and private sectors.

$\dfrac{TAX_{i,t}^P}{VAL_t^P} \Big/ \dfrac{TAX_{i,t}^F}{VAL_t^F}$ = proportional comparison of ratio of tax payments to value added between public enterprise and private sectors.

Later in this section, it will be indicated how the comparison of TAX/PRF ratios (tax payments as a proportion of accounting profit) may lead to imputation of an implicit tax subsidy to the public enterprise sector.

Tax categories (subscript i) whose coefficients one might wish to scrutinize under this heading include (i) direct taxes (comprising company/corporation income taxes, excess profits tax, payroll taxes, land and real estate taxes, licenses); (ii) taxes on domestically consumed goods and services other than import duties, sales and excise taxes, which are excluded here—first, because the same or larger amounts could be collected from final consumers if the commodities were imported in finished form and, second, because their point of collection is arbitrary (import duties could be collected from private importers and included in prices charged to public enterprises, and excises could be collected from private retailers, in both of which cases public enterprise tax payments would be correspondingly lower for institu-

---

[13] All indicators relating values in different time periods are assumed to be computed net of the effects of any discretionary tax rate changes.

tional reasons having nothing to do with operating efficiency); and (iii) export taxes and royalties on natural resource-based exports.

Increase in arrears of government payments for goods and services supplied by public enterprise. (Decrease = −.) This item, denoted ARR_t^P, could also be classified with public enterprise sector loans to government (subsection, "Lending to government by nonfinancial public enterprises," below). One can define several ratios as indicators of the public enterprise sector's exposure under conditions of fiscal stringency. For example, ARR_t^P/DEF_t denotes the proportion of the year t government deficit financed by increased arrears to public enterprises; and ARR_t^P/SAL_t^P represents the proportion of sales to government not compensated by timely payment, compared with the analogous ratio for the private sector, ARR_t^F/SAL_t^F.

Payments of return on investment. The key items here are:

INT_t^P = interest payments on government loans to public enterprises; and
DIV_t^P = dividend payments on government equity investment in the sector.

The point of departure in analyzing such payments is to compare them with the value of the investment on which they are earned. The obvious criterion value for the nominal return is unity plus the year's inflation rate, times the difference between the annualized social opportunity cost of the public capital employed by the public enterprise sector and its direct tax payments (tax payments are subtracted, because social opportunity cost, based on the social discount rate used in benefit-cost analysis of public investments, is computed gross of these whereas interest and dividend payments, of course, exclude them).

The objection may be interposed here that determination of the appropriate discount rate by which to compute social opportunity cost of use of public resources is subject to a considerable margin of uncertainty, and arguments are advanced for widely differing values. On the other hand, the consensus of modern social opportunity cost theorists is that the low rate of social time preference by virtue of which society collectively sets aside a much greater proportion of available resources to benefit future generations than the average citizen would agree to independently is not an appropriate discount rate for government expenditure.

The vast majority of estimates focusing on returns available from application of public capital to expenditure opportunities available at the margin yield values ranging from 10 percent to 20 percent in real terms (net of inflation). Since few public enterprises in mixed economies yield anything approaching such returns to their governments on commercial operations alone, the thrust of public enterprise evaluation against the criterion value in question is clear and a few percentage points of uncertainty in the social discount rate do not alter the conclusion that the public enterprise sector in most countries enjoys a hefty capital subsidy.[14]

The ideal measure of the capital stock to which the social discount rate is applied for purposes of calculating annualized opportunity cost is the net present value of the stream of social benefits obtainable from the assets in question under conditions of "normal" efficiency. Historical cost, even when inflated as a proxy for replacement cost, is only a rough index of this ideal measure, which treats all past investment as a sunk cost. There is much to be said for it in theory, but its estimation across the public enterprise sector as a whole poses insuperable problems. A more practicable candidate for denominator in the rate of return calculation, notwithstanding the major computational effort involved, is the constant-price value of the public enterprise sector's capital stock computed according to the methodology outlined in Appendix II. As noted in the subsection on the "Comparison of Adjusted Parameters with Criterion Values," above, for use in the present context, capital stock is computed gross of working capital (mean level during the period in question) and net of construction in progress or investment still in a start-up phase.

Specifically with regard to government equity investment, it could be argued that the criterion value for comparison with return on investment should include an element of compensation for the risk and uncertainty associated therewith. Opposing this would be the consideration that, particularly in the current inflationary environment, an equity investor expects part of his return by way of capital appreciation; hence, not even the most demanding finance minister would call for dividend payments corresponding to the full opportunity cost of government's equity.

This argument does not apply to loan capital. However, nominal financial charges that governments impose on their public enterprises are almost invariably below the social discount rate plus inflation, owing in large part to a widespread conception that one accelerates development by charging entities that carry out socially "desirable" activities less than they would have to pay to borrow on the open market, particularly considering the risk premium that the market

---

[14] Most countries have been the object of multiple efforts to estimate social discount rates, by staff of one or another creditor agency, technical assistance personnel, and local planners. In most cases there should be no difficulty in assembling a "consensus range" or mean of alternative estimates, and using such values for rough computations of social opportunity cost.

would have to collect from many of the activities in question. Thus, direct loans to public enterprises from government treasuries, as well as loans from government-controlled development banks and other financial intermediaries, more often than not carry nominal interest rates that are below the inflation rate and, hence, are negative in real terms.[15]

In most developing countries this picture is not confined to government-run credit facilities, since government regulation of the private financial sector holds nominal interest rates in the formal money market below levels that would prevail under competition, which one would expect to compensate for inflation and risk while approximating the real social opportunity cost of capital.

Flows to developing countries from public credit institutions likewise contain subsidy elements ranging up to and even exceeding 90 percent in the case of long-term (up to 50-year), low-interest (below 1 percent or even zero) loans when service obligations are discounted by anticipated export price inflation plus a real capital opportunity cost of 10 percent or more. Such institutions generally require that portion of their assistance destined for commercial-type activities of public enterprises to be on-lent by the host government on "economic" terms, but the outcome of a bargaining process in which most recipient governments (and, of course, the participating enterprises) strive to keep the on-lending terms relatively soft is normally an effective interest rate well below the social discount rate.

Flows from private foreign lenders usually carry terms much closer to the domestic opportunity cost of capital, however, even in this case, the following caveats apply: (1) such loans, particularly the subcategory of supplier credits, sometimes carry a hidden subsidy in the form of source government guarantees that soften the terms of repayment; (2) a portion of the true financing cost is sometimes hidden in inflated prices of capital equipment acquired under other than international competitive bidding arrangements; and (3) it is in this category that one most frequently encounters nonfungible transfers, altering the cost calculus as described in Appendix II. (Asset purchase costs are deducted from the value of capital stock, and annual interest and dividend payments are added to the product of the social discount rate times the residual capital stock.)

In conclusion, there is no mixed economy whose public enterprise

---

[15] It is appropriate to enter the caveat here that a fixed interest rate of, say, 12 percent or above on a long-term loan becomes a real burden as the rate of price inflation of the goods and services an enterprise sells to meet its debt service obligations drops toward zero. One supposes that most public enterprises will have access to means of refinancing their debt at lower terms under such circumstances.

sector would not display a substantial shortfall against the proposed criterion value.

Perusal of budgets and investment programs over a number of years in several countries reveals that early optimism about the proportion of these that could be financed out of cash returns on government's investment in public enterprises has faded. Today it is the rare national treasury that finances more than a trivial proportion of its investment budget from this source, other than via dividend payments more appropriately classified as royalties on natural resource-based output.

This suggests, as a second indicator with respect to cash returns on government investment in public enterprises, a comparison between actual outturn of $INT_t^P + DIV_t^P$ and planned or budgeted values, $INT_t^{P*} + DIV_t^{P*}$, suitably inflated to current prices. The latter figures may be available in summary form in annual budget and/or multiyear plan documents.

A related concept that applies to loan investment only is a comparison between the outturn of INT_t^P and the sum of products of loan balances outstanding times the respective contractual interest rates. Any discrepancy represents default of interest owed to government by the public enterprise sector.

Regardless of how far interest and dividend payments to government fall below the social opportunity cost criterion value, it may still make sense to examine a time series of the proportion that government is recovering in cash out of the annualized cost of its investment in the public enterprise sector. A marked trend upward or downward might be considered significant with respect to the authorities' diligence or lack thereof in imposing financial discipline on the sector.

It is worth repeating here that the present conceptual framework stops short of prescribing remedies for shortcomings in public enterprise performance, and specifically with regard to payments of return on investment, it does not advise that every government should as fast as possible reorganize its public enterprise sector to cover the full opportunity cost of past investment. Depending on factors specific to a given country, it may well be that social goals would best be served by, in effect, writing off much or all past investment in public enterprise while stiffening the criteria for approval of new investment proposals. Indeed many countries, both developing and industrial, are at one or another stage of implementing such a policy, and many are being supported in that direction by their international creditors. It is nevertheless the paper's thesis that evaluation of sectoral performance hitherto is a valid if not exclusive criterion for assessing the sector's likely contribution to achievement of macroeconomic policy objectives in future, and that measurement of current returns on past investment is a major component of such evaluation.

Redemption of capital. Under this heading, the following terms are defined:

AMR_t^P = amortization payments in year t on government loans to public enterprises; and

RED_t^P = transfers in redemption of government's equity investment in the sector.

The second of these terms represents a comparatively rare phenomenon, as the movement is overwhelmingly in the opposite direction—government increasing its equity (or providing outright grants in lieu of equity) either to assist in expansion or to cover operating deficits. Where an enterprise's cash flow would permit it to redeem shares without prejudice to financing its own socially beneficial expansion, most governments are inclined to channel the surplus into their own debt instruments or to tax it away via royalties, excess profits tax, etc.

Two indicators suggest themselves with respect to amortization of loan capital: first, a comparison of outturn with contractual obligations—payment arrears being represented by a negative result, $AMR_t^P - AMR_t^{P*} < 0$—suggests problems of cash flow, lax financial discipline, and the like. Second, the presence of significant discrepancies between AMR_t^P and depreciation allowances on account of the facilities financed by the public loans in question indicates either financing of medium- to long-term investments with excessively short-term capital or, conversely, a preferential arrangement that gives the borrowing enterprises financial leeway to increase investment out of cash flow or incur operating deficits. Either finding suggests an irregularity with respect to conventional standards; however, either practice may also be justified under special circumstances.

Lending to government by nonfinancial public enterprises. It is appropriate here to distinguish between medium- and long-term lending on the one hand, and purchases of treasury bills and other short-term instruments on the other hand as a component of normal liquidity management. To be sure, to any given program of medium-term and long-term lending mandated by government there will always be a corresponding equivalent rate of increase in purchase of short-term instruments, maintained over an adequate period of time.

Lending to government, denoted by LND_t^P, suggests no special indicator other than the fact that a significant positive value means one of two things: either (1) certain components of the sector, from which we exclude financial institutions for purposes of this heading, are in a cash surplus position that enables them to help finance other government programs, or else (2) fiscal stringency has led government, after exhausting the resources of the financial sector, to compel public enterprises to buy its bonds or otherwise lend to it against their commercial interest.

Case (1) may raise a question as to whether government should not be appropriating the surplus through special levies in lieu of indebting itself with the public enterprise sector. Alternatively, it may be a matter of particularly creditworthy enterprises, such as petroleum producers, mining concerns, or electric power and telecommunications companies, borrowing abroad in excess of the residual of their investment needs less internal cash flow; here, it often makes economic sense for the enterprise to go ahead and borrow as much as it can, meanwhile investing the surplus in general government obligations.

Implicit Transfers

Two items deserve mention under implicit financial transfers from the public enterprise sector to government.

Expenses and revenue losses arising from pursuit of noncommercial objectives. $EXP_{i,t}^P$ denotes the expense or revenue loss incurred by the public enterprise sector in year t as a result of pursuing, by government directive (explicit or implied), a given noncommercial objective, represented by the subscript i (see list on page 45 which is amplified in Appendix I).

A host of methodological issues arise in measuring the financial burden of pursuing noncommercial objectives. How to estimate prices that would have prevailed in the absence of inflation control measures? How to measure optimum food stocks from a commercial viewpoint, as opposed to stocks held on government directive to ensure an extra margin of security? What are the extra costs of a crash industrialization program initiated by government, as compared with the baseline investment program that the pre-existing public enterprise sector would have carried out in accordance with commercial objectives? What are the real differences in costs between operating in less developed regions benefiting from government preference and operating in locations that would be chosen on the basis of commercial criteria?

Moreover, there may be honest disagreement as to whether pursuit of a given objective does, in fact, impose a financial burden on a public enterprise. What, for example, is the cost of localizing a management position (assuming as the baseline alternative that a foreigner would have occupied the post in any private facility established in lieu of the public initiative)? Nominal emoluments are normally far lower. Who

would be bold enough to quantify the offsetting loss of revenue incurred as a result of the local manager's allegedly inferior experience,
skills, market contacts, etc.?

A standard approach to estimating EXP^P would be first to ask enterprise managers for documentary evidence concerning regulatory
controls imposed on them, on the one hand, and, on the other hand,
instructions received with respect to positive acts of resource allocation. The next step would be to sift through accounts to net out the
impact of controls and instructions that the managers claimed had
affected adversely their operating results. Such netting out involves
not only subtracting costs and revenues attributable to the relevant
measures, but also considering the disposition of the incremental operating surplus that would be generated by their cancellation.

For example, fiscal transfers identified above—tax payments or
returns on government investment—might well increase. Alternatively, if the effect of the netting out is to reduce a pre-existing deficit
rather than create or increase an operating surplus, an assumption is
required, preferably buttressed by advice of management, as to what
source(s) of deficit financing would most likely be released.

The exercise cannot, however, stop at documented measures of
control. Enterprise managers may well attribute a portion of any losses
to oral instructions, to decisions of their own in pursuit of general
policy guidelines, or perhaps merely to their own supposition as to
what course of action would be most in the public interest. These
attributions must be verified with government officials, who will often
counter that the enterprise managers are merely covering up for bad
business decisions or inept management. Ultimately some exercise of
the analyst's judgment cannot be avoided.

A few countries have progressed in government-public enterprise
relations to the point where, within the framework of a periodic (annual or multiannual) agreement,[16] government acknowledges responsibility for covering a certain level of losses which the enterprise
anticipates incurring in pursuing noncommercial objectives. Even where
this approach is adopted, however, the authorities who negotiate such
arrangements on government's behalf may not be free to acknowledge
the noneconomic motivations underlying certain instructions—for
example, using an enterprise's payroll as an instrument of political
patronage, as distinct from the broader goal of curbing unemployment in society at large—so that the analyst may be obliged to augment the estimates of the financial burden. Still, under the pressure

---

[16] Known as a *contrat de programme* or *contrat plan* in France and certain Francophone
African countries following the French model.

of negotiations leading to the agreement the parties normally gather
much data that are useful in the analysis.

Introducing the EXP^P term into the fiscal balance does not trigger
an offsetting entry in the reverse flow from government to the public
enterprise sector, although the sector may already be receiving sufficient cash or implicit tax subsidies to cover the sum of its EXP^Ps.

Below-market supply of goods and services to government. LOS_t^P ("LOS"
stands for "loss") symbolizes a positive difference (if any) between the
fair market or opportunity cost value of goods and services that the
public enterprise sector supplies to government in year t, and what
government actually pays for them. Having excluded the fair market
or opportunity cost value of transactions from fiscal impact, one is
obliged to enter this discrepancy as a flow from the sector. The criterion value is, of course, zero; any positive value of LOS^P is tantamount to imposition of an extralegal tax.

The reverse flow embodied in the accordance of preference to
public enterprises in government procurement may be more common,
however, cases of cereals marketing agencies supplying foodstuffs to
civil servants below purchase and handling cost are numerous.

Financial Flows from Government to the Public Enterprise Sector

Accounting Magnitudes

Explicit financial flows from government to the public enterprise
sector are grouped under three headings: (1) purchase of equity, (2)
debt transactions including return on loans (from the public enterprise sector to government), and (3) unrequited transfers (grants and
subsidies). Flows analogous to those in the subsection, "Financial Flows
from the Public Enterprise Sector to Government," carry the same
notation, except that the superscript "G" denotes payments by, or
changes in the financial assets of, government.

Purchase of equity (denoted by EQI_t^G). Two indicators are of interest
here: first, debt/equity ratios for the public enterprise sector as a
whole, various categories of enterprises, and the sector's current investment program or individual segments of it. Public enterprises and
their individual projects are frequently undercapitalized, as governments strive to carry out ambitious investments with a minimum com-
mitment of budget resources. Prudent debt/equity ratios differ sec-
torally and among categories of activities within a sector. Once a mean
criterion value has been determined for the set of activities currently
under implementation, divergence of EQI_t^G from that value (almost

invariably in a downward direction) increases the probability of future claims on the budget and the money market, unanticipated in the activities' initial planning, to forestall bankruptcy.

The second indicator pertains to the allocation of government transfers to public enterprises among equity, outright grants, and loans. Indiscriminate inflation of equity (or loan capital) on the occasion of every bailout operation enlarges the capital base against which returns are compared and may eventually create a misleading picture of low social profitability if the transfers merely served to compensate for pursuit of noncommercial objectives or were required during an atypical period of inferior management.

Debt transactions. Three items may be identified here.

LND_t^G denotes lending by government to the public enterprise sector. Relevant indicators are analogous to those under purchase of equity. In addition it is of interest to distinguish insofar as possible between external loans on-lent directly to public enterprises and all other government lending to the public enterprise sector. The first is a wash transaction with respect to its impact on the near-term fiscal balance, even though gross magnitudes are correspondingly enlarged and a government liability is created subject to some degree of probability that the exchequer will be called upon to make it good. (This latter point applies also to direct borrowings of public enterprises which are guaranteed by government, otherwise treated here as a monetary parameter under "The Monetary Impact of the Public Enterprise Sector" below.)

TAR_t^G denotes increase (decrease $= -$) in arrears of tax payments from the public enterprise sector to government. It enters into the fiscal balance equation only insofar as the corresponding liability has been included in the TAX^P expressions of the subsection "Financial Flows from the Public Enterprise Sector to Government," above, but even if it does not appear in the equation, it should be recorded as a memorandum item. A criterion value would be either zero or the ratio of increase in arrears to annual tax liabilities of a comparable segment of the private sector. An unfavorable comparison against the criterion value would cast the public enterprise sector in a burdensome light vis-à-vis the public finances.

AMR_t^G denotes amortization of government borrowings from the nonfinancial public enterprise sector. In some countries, it comprises redemption of government securities held by nonfinancial public enterprises; in other countries, redemption of public enterprise loans to government follows a more ad hoc pattern (i.e., government pays when, and only when, decision makers perceive the marginal social utility of doing so to be no less than that of any alternative expenditure). If amortization lags behind contractual schedules, the public enterprise sector is being penalized all the more for its close ties to government.

Interest on government borrowings (denoted by INT_t^G). Here one looks to see whether government is complying with its loan service obligations and what opportunity cost (by virtue of low—in real terms, typically negative—interest rates) government imposes on the public enterprise sector through compulsory borrowings.

Unrequited transfers (grants and subsidies) (denoted by SUB_t^G). This is a residual category grouping all transfers in cash or kind that do not qualify as payments for goods and services rendered, purchases of equity, or changes in liabilities. Given the heterogeneous nature of the animal, a varied set of analytical questions arises: what proportion, if any, of the transfers can be regarded as compensation for expenses and revenue losses incurred in pursuit of government-imposed noncommercial objectives? What rationale has been applied in allocating transfers to a given set of enterprises between SUB_t^G and EQI_t^G? In the preceding discussion of the latter component, reservations were expressed about the practice of loading transfers for extraneous purposes onto equity. The converse also applies—namely, that treating as "manna from heaven" what is essentially equity capital understates the asset value on which a positive real return should be earned.

It is, however, the implicit subsidy component of unrequited transfers that deserves the bulk of our analytical attention and to which the paper now turns.

Implicit Subsidies

Three items are identified here, of which the first two are tax subsidies. The first of these constitutes an implicit tax on the population that becomes an implicit subsidy to the public enterprise sector, because government allows the sector to retain it in lieu of handing it over to the treasury. The second implicit subsidy arises when government exempts public enterprises from taxation or levies lower taxes on them than on comparable units in the private sector. Finally, the third implicit subsidy arises because, as already noted, the public enterprise sector enjoys the use of public capital at a price well below its social opportunity cost.

Tax subsidies. The first entry under this heading is $SBT_{1,t}^G$ = implicit tax revenue retained by public enterprises, comprising payments to them by their customers—final consumers or other producers—which, as a result of some governmental policy or act of commission or omission, exceed baseline levels. The baseline here consists of revenues that would enable a public enterprise operating at a "normal" level of efficiency to cover exactly the opportunity cost of its capital—that is, to earn a "normal" profit only. Conversely, revenues—provided they are facilitated by governmental action—that enable such a public enterprise to incur a smaller deficit than would otherwise be the case, or even to earn normal profit or better, are treated as implicit tax receipts.

The justification for this is that the present paper focuses on payments in excess of economic cost that are extracted from the public via exercise of governmental power and are devoted to a governmental objective—namely, strengthening the financial position of public enterprises. Formally, if not politically, government could just as well have mandated the payments in question and directed the enterprises to remit the proceeds to it as conventional indirect tax revenue.

Implicit tax revenues are generated principally by two categories of government policy, the first normally pursued via acts of commission while the second may be associated with either acts of commission or omission. The first category consists of protection of enterprises against foreign and/or domestic competition, the second involves lax control over prices of natural monopolies.

For enterprises producing tradable goods and services, the baseline or zero-implicit-tax case holds where selling prices of output equal unit costs of inputs (which may be protected or taxed well above border price levels) plus unit value added (in the enterprises) reflecting a unit domestic resource cost (DRC) of earning or saving foreign exchange—units of local currency expended on local factor services consumed in producing one dollar of value added at border prices—equal to the shadow exchange rate.

In the case of nontradables, it is appropriate to distinguish goods and services whose production and distribution permit competition and the so-called natural monopolies. With the former, the baseline case corresponds to free competition, ensuring "normal" profits to firms operating at an efficiency level determined, by whatever means are available, to be "average" for the economy in question. Accepting the scope that public utility regulation allows for overinvestment and inefficient operation, the baseline case for natural monopolies is defined as a set of average prices such that production and consumption end up at approximately the level determined by the intersection between the demand curve and an average total cost curve considered by the regulatory authority to reflect reasonable efficiency. Determining such baseline prices is, of course, a standard task for regulatory entities, who have to judge what constitutes reasonable utilization of labor, capital, and purchased inputs to obtain a given level of output. Earning a level of average revenue that meets these criteria does not rule out the use of marginal cost pricing at the margin, since enterprises may still engage in sufficient inframarginal price discrimination to avoid losses or supernormal profits.

Once baseline prices are determined, the implicit tax revenue is given by the area of the rectangle defined by the intersection of the actual price line and the demand curve, and the horizontal line through the baseline price. Graphically, the implicit revenue, which then becomes an implicit subsidy to the public enterprise sector, equals the area bounded by $p_a A B p_b$ in Figure 1.

The second tax subsidy applicable here, which we term a "conventional" tax subsidy, is $SBT^G_{2,t}$, representing the value of any preferential tax treatment accorded to public enterprises. In some countries, varying proportions of the sector enjoy exemption from company tax, import duties, and/or other indirect taxes, or lower tax rates compared with the private sector as a whole. As in the computation of implicit tax revenue, it is necessary first to determine a baseline against which to measure the degree of preference involved.

This exercise is subject to two major complications. First, remaining within a partial equilibrium framework, the tax treatment of private companies often varies according to size, economic sector, and other characteristics. One might seek to establish the effective tax rates applied to the majority of private enterprises or to those enterprises accounting for the major share of the base for a given tax. Or one might calculate a mean yield from the application of a particular tax to private sector earnings or transactions.

Second, as one moves into a general equilibrium framework, it becomes necessary to take account of the fact that removal of tax subsidies from public enterprises would reduce the pressure on other points of the tax system, including taxation of private companies (another effect, assuming continuous behavioral functions, would be to stimulate supplemental expenditure). Thus, the baseline company tax against which the implicit subsidies should be measured is, in fact, lower than any that might be computed on the basis of de jure or de facto tax rates.

Any discrepancy between actual taxes paid by a public enterprise and the baseline, however determined, would then be considered an implicit subsidy from government to the enterprise (and would, of course, have to be balanced by expansion of enterprise direct tax payments as a corresponding entry under reverse flows).

It goes without saying that before computing conventional tax subsidies in the case of natural resource-based sectors, any portion of rents which is captured in the form of direct taxes rather than royalties and the like must be deducted from direct tax payments and treated as an implicit royalty.

The capital subsidy to public enterprise. This implicit subsidy, labeled

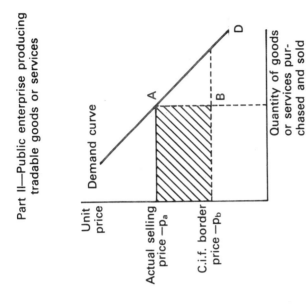

FIGURE 1— COLLECTION OF IMPLICIT TAX REVENUE BY PUBLIC ENTERPRISES

Part I—State-owned public utility (producing nontradable goods or services)

Unit price

Demand curve

A

Enterprise's long-run average total cost curve

Actual selling price —p_a

Baseline average selling price —p_b

B

D

Quantity of goods or services purchased and sold

Explanation: The baseline situation is defined as the establishment, by the regulatory authority, of an average selling price that enables the enterprise to cover the social opportunity cost of all factors, which includes earning a "normal" profit. In the actual situation shown, the regulatory authority is permitting the enterprise to charge a higher average selling price and thus to earn "supernormal" profit. The shaded area represents the implicit tax collected by the enterprise.

Part II—Public enterprise producing tradable goods or services

Unit price

Demand curve

A

Actual selling price —p_a

C.i.f. border price —p_b

B

D

Quantity of goods or services purchased and sold

Explanation: By levying an indirect tax equivalent to p_a-p_b on imports of the good or service in question, *or* through quantitative restrictions limiting the quantum of imports, the government has brought about an actual domestic selling price of p_a. As in Part I, the shaded area represents the implicit tax thereby levied on behalf of the public enterprise.

SBC_t^G, is essentially the difference between the criterion value for payment of returns on public investment and actual payments to government on account of interest and dividends, which was elaborated in the subsection "Payments of return on investment."As indicated in that discussion, most public enterprises enjoy a substantial subsidy on account of their use of the services of public capital; frequently, it exceeds the total of all other annual operating costs.

The approach followed here and in the subsection "Payments of return on investment" takes the history of government and financial sector capital infusions at face value and looks at the adequacy of the returns they are currently generating as compared with the social opportunity costs of those infusions.

An alternative approach, focusing exclusively on the capital stock's present earning power, would seek to provide a normative basis for evaluating the macroeconomic performance of the public enterprise sector's current management. The implicit subsidy calculated in this case measures the shortfall between what the sector is actually earning on its invested capital and what the analysts consider to be its true earning power, with due allowance made for the low or zero productivity of misguided past investment. In other words, with this approach, one seeks to avoid saddling current enterprise management with the responsibility for earning a return consonant with the social opportunity cost of capital on past losses in excess of reasonable start-up costs, as well as on politically and socially motivated expenditures of the past. Clearly, the process of netting out such expenditures is subject to a wide margin of uncertainty; but in some of the more blatant cases, reasonable observers might agree on the order of magnitude of the invested capital to be written down.

The question arises as to how adjustment of the "subsidy" entry in Table 1 to incorporate the implicit capital subsidy or attribution of a portion of before-tax profit to implicit tax revenue in the case of monopoly pricing would affect the national income aggregates discussed in "Summary Accounts of the Public Enterprise Sector."It turns out that these changes do not affect sectoral GDP at market prices, in the first case because introduction of a capital subsidy increases the financing charges/operating surplus pari passu, in the second case because treatment of part of profit/operating surplus as implicit indirect tax revenue merely shifts the sum in question from one component of value added/GDP to the other.

On the other hand, modification of either the subsidy or the indirect tax component affects the transition from market prices to factor incomes—upward adjustment of subsidies increasing GDP at factor cost and higher (implicit) indirect tax revenue decreasing it.

Adding a time dimension to analysis of the capital subsidy received by the public enterprise sector puts its importance, and the corresponding implicit fiscal burden on government, in even bolder relief. The discussion in this paper has hitherto been restricted to flows and stocks pertaining to a particular discrete period, typically one year, during which it is desired to evaluate the public enterprise sector's performance. However, the provision of public capital to enterprises is customarily a contractual arrangement in which government either binds itself explicitly to accept a specific rate of return over a period of years, sometimes indefinitely, or else renounces any entitlement to a specific return (case of equity capital) and, in many cases, by precedent as well as by current policy, signals to enterprise management that, far from expecting a financial return in the foreseeable future, it will be relieved if the enterprise can survive without periodic operating subsidies.

In either of these cases one can define the present value of an implicit stream of future subsidy payments to which government is committing itself, contractually or de facto. The stream consists of annual differences between the social opportunity cost of capital, as defined in "Payments of return on investment" above, and the interest payments stipulated in the loan agreement, or the expected flow of dividends in the case of equity capital. The social discount rate is applied to calculate present value. The ratio of present values of (1) the subsidy stream and (2) the disbursement stream of the loan or equity investment constitutes the grant element of the instrument in question. A new paper tabulates this grant element on varying assumptions about loan terms, and shows that explicit interest subsidies in Korea's direct official lending (not only to public enterprises) during the 1970s accounted for a minimum of half the central government budget deficit.[17]

Financial Flows Within the Public Enterprise Sector

As mentioned previously, intrasectoral flows constitute wash transactions when it comes to measuring the public enterprise sector's impact vis-à-vis government. However, they are of interest in assessing the fiscal impact of a subset of enterprises constituting on net either a source or an object of flows to or from the rest of the sector. This interest arises from a presumption that, in the case of enterprises serving as a net source of funds to others, the former are relieving government of a burden that would otherwise fall on itself. Con-

---

[17] Michael Wattleworth, "Credit Subsidies in Budgetary Lending" (unpublished, International Monetary Fund, May 1983).

versely, enterprises benefiting from the flows are viewed as diverting resources that could otherwise be channeled to the money market or the exchequer.

Three categories of flows, comprising (1) purchase of equity (EQI_t^I, with the superscript I symbolizing "intrasectoral"); (2) debt transactions (LND_t^I and AMR_t^I), and (3) payments of return on investment (INT_t^I and DIV_t^I), are discussed adequately in the two preceding subsections, and considerations distinguishing intrasectoral flows from those between the public enterprise sector and government do not require further elaboration. Conversely, category (4), cross-subsidies (SUB_t^I), comprising at once a payment for one set of enterprises and a receipt for another set, applies uniquely to intrasectoral flows.

Perhaps the outstanding current manifestation of cross-subsidies within the public enterprise sector is the supply of energy at below-market prices to energy-intensive manufacturing industries, notably fertilizer, other petrochemicals, and basic metals. Examples of this are found in both developing and industrial countries. The subsidized supply of fuel or feedstocks by state-controlled petroleum and natural gas companies ensures the solvency of many processing industries that could not otherwise meet international competition. In effect, the energy suppliers are relieving the government budget and/or the credit market of at least part of the burden they would otherwise have to bear to keep the enterprises in question afloat. The other side of the coin is that the recipient enterprises are in effect diverting revenues and investable funds that would otherwise accrue to the budget and credit institutions. (Assessing the implicit subsidy becomes subject to greater uncertainty in a situation of production restraint as marginal revenue drops substantially below market price.)

Fiscal Impact of the Public Enterprise Sector: Conclusion

Table 3 summarizes the 17 subheadings and 24 individual flows, explicit and implicit, identified in this subsection.

The nominal fiscal balance (net flow of resources from the public enterprise sector to government) is the sum of accounting magnitudes under (1) less the sum of those under (2). The real fiscal balance is found by adding the relevant implicit transfers and subsidies to (1) and (2), respectively.

Apart from these overall indicators of fiscal impact, other indicators may be obtained by comparing various components of the flows and subtotals thereof. Potentially significant indicators include the following:

$$SUB^G + SBT_1^G + SBT_2^G + SBC^G - (LOS^P + \Sigma\ EXP_i^P). \quad (1)$$

Table 3. Parameters of Public Enterprise Sector Fiscal Impact: A Listing

	Symbols[1]	
	Accounting magnitudes	Implicit transfers/ subsidies
Transfers from public enterprise sector to government		
Taxes and royalties (tax/tax category "i")	TAX_i^P	
Increase in arrears of government payments for goods and services supplied by public enterprises (decrease $= -$)	ARR^P	
Payments of return on investment		
Interest on government loans to public enterprises	INT^P	
Dividends on government equity investment	DIV^P	
Redemption of capital		
Amortization payments on government loans	AMR^P	
Redemption of government equity investment	RED^P	
Lending to government by nonfinancial public enterprises	LND^P	
Expenses and revenue losses arising from pursuit of noncommercial objectives (objective "i")		EXP_i^P
Losses from below-market sales of goods and services to government		LOS^P
Transfers from government to public enterprise sector		
Purchase of equity in public enterprises	EQI^G	
Debt transactions		
Lending by government to public enterprises	LND^G	
Increase in arrears of public enterprise tax payments (decrease $= -$)	TAR^G	
Repayment of government borrowings from public enterprise sector	AMR^G	
Interest payments on government borrowings	INT^G	
Unrequited transfers (grants and subsidies)	SUB^G	
Tax subsidies		
Implicit tax revenue retained by public enterprises		SBT_1^G
Conventional tax subsidies to public enterprises		SBT_2^G
Capital subsidies to public enterprises		SBC^G
Transfers within public enterprise sector		
Purchase of equity	EQI^I	
Debt transactions		
Loans	LND^I	
Repayments	AMR^I	
Payments of return on investment		
Interest	INT^I	
Dividends	DIV^I	
Cross-subsidies		SUB^I

[1] The subscript t ($=$ year) should be understood for all expressions.

This term represents the difference between the sum of explicit and implicit grants and subsidies from government to the public enterprise sector, and the sum of the sector's implicit transfers to government. If the first sum exceeds the second, one will most of the time be correct in asserting that the subsidies society is paying to the public enterprise sector exceed the costs that the sector is incurring in order to provide unrequited benefits to society. On the other hand, it would be a riskier proposition to assert the converse—namely, that if the first sum is less than the second, the sector is not recouping its full costs through subsidies, because vehicles of government transfer not included in the first sum—notably, purchase of equity and lending— are frequently tantamount to outright subsidies (the policymakers do not expect significant cash returns on, or redemption of, the investments, and/or effective machinery for realizing the same is lacking).

$$EQI^G + LND^G + AMR^G + INT^G + SUB^G - (INT^P$$
$$+ DIV^P + AMR^P + RED^P + LND^P). \quad (2)$$

The two sums comprising this difference represent the nominal flows between government and the public enterprise sector most likely to be estimated in government budget documents. Hence, the expression may be viewed as an approximation to the sector's budgetary impact determined by accessibility of data. It excludes, of course, the implicit transfers under (1) above, which means all the terms in (1) except SUB^G, that is, explicit grants and subsidies. It also excludes tax payments of public enterprises, changes in tax arrears, and changes in arrears of government payments to the sector, which budget documents seldom reveal.

This is the expression used by R.P. Short to measure budgetary "burden" in the following paper.

Anticipating the analysis of the following section on monetary impact, given what is already known in many countries about the implications of the central government's overall deficit for credit creation and the monetary expansion, comparison of the public enterprise sector's fiscal deficit with the overall government deficit provides an indicator of the proportion of those phenomena that can be traced back to fiscal pressures from the sector.

Monetary Impact of the Public Enterprise Sector

The focus under this heading is on the net increment in credit associated with operations of nonfinancial public enterprises and its impact on other monetary parameters, such as the money supply, the level of price inflation, the structure of interest rates, and the balance of payments. Financial public enterprises are excluded here, because they function primarily as vehicles, rather than users, of credit; although when a financial public enterprise gets into difficulty, the use of credit or budget resources to bail it out has the same monetary impact as a bailout of a nonfinancial enterprise.

First Level of Monetary Aggregates—Gross Use of Credit

Computation of Credit Accounted for by the Nonfinancial Public Enterprise Sector

The first crude measures of monetary impact are the shares of assets and liabilities of domestic financial institutions accounted for by the public enterprise sector.[18] It is convenient to distinguish among the central bank, other banks (whose deposits form part of the money supply), and nonbank financial institutions. Net credit outstanding directly to public enterprises is given by $(C_{cb}^P - D_{cb}^P) + (C_b^P D_b^P) + (C_{nb}^P - D_{nb}^P)$ where C represents credit outstanding, D represents deposits, the superscript P refers to the public enterprise sector, and the subscripts represent the central bank (cb), other banks (b), and nonbank financial institutions (nb), respectively. In some countries, either or both of C_{cb}^P and D_{cb}^P will be negligible or zero, as it is central bank policy not to deal directly with public enterprises. Corresponding to each absolute measure of C^P and D^P will be a proportion of total credit outstanding or deposits in a given category of institution accounted for by public enterprises. These proportions already merit some policy interest—a large public enterprise share on the credit side suggests crowding out of the private sector, a large share in deposits suggests a major public enterprise contribution to financing the rest of the economy.

Apart from the financial sector's direct lending to public enterprises, one must take into account recourse that government and private nonfinancial enterprises have to financial institutions in order to finance (1) net government loans and transfers to public enterprises and (2) arrears in public enterprise payments to the private nonfi-

---

[18] Banking statistics in many countries classify all nonfinancial public enterprises, or all but a small selection of them, in the private sector. Collection of this data will thus not always be feasible initially and will often require a reform of current reporting procedures. Implied in the main theses of the present paper is the premise that sound financial management calls for such a reform, and governments should be pressed to institute it.

nancial sector.[19] We denote (1) by C_G^P and (2) by A^P (A denotes arrears).

In the extreme case where one can assume that a government would reduce its deficit financing pari passu with a reduction in loans or subsidies to public enterprises, the volume of these transfers, identified in the analysis of the fiscal impact (preceding subsection), translates into an equivalent amount of credit. In the more realistic case, where the disutility associated with resort to deficit financing and consequent inflation strengthens the authorities' resistance to demands A, B, and C for each unavoidable increase in demand D, one estimates a coefficient, say g, less than unity, giving the proportion by which the transfers in question augment the government's deficit and thus its resort to credit.

The amount of financial sector credit accounted for by the public enterprise sector can now be defined as:

$$X^P = (C_{cb}^P - D_{cb}^P) + (C_b^P - D_{cb}^P)$$
$$+ (C_{nb}^P - D_{nb}^P) + gC_G^P + A^P. \quad (3)$$

The sector's proportional share may be denoted $\dfrac{X^P}{X}$; residual shares are accounted for by government and the private sector, direct credit to which is adjusted downward to account for the amounts gC_G^P and A^P, respectively, which are attributed to public enterprise operations.

Public Enterprise Sector's Share in Real Credit Expansion

Once absolute credit levels accounted for by public enterprises have been assessed, the next step is to examine the sector's share in real credit expansion during a given period, ranging from, say, one quarter to a year or more. Expansion of total credit from financial institutions is denoted by $X_t - X_{t-1}$ and in real terms by $\dfrac{X_t}{1+p} - X_{t-1}$ with p representing the relevant inflation rate during period t. Real expansion of credit accounted for directly and indirectly by public enterprises

---

[19] One might also argue that public enterprises pose an indirect demand for credit insofar as private suppliers to (and purchasers from) them utilize credit to finance the corresponding portion of their transactions, quite apart from any requirement posed by payments arrears. By looking only at arrears, one is in effect comparing the existing situation with a baseline need for credit to finance investment and current transactions associated with the given level of output, with or without participation by public enterprises, subject to a "normal" level of arrears.

is given by

$$\frac{X_t^P}{1+\dot{p}} - X_{t-1}^P \tag{4}$$

The share of public enterprises in total credit expansion from $t-1$ to t is then given by

$$s_t^P = \frac{\dfrac{X_t^P}{1+\dot{p}_t} - X_{t-1}^P}{\dfrac{X_t}{1+\dot{p}_t} - X_{t-1}} \tag{5}$$

One's policy-attuned ears perk up on hearing that public enterprises in Country A absorbed s^P percent of the real increase in credit during year t, which together with direct government use (excluding the share accounted for by gC_G^P) of s^G percent, left only s^R percent for the private sector. We are especially disturbed if, by chance, s^R turns out to be negative, which is perfectly possible—in other words, while financial sector credit expanded in real terms, credit to the private sector increased less rapidly than the price level. Short of this extreme case, any excess of the public enterprise sector's marginal share in real credit expansion, s^P, over the proportional share $\dfrac{X^P}{X}$ may be indicative of growing pressure on the credit markets from the side of public enterprises.

Classified Loans to the Public Enterprise Sector

Another set of parameters of policy interest are those relating to amounts and proportions of loans outstanding to public enterprises that are "classified" or "graded" by management or outside examiners as being of doubtful collectibility. Monetary complications arise if public enterprises are threatening the solvency of financial institutions or merely constraining their flexibility while government delays making good on explicit or implicit guarantees.[20]

The Impact of the Public Enterprise Sector on Financial Institutions' Assets and Liabilities

Turning from the gross parameters to the sector's net impact on financial institutions' assets and liabilities, estimating the latter be-

---

[20] One does not envisage outsiders sifting through loan portfolios to tabulate these data, but it is among the information that Ministry of Finance control units should be collecting, interpreting, and supplying on an aggregated basis to international creditors. Local bank officials, frustrated by slow turnover of the relevant portions of their loan portfolios, are often eager to collaborate with the authorities in this respect.

comes an ambiguous exercise. Short of general equilibrium modeling, the neutral course is to assume a break-even baseline, with capital costs covered, and to focus attention on operating deficits. An increment of ΔA in the aggregate operating deficit may inflate X^P by anywhere between zero and ΔA. The extreme value of zero would prevail if monetary authorities and financial institutions collaborated to hold the nonfinancial public enterprise sector, the government as one of its creditors, and the sector's private suppliers to a firm credit ceiling such that any increase in sectoral demand for credit occasioned by the incremental deficit was exactly offset by a decrease in the allocation of credit for public enterprise investment, working capital, etc. This implies that banks and other financial institutions would hold the line against reducing their loans to other borrowers apart from public enterprise creditors.

At the opposite extreme, the increment in the operating deficit induces some combination, equal to ΔA, of new deposits, credit diversion, and credit creation. New deposits would likely account for only a small fraction of ΔA, and that only if the money market were sufficiently free so that an increase in the effective demand for credit—assuming that public enterprises, with their government backing, constitute such demand—could evoke a rise in the expected return from holding financial assets.

Any of the three categories of financial institutions can divert credit from their other borrowers in order to increase the relevant C^P term. The central bank can raise C_{cb}^P at will through credit creation. The most plausible assumption about banks and other institutions is that they will lend to the maximum permitted by the monetary authorities in the absence of the incremental deficit. Thus C_{nb}^P can rise only through additional deposits or credit diversion, while C_b^P can increase through either of those two mechanisms or, to the extent the central bank rediscounts the public enterprise paper, through credit creation.

In conclusion, only by collecting evidence at the microeconomic level regarding the behavior of the group of public enterprises accounting for the bulk of the aggregate operating deficit, together with that of their creditors; or, alternatively, via econometric modeling from time series with public enterprise deficits as the exogenous variable of primary interest;[21] or, even better, using a combination of the two approaches, can one estimate the impact of sectoral operating

---

[21] In the following paper in this volume, R.P. Short conducts an interesting exercise along these lines, obtaining a regression coefficient of near unity in relating growth in total credit to growth of credit to the public enterprise sector on a cross-country basis. Short interprets this, with reservations, as suggesting that public enterprise credit growth is almost fully passed through into credit creation.

deficits on total credit outstanding and its allocation between public enterprises and other borrowers.

Second Level of Monetary Aggregates—Money Supply, Level of Inflation, and Interest Rate Structure

Policy interest of a whole new order of magnitude attaches to appraisal of the nonfinancial public enterprise sector's impact on these parameters. There are, of course, no direct measures of sectoral impact as there are of the sector's participation in credit outstanding. Hence, one cannot avoid modeling (at least implicitly) the baseline alternative(s) and, as per the subsection, "First Level of Monetary Aggregates: Gross Use of Credit" above, attributing the credit by which deficits are financed among (1) new deposits, (2) credit diversion, and (3) credit creation. New deposits (ΔD), unless neutralized by action of the monetary authority, lead to expansion of the reserve base, and thus of the money supply, according to the familiar money multiplier (reciprocal of the reserve ratio), k.[22] Credit diversion, on the other hand, has no direct impact on the money supply; in the medium and long term, repercussions may follow from its impact on resource allocation if relatively efficient activities are deprived of credit in order to finance public enterprise operating deficits.

Finally, credit creation arises from the monetary authority's action in financing public enterprise deficits with high-powered money (ΔH)—that is, infusions leading to a one-for-one increase in bank reserves—whether via government or the banking system. Here again, the money multiplier comes into action.

The increment in money supply (ΔM) caused by a unit increment in public enterprise operating deficits is now seen to equal $k(\Delta D + \Delta H)$. Of the two terms in parentheses, ΔH will almost invariably be dominant.

Turning to the level of inflation, the price index of output produced by the public enterprises themselves can be computed as an initial, essentially trivial, measure of sector impact. Such indices are readily available for individual enterprises, especially public utilities and major transport enterprises such as railroads, and the managements of nearly all public enterprises will (or should) have a good idea as to

---

[22] The previous observation that the impact of public enterprise deficits in generating new deposits is likely to be minimal deserves re-emphasis here. Indeed, wherever regulation of the money market is such that formal sector interest rates are not free to respond to higher effective demand for credit, an increase in public enterprise operating deficits is likely to reduce the demand for real cash balances by aggravating inflationary expectations.

the trend of their output prices. The measure is trivial, however, because the force of the sector's impact on the overall price level comes via the impact of its operating deficits on money supply, not the weight of its output in any general price index.

The impact on prices of any increase in money supply is heavily influenced by the degree of openness of the economy. At one extreme, in an economy with a high propensity to import that is not frustrated by quantitative restrictions, the purchasing power generated by the credit expansion quickly evaporates in the form of imports, and the mean additional demand in effect during any given period of time is considerably less than it would be in an economy where the authorities have imposed an absolute ceiling on imports in accordance with projections of available foreign exchange. The extreme of this latter case is represented by countries that maintain constant exchange rates during periods when their inflation rates greatly exceed the rise of prices (expressed in foreign currency units) of their imports, devaluation being one means of accelerating the evaporation of purchasing power without a commensurate rise in import ceilings. (The effect of the devaluation-induced rise in nominal c.i.f. values by way of offsetting the anti-inflationary impact of the leakage is normally trivial, since the imports already carry scarcity values far in excess of their c.i.f. prices.)

Computing Increment in Mean Level of Money Supply

Of interest in analyzing inflationary impact is the relationship between an injection of money (ΔM) at a given point in time and the mean level of the money supply prevailing during the subsequent period whose incremental inflation is to be measured. With instantaneous leakage of ΔM into imports, the level of the money supply that would have prevailed without the injection in question, which is denoted by M, continues to prevail in spite of the injection. Conversely, with zero leakage the mean level of money ($\overline{M}$) during the period following the injection is equal to $M + \Delta M$. The more general case features incremental imports of ΔI, which can also be interpreted to contain an element of capital outflow on the assumption that income receivers have a propensity to invest abroad out of incremental income. At the end of the period, money supply is given by $M + \Delta M - \Delta I$. On the simplifying assumption that the leakage into imports and capital outflow is spread evenly over the period, the mean level of money during the period would be given by

$$\overline{M} = \frac{(M + \Delta M) + (M + \Delta M - \Delta I)}{2} = M + \Delta M - \frac{\Delta I}{2}. \quad (6)$$

As a standard pattern of financing public enterprise deficits it is convenient to assume, for purposes of monetary analysis, a total injection of one unit of credit (ΔX^P) during a given year, spread equally among v "income periods," v representing the income velocity of money.[23] Thus, $1/v$ amount of credit is injected at the outset of each period. By virtue of the definition of an income period, the amount of income generated in the first period by this infusion equals the amount of the infusion, *less* the portion of it leaking out via imports (and possibly also capital outflow—henceforward "imports" will be used as a proxy for both). Incremental imports are given by a constant marginal propensity to import (m) times incremental income, which is now seen to equal $\Delta y = 1/v - m\Delta y$. Thus $\Delta y(1+m) = \frac{1}{v}$, $\Delta I = \frac{m}{v(1+m)}$, and the increment in money as of the end of the period, following leakage of ΔI worth of imports, is $1/v -$

$$\frac{m}{v(1+m)} = \frac{1}{v}\left(1 - \frac{m}{1+m}\right) = \frac{1}{v}(1 + m)^{-1}.$$

It can easily be shown that the increment in money at the end of period t following infusion of $1/v$ amount of credit at the beginning of a period defined as No. 1, assuming no further infusions in subsequent periods, is $\frac{1}{v}(1+m)^{-t}$. Taking into account the infusions in succeeding periods, the increment in money at the end of each period t consists of the residual—whatever portion has not yet leaked out via imports—of that period's and each preceding period's infusions. These residuals comprise a geometric progression whose sum can be written:

$$\Delta M_t = \frac{1 - (1+m)^{-t}}{m}. \tag{7}$$

The next step is to calculate the increment in *average* money supply during the year, arising from credit creation to finance public enterprise deficits. For this purpose one first seeks the sum of successive money increments at the end of all v periods in the year; this is done by summing expression (7) over v, yielding another geometric progression, which can be written:

$$\sum_{t=1}^{v} \Delta M_t = \frac{v}{m} - \frac{1 - (1+m)^{-v}}{m^2} \tag{8}$$

The best measure of the increment in average money supply is then

---

[23] This expository device was utilized in early versions of the Polak model of money, income, and imports. See, for example, J.J. Polak and Lorette Boissonneault, "Monetary Analysis of Income and Imports and Its Statistical Application," International Monetary Fund, *Staff Papers*, Vol. 7 (April 1960), pp. 349–415.

the overall mean of the means of money supply values at the beginning
and end of successive income periods, which may be written thus:

$$\frac{1}{v}\left(\frac{\Delta M_0 + \Delta M_1}{2} + \frac{\Delta M_1 + \Delta M_2}{2} + \dots + \frac{\Delta M_{v-1} + \Delta M_v}{2}\right) =$$
$$\frac{1}{v}\left(\frac{\Delta M_0}{2} + \Delta M_1 + \Delta M_2 + \Delta M_3 + \Delta M_4 + \dots + \Delta M_{v-1} + \frac{\Delta M_v}{2}\right). \quad (9)$$

In other words intrayear values receive double weights as compared
with successive year-end values, namely, ΔM_0 and ΔM_v.

The term ΔM_0 is zero, since the relevant credit infusions begin only
after the end of the preceding year. Thus the only adjustment that
need be made in expression (8) in order to obtain (9), apart from
dividing by v, is to subtract half of ΔM_v, namely, $\dfrac{1 - (1+m)^{-v}}{2m}$. The
increment in average money supply during year t attributable to public
enterprise credit infusions is thus given by:

$$\overset{*}{\Delta}\overline{M}_t = \frac{1}{m} - \frac{[1 - (1+m)^{-v}]\left(\dfrac{1}{m} + \dfrac{1}{2}\right)}{mv} \quad (10)$$

The asterisk atop the Δ in expression (10) denotes an incremental
value attributable to expansion solely of credit to public enterprises;
this notation will be used for other variables similarly affected by the
credit expansion in question.

Computing Increment in Prices

A simple quantity theory model will be applied in analyzing the
impact of public enterprise sector credit expansion on inflation. The
model is based on the identity $\overline{M}v = \overline{p}Q$, where $\overline{M}$ denotes the average
level of money supply during a year, v the income velocity of money,
$\overline{p}$ the average price index during the year, and Q the year's GDP at
prices of the year serving as the base for the price index.

The model's key assumption is that v remains constant—in other
words, one abstracts from dynamic effects that might cause the marginal income velocity applicable to ΔM to differ from the average
value, v, applicable to M.

With v constant, the following identity holds for the case where an
increment in public enterprise sector credit has had the indicated
effects ($\overset{*}{\Delta}$ terms) on average money supply, the average price index
and GDP:

$$(\overline{M}_t + \overset{*}{\Delta}\overline{M}_t)v = (\overline{p}_t + \overset{*}{\Delta}\overline{p}_t)(Q_t + \overset{*}{\Delta}Q_t). \quad (11)$$

This identity is then divided by the analogous one applying in the absence of the increment in public enterprise sector credit, namely, $\overline{M}_t v = \overline{p}_t Q_t$; the v's cancel out, as do the unity terms,

$$\frac{\overline{M}_t}{\overline{M}_t} \text{ and } \frac{\overline{p}_t Q_t}{\overline{p}_t Q_t}$$

on both sides of the new equation, which now reads

$$\frac{\overset{*}{\Delta}\overline{p}_t}{\overline{p}_t} \cdot \frac{Q_t + \overset{*}{\Delta}Q_t}{Q_t} + \frac{\overset{*}{\Delta}Q_t}{Q_t} = \frac{\overset{*}{\Delta}\overline{M}_t}{\overline{M}_t} \qquad (12)$$

It is clear on inspection of equation (12) that, should $\overset{*}{\Delta}Q_t$ equal zero—that is, expansion of public enterprise sector credit brings no change in real output—then the proportional increment in average prices is identical to that in average money supply. It may be argued that some enterprises will have to cease production and discharge their labor forces if their deficits are not financed. Conversely, in many countries improved trade and incentive policies would facilitate re-employment of the public enterprise labor and pick up the slack in production within a short time.

In order to compute the impact of the public enterprise sector credit expansion on the price level over the course of a full year, the term representing the increment in the average price level must be modified accordingly. It would be consistent with the assumption of equal amounts of credit creation in each income period to treat $\overset{*}{\Delta}\overline{p}_t$ as simply half of the full-year price level increment, $\overset{*}{\Delta}p_t$.

Accordingly equation (12) can be written:

$$\overset{*}{\Delta}p_t = 2\overline{p}_t \cdot \frac{\dfrac{Q_t \overset{*}{\Delta}\overline{M}_t}{\overline{M}_t} - \overset{*}{\Delta}Q_t}{Q_t + \overset{*}{\Delta}Q_t} \qquad (13)$$

Useful indicators of inflationary impact are (1) the ratio of $\overset{*}{\Delta}p_t$ to p_{t-1}, showing the proportional increase over the end-of-last-year index that can be attributed to the public enterprise sector credit expansion and (2) $\overset{*}{\Delta}p_t$ as a ratio to year t's total increase, namely, $p_t - p_{t-1} + \overset{*}{\Delta}p_t$, showing the proportion of the year's inflation that can be so attributed.[24]

---

[24] It will be recalled that p_t represents the price index that would prevail at the end of year t in the absence of the given increment in public enterprise sector credit expansion, hence $\overset{*}{\Delta}p_t$ bears no relation to the difference between p_t and p_{t-1} and is supplemental to it.

In many countries, more sophisticated models have been applied, using time series data to relate public enterprise deficits to money supply and inflation, or simply to relate money supply to inflation. Such models can be adapted to the pattern of inflationary expectations, lag structures, and other dynamic characteristics of a particular economy to yield more reliable estimates than the naive predictions of a simple quantity theory model.

One such exercise that is of more than passing interest here—because it examines the impact of price controls on operating deficits, credit creation, and ultimately inflation with respect to both public enterprises and private firms—was reported in an article on Argentina by Chu and Feltenstein.[25] Government transfers to public enterprises translated one-for-one into high-powered money through central bank financing of the government deficit, while private losses were financed by the commercial banks and were not, as a general rule, rediscounted by the central bank. Hence, the Chu and Feltenstein data suggest that the public enterprise transfers were proportionately ten times as inflationary per unit of transfer as the private losses; however, since the latter were so much larger in aggregate, they contributed 2.3 times as much as the former to Argentina's 15 percent average quarterly inflation rate during 1965–76.[26]

Impact on Interest Rate Structure

In conclusion, the possible impact of operating deficits of public enterprises on interest rate structure is worthy of passing mention. In the event—more common in industrial than in developing countries—that nominal rates are allowed to respond to modest shifts in demand and supply schedules in the formal money market, the occurrence of public enterprise deficits and the corresponding upward shift of the credit demand curve would force the rates upward. To estimate this effect, one would look primarily at cross–section data on the elasticities of credit supply and demand with respect to perceived financial returns. Over the medium to long term, one would have to take into account feedback from inflation fueled by the public enterprise deficits.

---

[25] Ke-Young Chu and Andrew Feltenstein, "Relative Price Distortions and Inflation: The Case of Argentina, 1963–76," International Monetary Fund, *Staff Papers*, Vol. 25 (September 1978), pp. 452–93.

[26] Ratios computed from the Chu-Feltenstein simulation exercise are reported on page 484 of their article. Reducing simulated quarterly public enterprise transfers of 0.04 billion pesos to zero, ceteris paribus, knocks 2.97 points off the simulated quarterly inflation rate, while a similar elimination of simulated private losses of 0.90 billion pesos knocks off 6.80 points; 2.97/.04 divided by 6.80/.90 equals approximately ten, and 6.80/2.97 = 2.29.

Balance of Payments

A naive approach to estimating the impact of the public enterprise sector on the balance of payments would be to attempt to draw up a balance of credits and debits on current and capital accounts for which the components of the sector are directly responsible. Apart from being an extremely tedious assignment this would lead the analyst into a maze of classification problems. What to do about goods and services purchased from a private importer? What about goods purchased from a local private assembler who embellishes imported inputs with negative value added? What about production of tradables that happen to be consumed domestically in one year and exported the next?

These issues illustrate why attempting to draw such a foreign exchange balance for an industry or a sector classified along other lines is not an economically meaningful exercise. A country's most efficient public enterprises and/or those whose expansion would yield the highest social benefit may be public utilities earning no foreign exchange on their own account while expending large sums on imported inputs. Instead, what is of interest is whether an industry or sector yields sufficient benefits to cover its social opportunity costs, with tradable inputs and outputs valued at border prices. That issue was already covered in "Summary Accounts of the Public Enterprise Sector" in connection with the public enterprise sector's contribution to GDP.

Balance on Capital Account

The capital account is arguably an exception to the stricture against attempting to compute a public enterprise sector balance of payments. It will often be of interest to determine whether the sector is contributing a net inflow or outflow of capital. Inflow arises primarily from borrowing, typically medium-to-long-term from official lending agencies, commercial banks, and suppliers, normally backed by host government guarantees. Additionally, petroleum and minerals exporters, power companies, and public enterprises generally in countries regarded as particularly creditworthy have also borrowed internationally at the short end of the spectrum. Foreign equity investment is effectively limited to enterprises with a reasonably assured export market, or situations where the foreign partner derives a satisfactory return from supplying goods and services to the enterprise, and hence can afford to take a nominal equity whose return is uncertain.

Capital outflow arises primarily from repayment of borrowings, though again petroleum and minerals exporters and a few other well-positioned enterprises have transferred funds either to take advantage of interest rate differentials and other short-term earnings opportunities, or even as direct foreign investment. Notwithstanding government's nominal control over the sector, public enterprises engaging in such operations often find it advantageous to disguise them via transfer pricing, and measurement of the flows by outsiders is subject to considerable uncertainty.

Nevertheless, where public enterprises are sufficiently active in the capital market to affect the outcome of government stabilization policies, an attempt should be made to determine the direction of the net flow and measure it.

Focusing on medium-to-long-term debt capital, a finding that, for example, the public enterprise sector had switched from a position of net inflow to one where amortization payments strongly outweighed loan disbursements, with a concomitant negative impact on the balance of payments, might reflect a relatively stagnant position calling for reform measures. Yet such a conclusion is by no means automatic, since the imbalance in question could also reflect a process of the state divesting itself of those enterprises strong enough to continue borrowing, or a policy of suspending new borrowing to allow time to digest a spate of ill-advised investments.

Import Generation from Credit Created to Finance Public Enterprise Deficits

In many countries the most significant element in the public enterprise sector's balance of payments impact is the flow of payments associated with the creation of credit to finance operating deficits, if any. The subsection "Second Level of Monetary Aggregates—Money Supply, Level of Inflation, and Interest Rate Structure," above, examined the case of a strict regime of import and exchange controls under which the government prevents incremental credit from leaking into international payments. The converse situation of an open economy lends itself to analysis via the Polak model of money, income, and the balance of payments, which adds the assumption of a constant propensity to import (marginal = average) to the simple quantity theory's assumption of constant income velocity.

The rate of generation of imports resulting from a unit expansion of credit at the beginning of a period is determined by a coefficient mv, equal to the product of the propensity to import and income velocity of money, which in turn is equal to imports divided by money supply (the GDP expression in the denominator of the import propensity and the numerator of the velocity term cancel out). For example, import generation during the first year following the injection equals $\frac{mv}{1+mv}$.[27]

[27] J.J. Polak and Victor Argy, "Credit Policy and the Balance of Payments," International Monetary Fund, *Staff Papers*, Vol. 18 (March 1971), p. 3.

For analysis of the impact of deficit financing measured over a period of one year, which will be the normal application of this approach, it is useful to derive coefficients giving import generation during the same year (while the deficit in question is also being financed) and then during subsequent years (without taking into account financing of new deficits in those later years). This is done on the basis of the simplifying (but reasonable) assumption that equal increments of credit/ money are created in each of v "income periods" during the given year, summing to one unit. The relevant formulas are shown in Table 4.

With increasing values of n, the summation of the formulas for years 0 through n rapidly approaches 1.0. For typical developing country values of mv, additional imports/reserve loss cumulate to at least 82 percent of ΔM after two years (that is, by the end of year 1) and 94 percent after three years.[28]

Table 4. Formulas for Polak Import Generation Coefficients[1]

Year	
0	$\dfrac{1}{mv}[mv - (1 - (1+m)^{-v})]$
1	$\dfrac{1}{mv}(1 - (1+m)^{-v})^2$
2	$\dfrac{1}{mv}(1+m)^{-v}(1 - (1+m)^{-v})^2$
$n\ (\geqslant 1)$	$\dfrac{1}{mv}(1+m)^{-(n-1)v}(1 - (1+m)^{-v})^2$

Source: J. J. Polak and Lorette Boissonneault, "Monetary Analysis of Income and Imports and its Statistical Application," International Monetary Fund, *Staff Papers*, Vol. 7 (April 1960), p. 356.

[1] The formula for each year gives the coefficient of import generation for that year caused by creation of one unit of credit/money during year 0 distributed equally among v income periods of year 0, propensity to import and income velocity of money supply being denoted by m and v, respectively.

---

[28] Taking the first 27 developing countries (alphabetical order) for which import values in local currency (line 98c) are available in the country pages of the International Monetary Fund's 1981 *International Financial Statistics Yearbook*, the ratio of imports to the average level of money (line 34, average of successive end-of-year values) in the latest year for which both figures are given exceeds 1.0 in 20 cases, implying first-year import generation exceeding 40 percent of ΔM and cumulative generation over three years exceeding 90 percent. Most of the countries with ratios below 1.0 fall into special categories, such as large economic scale (Brazil, India), strict exchange controls/ high protection (Algeria, Ghana, India), or isolation (the Central African Republic).

APPENDIX I

Assessing the Impact of Public Enterprise on Attainment of Noncommercial Objectives

Whatever measurements made pursuant to Section V may tell one about the impact of Country A's public enterprise sector on economic aggregates, including particularly fiscal and monetary magnitudes, even if one succeeds in conducting a general equilibrium analysis that compares observed parameters with those of a baseline alternative, the elements required for a definitive policy prescription will not be complete until the sector's impact on attainment of government's noncommercial objectives has also been assessed. Actual policy decisions, even apparent nondecisions that result in maintenance of the status quo, are the outcome of a (normally more implicit than explicit) process of weighing costs and benefits associated with the impact of alternative courses of action on a wide range of objectives. Depending on the structure of the objective function (s) of Country A's decision makers (i.e., the value of the weights attached to some unit of advancement of each objective), perfectly rational behavior on their part may be to choose alternatives that appear to conflict with standard goals of fiscal and monetary policy.

There can be no substitutes for adequately trained local officials in the task of analyzing implicit objective functions and measuring the public enterprise sector's impact on their fulfillment if such work is ultimately to influence the future choices of a country's policymakers. On the other hand, outsiders who aspire to conduct the more straightforward computations of Section V, and thereby to create presumptive evidence for the desirability of certain policy changes, perhaps reinforced by conditionality of external assistance, should be aware of these more subjective elements in the policy equation and should be prepared to exhort their local counterparts to undertake the necessary work on them.

In this spirit, the present appendix sets forth a taxonomy of noncommercial objectives; indicates in what ways public enterprises are considered by many governments to be effective vehicles for promoting them; suggests conditions under which some objectives might be as well (or even better) served by an alternative industrial organization; and, in some cases, touches on a possible approach to assessing the public enterprise sector's impact on the objectives. Objectives are organized under five headings: (1) economic stabilization, (2) economic growth, (3) income redistribution, (4) localization/indigenization, and (5) miscellaneous.

Economic Stabilization

Control of Inflation

Policymakers in many countries believe that government's more direct control over the pricing decisions of public enterprises gives it a better handle on controlling inflation than is available to it through regulation of the private sector. While admitting the inflationary impact of financing, with high-powered money, public enterprise operating deficits that result from price control, advocates of this position argue that quiet restraint of public enterprise pricing, avoiding the fanfare and speculation that accompany broad-based price ceilings, retards inflationary expectations, thus limiting the dynamics of the process. If such an effect is, indeed, present, it will be difficult to spot through partial equilibrium comparison of public enterprise aggregates with criterion values, though it will still come out in an appropriate general equilibrium model.

On the other hand, the Chu and Feltenstein study of Argentina cited in the subsection "Monetary Impact of the Public Enterprise Sector" illustrates how the initial objectives of price control can be achieved through the private sector, as long as compensatory financing is available from the banking system (to be sure, ultimately undermining the anti-inflation objective); moreover, if the supply of commodities is insufficient to meet the demand at controlled prices and unless government's enforcement network can monitor each point of sale to final users, exchange will eventually take place at scarcity-determined prices, regardless of what role public enterprises have played in production and prior stages of distribution.

Subject to these observations, analysis of the public enterprise sector's impact on inflation flows from the aggregates discussed in "Monetary Impact of the Public Enterprise Sector."

Food Security

A prime objective of virtually every government is to ensure that the demand of the population for basic foodstuffs, at price levels perceived as politically acceptable, is met. Political pressures from the producer side counterbalance, to some extent, those emanating from the consumers, and some policymakers are aware of a positive functional relationship between producer prices, on the one hand, and the domestic supply (net of imports), on the other. These conflicting pressures lead many governments into price control measures and other marketing policies that put a financial squeeze on one or more components of the production/marketing system—sellers of inputs, producers using significant quantities of purchased inputs, transporters, processing units, marketing boards, wholesalers, retailers, and/or other categories of intermediaries between producers and final consumers.

Food security issues may be regarded as a subset of those falling within the ambit of anti-inflation policy; however, they merit separate identification in the present context, both by virtue of special characteristics of the public enterprises (notably central agencies for input supply and/or commodity purchasing and marketing) that bear the financial brunt of government policies in the sector and because of the emphasis which even short-term policies normally place on the supply side, drawing on imports to close the gap. By contrast, price control policy in other sectors traditionally pays less heed, at least in the short run, to ensuring supplies that will clear the market at the target price, with the result that controls invariably engender nonprice rationing.

Some governments meet their food price and supply objectives by operating through private, rather than public, enterprises. The approach is normally to (1) prevent monopolization or the operation of domestic cartels in importation and exportation of foodstuffs, and (2) subsidize imports or exports (depending on the domestic demand/supply balance in a given period) with as much cash on the barrel as is needed to maintain the desired retail price ceiling or producer price floor. Reports on some countries by outside observers have taken the position that such an arrangement would evoke more production and reduce effective consumer prices with little, if any, additional fiscal burden as compared with the present situation of intervention by state-controlled marketing agencies.

Noting the opposite stand taken by other observers who attribute certain recorded supply disturbances to unbridled speculation by private agents, the present paper takes no position on the merits of the case. Rather, it contents itself with noting that the issue of food security does not necessarily overlap with that of public enterprise; conversely, where such overlap occurs, the crucial question is the comparative efficiency of the public sector as entrepreneur and manager in this particular activity.

Dampening Economic Downturns

The principle underlying this objective is that by virtue of its control over public enterprises, government can direct them into countercyclical measures consistent with its efforts to maintain output and employment in times of recession. In other words, public enterprises can be relied on more consistently than private firms, notwithstanding the regulation to which the latter can be subjected, to maintain production, build up inventories, and/or, regardless of the course of their production, keep staff on the payroll in the face of slack demand.

As with virtually all noncommercial objectives, this one worsens the enterprises' financial position and aggravates the sector's fiscal and monetary impact. This becomes especially clear when one examines cases where a failing private enterprise has been nationalized to prevent it from closing its doors and releasing its labor force. A particular case in point is the Bolivian tin industry, where the continuing deficits of such enterprises pose major fiscal and monetary burdens.

To assess the public enterprise sector's performance in preserving jobs, which is clearly its prime counterrecessionary contribution, one estimates the fluctuation in employment that would have characterized the units in question had they been under private control. (For this purpose one may apply a coefficient derived from observing the modern private sector's employment response to business downturns.)

The culmination of this evaluation is a general equilibrium model in which a coefficient of benefit (in monetary terms) is multiplied by person-months of employment preserved by the public enterprise sector. Determining the coefficient is tantamount to a wild exercise of value judgment in which one estimates the probability that unemployment beyond a certain level will cause political disruption and multiplies it by an estimate of the economic cost of the disruption. The opposite side of the balance sheet will contain cost parameters corresponding to the fiscal and monetary impact of the deficits incurred by virtue of preserving the jobs. (In some situations, one might argue that it should also account for output sacrificed because the employment policy in question raises the cost of labor to other producers.)

Whatever the balance of economic costs and benefits, situations will be encountered where the national political leadership weighs the avoidance of political disruption so heavily as to offset virtually any conceivable increment to the budget deficit and inflation associated with preserving modern-sector jobs.

Economic Growth

Increasing Investment, Output, Exports, Income, and Employment

For this subset of objectives, emphasis is placed on the absolute levels of the parameters in question rather than on the locus of control of economic activity or its distributional impact.

The possibility that greater reliance on public enterprise would increase output, income, and employment, as compared with a baseline alternative, depends on whether such a policy would (1) raise investment; (2) affect the sectoral composition of output so as to maximize backward and forward "linkage" effects; and/or (3) utilize capital stock more efficiently and/or employ more workers per unit of investment.

Taking the third possibility first, it turns out that relatively efficient utilization of capital stock has not been a hallmark of public enterprise in most mixed economies, and this has been reflected in the operating deficits and implicit capital subsidies discussed in the subsection on the "Fiscal Impact of the Public Enterprise Sector." Some public enterprises have attained higher employee/capital ratios than is characteristic of some private firms in the same industries, but more often than not this has been the result of political patronage, which is, again, the antithesis of efficiency. On the other hand, many instances have been documented where, precisely because of their access to subsidized capital, public enterprises have chosen more capital-intensive technology than was suitable for the country's factor proportions. Whether or not these enterprises were then obliged to employ redundant workers, forcing up the employee/capital ratio, efficiency was impaired.

Turning to linkages, many governments have acted on the supposition that these are enhanced by promoting basic industries, such as iron and steel and heavy chemicals, as well as industries that process the output of the country's primary producing sectors—notably, agriculture, livestock, forestry, hard minerals, and hydrocarbons—over and above the levels of investment that would occur without direct government intervention. On the other hand, some countries have found more effective, largely skill-related linkages in export-oriented light manufacture utilizing imported inputs where ability to respond more rapidly and flexibly to changing market opportunities appears to give private enterprise a comparative advantage.

A policy favoring public enterprise may raise the investment rate in one of two ways—first, it may steer into investment domestic savings that, for want of private investment demand (lack of entrepreneurs, unfavorable business outlook, or what not), would not translate into a similar investment rate through the private sector. In other words, if steered into private hands by public credit institutions or other intermediaries, the given volume of resources would largely displace the financing of private investment through other resources, and the economy would end up with a higher consumption/savings ratio than under a public enterprise orientation. Second, the policy may open up channels for a larger inflow of foreign capital than the sources of such capital would choose to make available for on-lending to private investors. Whether the stepped-up investment rate makes output, income, and employment over the long run higher than they would have been in the baseline case depends on the efficiency of the investment as well as on the debt service burden generated by the increased capital inflow.

To evaluate the impact of public enterprise under these headings without recourse to a general equilibrium model, one may compare (1) social rates of return, with nominal values of tradable goods and services being adjusted for border prices, along with (2) capital/value added, and (3) employment/capital ratios between public enterprise and private firms that are analogous in other respects. Also relevant are characteristics of the currently unsatisfied private demand for credit, and the willingness of foreign capital sources to channel funds to the local private sector through financial institutions, as opposed to lending to public enterprises.

Accelerating Industrialization

As a rationale for the establishment of public enterprises in the manufacturing sector, of greater importance than any ideological preference for state *versus* private ownership has been, in many countries, the perception that private capital and entrepreneurship were not mobilizing as rapidly as desirable, from the viewpoint of social objectives—and indeed, given various and sundry constraints, could not be expected to do so—to exploit socially profitable investment and production opportunities, especially in the field of import substitution.

By international standards, many of the facilities established in this area by the public sector have been too small to exploit the economies of scale associated with modern technology, and many have operated at only a small fraction of even the limited capacity with which they were established. High average production costs resulting from these (and other) circumstances have engendered financial deficits for many such enterprises, creating yet another source of pressure on government budgets and credit markets.

On the other hand, the problem is not generic to public enterprises. Government policy has drawn large sums of private capital into inefficient import-substitution industries, which have not always received, *ex post facto*, the degree of protection required to support selling prices that would cover costs.[29]

---

[29] A common manifestation of financially inadequate protection *ex post facto* is that firms are given promises of restrictions on domestic competition that are subsequently not honored, whether for good reasons—desire to reduce costs, create pressure to export, etc.—or bad (bribery by competitors).

Before the problem is made to look too much like that faced under the earlier topic of price control, it should be noted that the economist's optimizing concern here approaches the price issue from the opposite direction, seeking to avoid the distortions that arise where resources are allocated to high-cost activities when improved policies would allocate them to efficient uses and thereby accelerate the growth of output and employment. It is this concern that leads one to reject additional protection as a necessarily desirable solution to the financial strains encountered by public and/or private enterprises in this area.

Likewise, the absence of such strains in import-substituting public enterprises, if achieved by high effective protection that distorts the economy's cost structure and discourages export-led growth, should not be taken to mean that the enterprises in question pose no problem from the viewpoint of macroeconomic policy. A de facto policy of ensuring financial viability for a wide range of industries with very high unit domestic resource costs, even negative value added at border prices, certainly qualifies as a macroeconomic policy, and one highly counterproductive from the viewpoint of long-term economic and political stability.

Income Redistribution

Promotion of Small-Scale Producers Through Credit

This objective comes first under the heading of income redistribution because it has loomed large in the financial position of public credit institutions in many countries. The problem arises when governments—often aided and abetted by donor agencies—direct credit institutions to finance provision of capital equipment, current inputs and/or working capital to farmers, artisans, and other small-scale producers whose collateral, if any, cannot be readily converted into cash. The borrowers are not oblivious to the difficulties, whether economic or political, that creditors would face in trying to foreclose on and sell their land or movable assets, and except where management conveys a credible threat of cutting off future credit (which has often proven an elusive goal) and, moreover, the net present value of the future credit exceeds that of the current amounts due, the institutions in question have encountered serious problems of arrears and defaults.[30]

Insofar as an initial government subvention leaks out, is not replenished, and the program winds down, continuing fiscal implications are absent. But where the government faces political pressure to continue lending, as in the case of agricultural credit that is cast as seasonal crop finance, the repayment shortfall may engender ongoing fiscal pressure.

In many countries, the problem is assailed as a reflection of weak management of public credit institutions and perhaps also as a slackening of

---

[30] The issue considered here does not arise, or assumes considerably less importance, to the extent that geographical or technological factors enable the credit-providing agency to appropriate a substantial share of the borrowers' output and to deduct loan service payments before passing on the net proceeds.

political discipline when governments hesitate to crack down on a large mass of low-income defaulters. The policy discussion revolves around ways and means of improving management and stiffening politicians' backbones. However, even if implementation of the policy were entrusted to the private money market, institutions in the formal sector would ordinarily seek government guarantees before intervening in markets with dubious collateral, and continuation of the program would involve a fiscal burden.

Once more the quintessential public enterprise issue is whether social objectives are enhanced by entrusting the activity to public institutions as opposed to working out some cost reimbursement and loan guarantee arrangement with private agencies.[31]

Other Modes of Vertical Income Redistribution

The public enterprise mode of industrial organization can contribute to achievement of income distribution goals because sectors of investment can be chosen and employment configurations designed so that disposable income flows are targeted at particular segments of the population.

On the other hand, critiques of public enterprise performance in some countries have alleged that, by appropriating an undue share of the nation's fiscal and credit resources for a small set of highly capital-intensive, corruptly installed, and/or badly managed public enterprises, governments, while undoubtedly raising the disposable incomes of a small privileged class of managers and workers, have retarded the creation and expansion of a much bigger set of small- and medium-sized private businesses that would have drawn a larger segment of the labor force into modern economic activity and thus would, in the final analysis, have made for a lower Gini coefficient of income inequality. While these allegations certainly do not apply to every country, they raise a set of issues that must be addressed in measuring the distributional impact of public enterprise. Given the extensive overlap between the issues of employment creation and income distribution, the parameters to be evaluated under the present heading include those listed above under "Economic Growth," notably comparative capital/value added and employment/capital ratios, and characteristics of the unsatisfied private demand for credit.

Geographical Redistribution (Promoting Regional Equity)

Once again, a public enterprise-oriented policy confers direct control over the locations whose populations are to benefit from an expansion of economic activity.

The appropriate baseline with which to compare the contribution of public enterprise toward regional equity is a program of subsidies and other incentives by which government would seek to attract private investment, domestic

---

[31] Some countries have pursued yet another alternative—that of strengthening the informal financial sector to satisfy small producers' credit needs at less "usurious" interest rates than frequently characterize this market at present. While the fiscal and monetary burdens of such an approach are minimal, its capacity to meet the relevant demand is a subject of debate that cannot be resolved here.

or foreign, into less developed regions. Public enterprise will come out ahead in the comparison if its fiscal impact is less burdensome than the incentives government would have had to offer private firms to generate the same disposable income. In the absence of a negotiating record that shows just what private investors asked in order to locate in a region, this exercise will unavoidably involve a greater or lesser degree of speculation.

In the event public enterprise is shown to have pumped X amount of disposable income into a region at lower social cost than might have been expected from the baseline alternative, the question of negative, zero, or positive net present value will still remain. An approach that has won considerable favor in recent years is the revealed preference method expounded in the United Nations Industrial Development Organization (UNIDO) project evaluation guidelines, whereby the analyst assesses the implicit weight given by policymakers to an increment of disposable income in Region A as opposed to Region B by examining their past or present choices among investment alternatives.[32] This paper will not tarry on this point, which is tangential to the intrinsic social efficiency of public enterprises.

Localization/Indigenization

Supply Sources

The principle here is to ensure production locally of certain goods and services that are regarded as "strategic" to the economy, the defense effort, or whatever, and in which the private sector evinces little interest or demands excessive subsidies. The key question in evaluation: have the state-controlled producers succeeded in generating sufficient local value added, measured at border prices, to make the country's dependence on imported inputs less of a problem than its previous dependence on imports of the final product was perceived to be?

Asset Ownership and Control

Here the objective is to displace or forestall foreign ownership and control of existing and potential productive facilities. The current government's intention may be to leave the facilities in state hands indefinitely or to turn them over to local private ownership as and when the government considers the private sector "ready" to receive them. ("Readiness" may be measured in the proportion of share value, on whatever basis estimated, that local private investors are able and willing to put up out of their own resources, which should not exceed a "reasonable" amount of debt capital; it may also relate to government's perception of the availability of private managerial talent.) Among criteria for performance evaluation: does government exercise de facto control over the facilities in question, or is it effectively at the mercy of foreign managers and suppliers, its nominal partners in a joint venture? What is the record of divestiture of state-owned facilities to local private investors? To what extent are the latter merely "fronting" for foreigners?

---

[32] United Nations Industrial Development Organization, *Guidelines for Project Evaluation* (New York, 1972). See especially Chapters 7, 11, and 12.

Jobs

Some governments consider labor legislation and immigration control over employment of foreign manpower by private firms to be an inadequate mechanism for ensuring citizens access to skilled and white-collar positions. Accordingly, public enterprise is viewed as a vehicle for accelerated training and promotion of citizen labor. Partial evaluation of its performance in this regard may be achieved by comparing the relevant cadres of analogous enterprises under public and private (domestic or foreign) control. The far more complex general equilibrium issue is: which mode of industrial organization ultimately prepares more citizens for effective economic participation at middle and upper levels? Should the allegation prove correct that public enterprise in some countries crowds out more value added under the aegis of small- and medium-sized private business than it generates itself, the case for the public enterprise regime as a superior contributor to human capital formation in those countries would be weakened.

National Policymaking

The fact that this is the most nebulous of the subobjectives under localization does not gainsay its importance as a rationale for resort to public enterprise, based on the perception that concentration in the foreign headquarters of multinational firms of authority over investment, employment, procurement, production, pricing, and marketing decisions of major local enterprises heavily circumscribes the ability of the government to determine macroeconomic policies in these areas. This concern is cited when certain areas of production are closed to foreign investment, and it also partly motivates a policy on the part of some governments to resist the establishment of branches and wholly owned subsidiaries of foreign companies in favor of joint ventures with sufficient public sector participation to qualify as public enterprises. To evaluate achievement of the objective, one reviews the performance of the enterprises in whose establishment this concern has been a motivating factor and considers how they might have acted differently in the areas listed above, had they responded solely to interests of multinationals.

The mere fact that an enterprise qualifies as public in no way guarantees that its performance adheres more closely to government policy guidelines (with the degree of ambiguity that often attaches to identifying what these are) than would have that of a multinational subsidiary. An extensive and rapidly growing literature dealing with the behavior of public enterprise managers points to many dichotomies between their interests and government's policy concerns.

Miscellaneous Objectives

Concluding the discussion of noncommercial objectives supposedly served by the establishment of public enterprises are two that figure less often in explicit rationalizations, while carrying weight from time to time in some countries.

Ensuring Government Access to Market Information for Regulatory Purposes

The principle here is that government, by entering certain lines of production on its own account, acquires hard data about costs and selling prices with which to design more enlightened price control measures and other regulatory policies vis-à-vis the remaining enterprises in an industry. For purposes of evaluation, the analyst would require access to the flow of information from the public enterprises in question to the regulatory authorities and would have to judge the effectiveness of its use by the latter. Once again the fact that a public enterprise may have access to "inside" information pertaining to its industry does not guarantee that management will consider it in its own interest to reveal the complete picture to government regulators.

Improving Working Conditions

With this variant of subobjectives relating to employment, a government seeks to provide better working conditions for the labor force in a given line of production than those prevailing under private management or thought likely to prevail should an industry be left to develop under private auspices. To be sure, such magnanimity vis-à-vis the proletariat is likely to bear a fiscal, and even a monetary, cost. Evaluation of performance is a relatively simple matter of comparing terms and conditions of service and work environment of the public enterprise in question with a sample of private firms of comparable size. Intensified regulation of the private sector in this area should not be overlooked as a baseline alternative.

Concluding Note to Appendix I

It is virtually axiomatic that a given number of economists will produce at least as many different typologies of public enterprise noncommercial objectives. One prepared some seven years before the present paper is of particular interest because its author went to the trouble of drawing up a matrix of information requirements associated with assessing attainment of the objectives.[33] The matrix is reproduced on pages 102–103 as Table 5.

---

[33] Alan A. Tait, "The Fiscal Policy Objectives of Nonfinancial Public Enterprises and Their Information Requirements: A Simple Taxonomy Suggested" (unpublished, International Monetary Fund, 1977).

Objectives

Economic

Allocation

1. Decreasing costs

2. Monopoly

3. Externalities

4. Generate surplus funds

5. Transfer private profits to the Exchequer

Distribution

6. Horizontal

7. Vertical

Stabilization

8. Employment

9. Prices

Growth

10. Help weak and/or declining industries

11. Deal with lumpiness of investment

12. Advance research and development

13. Improve industrial relations

14. Promote international economic cooperation

Balance of payments

15. Import substitution

16. Export expansion

Political

17. Strategic industry

18. Commanding heights of the economy

Table 5. Nonfinancial Public Enterprises: Objectives and Evaluation

Types of Information Required

	Financial	Percent market controlled	Number of employees	Depletion rates	Price indices and weights	Domestic supply as percent of imports	Household budget surveys	Commodity price changes (including black market prices)	Number of new employees	Local unemployment	Migration	National Plan	1-0 Sector	Patents and royalties	Days lost through stoppages	Capacity to ship imports	Cost-benefit analysis	Public sector borrowing requirement	Wage rates	Wages paid
	a	b	c	d	e	f	g	h	i	j	k	l	m	n	o	p	q	r	s	t
1.	✓							✓												
2.	✓	✓						✓												
3.	✓	✓	✓	✓		✓											✓			✓
4.	✓					✓												✓		
5.	✓	✓																✓		
6.	✓				✓		✓	✓									✓		✓	
7.	✓				✓		✓	✓									✓		✓	
8.	✓								✓	✓	✓		✓					✓	✓	✓
9.	✓				✓		✓	✓										✓	✓	✓
10.	✓	✓	✓			✓			✓	✓			✓		✓		✓			
11.	✓											✓	✓							
12.	✓												✓	✓						
13.	✓		✓						✓	✓									✓	
14.	✓											✓								
15.	✓	✓				✓														
16.	✓											✓								
17.	✓												✓			✓				
18.	✓	✓	✓								✓	✓								

Source: Alan A. Tait, "The Fiscal Policy Objectives of Nonfinancial Public Enterprises and Their Information Requirements: A Simple Taxonomy Suggested" (unpublished, International Monetary Fund, 1977).

APPENDIX II

Computation of Public Enterprise Sector Capital Stock as Determinant of Annualized Opportunity Cost of Capital

Evaluation of the public enterprise sector's performance in covering the social opportunity cost of its capital, and measurement of the subsidy involved where this cost is not covered, presuppose estimation of the sector's capital stock.

The first step in deriving such an estimate is to compile a series on annual gross capital formation, revaluing each year's historical value by the quotient of the relevant price index for the latest year (the year in whose prices capital stock is to be expressed) divided by the index of the investment year in question. If separate price indices are available for components of capital formation (construction, machinery imports, vehicles, etc.), then those should be used for the revaluation. A wholesale price index would be most appropriate for revaluing inventory changes. In some countries, one will have to be content with using a crude consumer price index for the entire exercise.

A series of annual capital depreciation is now needed in order to arrive at a net capital stock. Revaluing the data for each year of the historical series would be extremely cumbersome. A suggested alternative approach is to break down the constant-price capital formation series by broad asset class and to apply a perpetual inventory technique to each class according to its mean economic life. Such an approach has been used by Harberger to calculate the return on national capital stocks of a number of countries.[34] A minimum breakdown (used by Harberger) would distinguish between buildings, machinery and equipment, and inventory; data in some countries would permit a more detailed classification, separating out, for example, vehicles. Harberger assumes mean asset lives of 40 years for buildings and 12½ years for machinery and equipment, yielding annual depreciation rates of 2½ percent and 8 percent, respectively.

The trick in applying this approach is to obtain a plausible estimate for the capital stock in some initial year. The longer the investment series, and thus the earlier that year, the less any overestimation or underestimation of capital stock at that point will influence the current estimate, since more of the former will have depreciated out of existence. In some countries, the public enterprise

---

[34] Arnold C. Harberger, "On Estimating the Rate of Return to Capital in Colombia," *Project Evaluation: Collected Papers* (London and Chicago, 1972), pp. 132–56; Arnold C. Harberger and Daniel L. Wisecarver, "Private and Social Rates of Return to Capital in Uruguay," *Economic Development and Cultural Change*, Vol. 25 (April 1977), pp. 411–45; Arnold C. Harberger, "Perspectives on Capital and Technology in Less-Developed Countries," in M.J. Artis and A.R. Nobay (eds.), *Contemporary Economic Analysis* (Croom-Helm, London, 1978), pp. 15–40. The latter paper applies the procedure to 18 countries, of which 11 (including Greece and Portugal) qualify as less-developed countries.

sector has mushroomed to such an extent in recent years that current capital stock is overwhelmingly determined by investment series going back only a short time. Where this is not so and annual investment data are not readily available for earlier years, one can follow Harberger in picking a period of, say, three years when there are reasons for presuming that value added in the public enterprise sector and capital stock of the different asset classes all grew at approximately the same rate.

In this case, the equation $I_t = (d + r) K_{t-1}$ holds (reflecting investment's two components, (1) replacement, and (2) augmentation of capital stock), where t denotes the middle year of the period, I denotes annual investment in a given asset class, K denotes the year-end stock of that class, d denotes the relevant depreciation rate, and r denotes the common growth rate of value added and capital stock during the three-year period only (values of r for subsequent periods are irrelevant). To eliminate the effects of random fluctuations in investment, one averages I over the three-year period. Then capital stock of the class in question at the end of year t equals $\dfrac{I_{t+1}}{d + r}$, stock at the end of year $t + 1$ equals $(1 - d)$ times stock at the end of year t plus investment during $t + 1$, that is,

$$K_{t+1} = (1 - d)\frac{I_{t+1}}{d + r} + I_{t+1} = \left(\frac{1 - d}{d + r} + 1\right)I_{t+1} = \frac{1 + r}{d + r}I_{t+1},$$

and values of capital stock emerge readily as functions of d, r (during the initial period), and successive values of I.

The gross capital formation series may require adjustment insofar as it was financed by an inflow of foreign capital, say X foreign currency units, tied so closely to the investment(s) in question that, had those investments not been carried out, the total inflow would have been X units less. (To allow for the possibility that inflows in later periods might have been correspondingly higher to compensate for omission of X in an earlier period, we must convert the comparison to present value terms, discounting foreign capital inflows at the social discount rate.)

In this case, the correct measure of the annualized social opportunity cost of the capital in question is not the product of its constant-price depreciated value and the social discount rate, which costs each unit of capital at the return it would have yielded in the investment opportunity forgone at the margin. Rather, the correct measure of annualized cost is the annual interest or dividend payment made to the investor or provider of funds by way of servicing the capital transfer in question. When the annualized cost of the relevant assets is taken into account in this way, the corresponding asset value must be subtracted from the remaining capital stock by which the discount rate is to be multiplied.

For example, if the transfer comprises a "soft" loan bearing interest well below the recipient country's social discount rate—and of course the longer the amortization period at any given interest rate meeting this condition, the softer the loan, in other words the larger its grant element—then the annual interest payment is correspondingly well below the product of asset value and the social discount rate, and the procedure outlined here makes for a lower annualized social opportunity cost than would prevail were all investment resources fungible.[35]

---

[35] This discussion should not be interpreted to mean that tied inflows are desirable because their social opportunity cost is less than that of fungible inflows. What matters is the productivity of the projects in which the resources are invested. An inflow tied to the source's inappropriate equipment often turns out to be very costly in relation to value added.

APPENDIX III

Quality of Investment Decision Making: An Indirect Indicator of Public Enterprise Sector Impact

The need to define this final area of macroeconomic performance of the public enterprise sector arises because reports have been published alleging that declared pursuit of either commercial or noncommercial objectives cannot always be taken at face value.

The discussion in the main body of this paper proceeds on the assumption that policy decisions with regard to the establishment and operation of public enterprises are made in accordance with sincere perceptions of national interest on the part of the authorities. Thus, even where public enterprise operations impose substantial fiscal and monetary burdens, the paper assumes that the sector plays the role it does because the authorities have concluded rationally that the social benefits gained thereby are bona fide and more than offset the costs.

The reports in question allege, on the other hand, that corruption has served, in some situations, as a primary motive in the establishment of certain public enterprises other than public utilities and natural monopolies. In essence, it is charged, establishment of these entities represented a move by one or more politicians and/or officials to tap into a circuit of transactions occasioned by the sale of goods and services and to divert a portion of it to the consumption and aggrandizement of self, family, and friends. It is noted that the initiative for establishment often originated with the private sector in the form of promotors, suppliers, and other interests who have been rewarded with a share of the "take." Under one frequently cited scenario, foreign suppliers are said to have induced officials to establish public enterprises as customers for their wares, notably factory machinery. In return for a kickback, the officials have supposedly arranged public financing, local and foreign (the latter on the strength of government guarantees), and enacted measures of protection against domestic and foreign competition. Apart from obvious social costs imposed by such practices it is alleged that they have undermined international competitiveness and choked off industrial growth via balance of payments pressures.

Sociologists focusing on the study of political elites and the bureaucracy build scientific models that predict the response of officials, under specified circumstances, in situations offering such temptations. They add the obvious caveat that corruption is neither limited to the formulation of public enterprise policy, nor more characteristic of it than of other governmental functions.

The present discussion takes no position regarding the truth of the allegations in question. However, should they turn out to be correct in certain situations, it could be argued that economists would mislead by confining their attention to measuring the public enterprise sector's attainment of putative goals that had little to do with decisions bearing on its organization. In such cases, it would be incumbent on them to seek indicators bearing on the overall quality of the decision-making process with respect to establishment and expansion of public enterprises. In this vein, questions such as the following would have to be addressed.

● *Choices among alternative uses of resources*

How serious an attempt is made to weigh alternative strategies for, and configurations of, the public enterprise sector according to commercial and noncommercial objectives? Are scarce resources expended in collecting relevant data and commissioning studies by bona fide, disinterested experts? Do the authorities appear to give serious weight to the findings of such studies and recommendations by their technical staffs? Conversely, do the authorities' consultations regarding alternative courses of action appear to be limited to promoters and would-be suppliers? Are feasibility studies at best perfunctory, at worse merely disguised sales pitches?

● *Design of investments*

Once it has been effectively decided to proceed with a certain category of activity under the aegis of public enterprise, how serious is the consideration given to different technologies of production, and different institutional and legal arrangements for implementation? How serious an effort is made to minimize costs for a given level of output? Is competitive tendering provided for? Conversely, do the authorities seem to rush into approval of a design that suits the convenience of a particular supplier rather than offering economies to the host country?

● *Investment execution*

Are standard arrangements made for supervision of procurement, execution of construction contracts, etc.? How severe are the cost overruns and start-up difficulties encountered? Does equipment perform according to specifications and, if not, what is done about it? When the problems encountered are so severe—leading in the extreme to project collapse—as to raise the possibility of fraud in project choice and design, is the matter brought out into the open and investigated, or is it swept under the rug to avoid embarrassment to culpable politicians and officials?

REFERENCES

Chu, Ke-Young, and Andrew Feltenstein, "Relative Price Distortions and Inflation: The Case of Argentina, 1963–76," *Staff Papers*, International Monetary Fund (Washington), Vol. 25 (September 1978), pp. 452–93.

Gillis, Malcolm, "The Role of State Enterprises in Economic Development," *Social Research* (New York), Vol. 47 (Summer 1980), pp. 248–89.

Goode, Richard, "Nonfinancial Public Enterprises" (unpublished, International Monetary Fund, May 15, 1980).

Harberger, Arnold C., "On Estimating the Rate of Return to Capital in Colombia," in *Project Evaluation: Collected Papers* (Chicago: Markham, 1972), pp. 132–56.

————, "Perspectives on Capital and Technology in Less-Developed Countries," in *Contemporary Economic Analysis*, ed. by M.J. Artis and A.R. Nobay (London: Croom-Helm, 1978).

————, and Daniel L. Wisecarver, "Private and Social Rates of Return to Capital in Uruguay," in *Economic Development and Cultural Change* (Chicago), Vol. 25 (April 1977), pp. 411–45.

International Monetary Fund, *A Manual on Government Finance Statistics* (Draft) (Washington: IMF, 1974).

————, *International Financial Statistics Yearbook* (Washington: IMF, 1981).

Mali, Republic of, Ministère de Tutelle des Sociétés et Entreprises d'Etat, *Analyse de la Situation Financière du Secteur d'Etat au 31 Décembre 1976* (Bamako: October 1977).

Polak, J.J., and Victor Argy, "Credit Policy and the Balance of Payments," *Staff Papers*, International Monetary Fund (Washington), Vol. 18 (March 1971), pp. 1–24.

————, and Lorette Boissonneault, "Monetary Analysis of Income and Imports and Its Statistical Application," *Staff Papers*, International Monetary Fund (Washington), Vol. 7 (April 1960), pp. 349–415.

Tait, Alan A., "The Fiscal Policy Objectives of Nonfinancial Public Enterprises and Their Information Requirements: A Simple Taxonomy Suggested" (unpublished, International Monetary Fund, 1977).

United Nations Industrial Development Organization, *Guidelines for Project Evaluation* (New York: UN, 1972).

United Nations Statistical Office, *A System of National Accounts* (New York: UN, 1968).

Wattleworth, Michael, "Credit Subsidies in Budgetary Lending" (unpublished, International Monetary Fund, May 1983).

The Role of Public Enterprises: An International Statistical Comparison

R. P. SHORT*

There is a growing awareness that public enterprises can be a major source of macroeconomic problems. One consequence is that programs of the International Monetary Fund often contain undertakings relating to the public enterprise sector or to particular units within that sector.[1] There is, however, a shortage of analytical work on the macroeconomic role and impact of public enterprises. A principal reason for this is the scarcity and inadequacy of data on public enterprises.

As a preliminary to such work, this paper provides statistical information on important macroeconomic dimensions of public enterprise operations. Data are presented for almost 90 countries, including both industrial and developing countries and countries with a range of political philosophies regarding public ownership. The major exclusions are many Middle Eastern countries and most centrally planned economies in Europe and Asia.

In Section I, some of the problems that arise in compiling consistent data for public enterprises are discussed. In Section II, data on important characteristics of public enterprise sectors are presented. Fi-

*The research for this paper was largely undertaken in 1980–82 while the author was a staff member of the International Monetary Fund. Mr. Short is presently an Economic Advisor in H. M. Treasury, London. The views are his own, they do not necessarily represent those of the Fund or the Treasury.

[1] W.A. Beveridge and Margaret R. Kelly, "Fiscal Content of Financial Programs Supported by Stand-By Arrangements in the Upper Credit Tranches, 1969–78," *Staff Papers*, International Monetary Fund (Washington), Vol. 27 (June 1980), pp. 205–49.

nally, in Section III, statistics are provided on major indicators of the macroeconomic impact and performance of public enterprises—the level and composition of their overall financial balances and the financing they obtain from, in particular, the government and the banking system. A summary is provided in Section IV.

I. PROBLEMS OF DEFINITION AND AVAILABILITY OF DATA

Public enterprises have two defining characteristics: they are government owned and controlled; and they are engaged in business activities. Ideally, when making statistical comparisons, these characteristics should be given a precise and consistent meaning, but, in practice, this is difficult to do.

This is partly because it is difficult to draw a clear-cut and economically useful boundary around the public enterprise sector, especially as, in most countries, virtually all enterprises are subject to some degree of government control.[2] However, more important, it is because of data problems. None of the international organizations publishes comprehensive information on public enterprises and statistical sources for individual countries generally do not separately identify public enterprise operations. Moreover, there are differences between countries—and sometimes even between different sources for the same country—in the exact definition of the public enterprise sector used for statistical purposes.

In preparing the data for this paper, an attempt was made to adjust the statistics to a common definition that appeared suitable for statistical analysis. This met with only partial success. However, as much of the basic information has not previously been brought together, it was decided to err on the side of comprehensiveness rather than comparability in choosing which statistics to include.

The problems in obtaining consistent statistics are discussed in the remainder of this section. Details of the coverage and sources of the data are given in the Appendix.

As far as possible, ownership/control was taken to mean that the government is able to control management decisions by virtue of its ownership stake alone. This will be true if the enterprise is directly operated by a government department or, in the case of a separate

---

[2] Problems of definition are discussed by, for example, Leroy P. Jones in *Public Enterprise and Economic Development: The Korean Case* (Seoul: Korean Development Institute, 1975), pp. 22–42, and by Andreja Böhm in "The Concept, Definition and Classification of Public Enterprises," *Public Enterprise*, Vol. 1, No. 4 (1981), pp. 72–78.

enterprise, if the government holds a majority of its shares, either directly, or indirectly through another public enterprise. A smaller shareholding may be sufficient to give the government effective control, but this will depend on the distribution of the ownership of the remaining shares.

For many countries, little information is provided on the criteria used in classifying enterprises under the public enterprise sector. However, where an explicit definition is given, this is most often based on majority ownership as, for example, for Finland and Botswana. For a few countries, for example, Tunisia, some enterprises with minority government shareholdings are also included in public enterprise statistics. It is possible that these holdings are sufficient to enable the government to exercise effective control, but this cannot easily be determined.

More of a problem is that, for a large number of countries, a narrower definition than majority ownership is used for statistical purposes. There are three main reasons for this. First, for several countries, public enterprise statistics cover only enterprises with particular legal forms.[3] Most countries include public corporations in their statistics. However, some, for example, Malawi, exclude departmental undertakings, and some, for example, Sudan, exclude publicly owned companies. Second, for many countries, for example, Turkey, public enterprise statistics exclude enterprises owned by regional and local governments. Third, for several countries, statistics are only readily available for a number of the most important enterprises. These may be, for example, those subject to budgetary control, as in Mexico, or the largest, as in Mali, or those in receipt of government transfers.

The impact of these omissions varies widely. Excluded departmental undertakings are generally not significant in quantitative terms, although they include postal services, ports, and/or airports in a few countries and limited industrial or agricultural activities, such as printing or forestry, in several more. Also, in a number of cases, it was possible to obtain figures for these enterprises from government accounts. The omission of public enterprises owned by regional or local governments may be significant in some cases, especially in the larger developing countries of South America and Europe. However, in most

---

[3] There are three main legal forms that may be taken by a public enterprise: (1) it may be a departmental undertaking, that is, it is operated by a government department with finances and accounts at least partly integrated with those of the government; (2) it may be a public corporation, that is, a corporation operating under a special law that may lay down particular conditions, for example, that it should be wholly government owned or that control should be exercised in particular ways; or (3) it may be a publicly owned company, that is, a company operating under private law in which the government has a controlling ownership stake.

countries where such enterprises are excluded from the statistics, their operations are mainly confined to limited public utility, transport, and marketing activities. These are probably small compared with those of enterprises owned by the national government. The most serious omissions are publicly owned companies, especially indirectly held ones, and cases where only major enterprises are included in the statistics. Impressionistic evidence suggests that such exclusions are significant in quantitative terms in several countries. In a few cases, for example, Mexico, it was possible to obtain an estimate of the importance of these enterprises using other statistical sources, but in most cases it was not feasible to adjust the statistics in this way.

These omissions limit the comparability of the data in the tables. However, the particular definitions used in individual countries often correspond to ways of classifying public enterprises that are useful for analyzing their role.

First, an important distinction between public enterprises arises from the extent and nature of the control actually exercised by the government. It is this that mainly determines the economic impact of public ownership and, particularly between countries but also often within countries, there are substantial differences between public enterprises in this respect. Actual control is extremely difficult to measure and is not a suitable basis for a statistical definition for use in international comparisons. Nevertheless, at least implicitly, it is often a factor in classifying enterprises as public enterprises for statistical purposes. This is likely to be true when the enterprises included in statistics are only those subject to budgetary control. It may also be true when the legal form is a factor in defining the public enterprise sector; for example, publicly owned companies, especially indirectly held ones, are often subject to less control than other forms of public enterprise.

Second, in several developing countries, the number of public enterprises is large, sometimes exceeding 100. It is difficult, if not impossible, for the government to exercise effective control over such a large number of enterprises, especially in countries with weak administrative capacities. The controllable public enterprise sector may, therefore, be better represented by a few of the larger enterprises.

Third, the distinction between enterprises owned by different levels of government is also important. Because of the dispersion of control and the large number of enterprises, it will be more difficult to use the public enterprise sector as a macroeconomic policy tool when the local or regional element is substantial.

As far as possible, the business characteristic of public enterprises was taken to mean that the organization's output is sold and is of a type for which, in most countries, revenue is expected to cover a substantial proportion of costs. This condition is intended to restrict coverage to activities for which a market test is a major consideration in judging performance and to exclude public goods and merit goods. Attention was also confined to nonfinancial enterprises because financial enterprises have a special role in macroeconomic policy that requires separate analysis.

Most countries use some kind of business criterion in defining the public enterprise sector, although this is generally implicit and follows from only including organizations with accounts of a commercial nature. A few restrict the coverage of their statistics to only certain types of economic activity; for example, France only includes monopoly enterprises in basic industries. However, most differences in coverage between countries reflect institutional differences in the extent to which certain activities are organized in enterprise form or operated on a commercial basis. In particular, a number of countries include activities with public or merit good characteristics in their public enterprise statistics; for example, public hospitals in Belgium, toll roads in Austria, and broadcasting services in many countries. On the whole, these differences are probably not of major quantitative importance. Also, in a few cases, disaggregated data were available to enable such activities to be excluded from the figures.

Nonfinancial public enterprises are identified separately in the statistics of most countries. However, in a few cases, for example, the United Kingdom, the only figures available include financial as well as nonfinancial enterprises. As the quantitative importance of financial public enterprises for many of the variables used in this paper, most notably capital formation, is likely to be small, this is probably not a serious problem. There are also some hybrid cases of enterprises engaged in both business and financial activities. Public agricultural and industrial development corporations, which are common in developing countries, are a prime example. Individual country practice was followed in deciding whether to classify these as public enterprises.

The differences in coverage noted above should be borne in mind when considering the figures.[4] Overall, it seems unlikely that they seriously distort the general picture given by the tables, although they probably mean that the size and impact of the public enterprise sector is understated, at least on average. These differences are most relevant when comparisons are made between individual countries. They are of less significance when considering averages for broad areas or trends over time.

---

[4] Cases where the coverage of the figures is significantly different from the common definition are footnoted in the tables.

II. SIZE AND CHARACTERISTICS OF THE PUBLIC ENTERPRISE SECTOR

Size of the Public Enterprise Sector

The quantitative importance of public enterprises is clear from Table 1, which shows two measures of the size of the public enterprise sector: the percentage shares of public enterprises in gross domestic product (GDP) and in gross fixed capital formation. In the mid-1970s, public enterprises accounted for an average[5] of 13½ percent of capital formation for the countries for which investment figures are available; excluding the United States, whose share is untypically low, the average share exceeded 16½ percent. They accounted for an average of 9½ percent of GDP for the smaller group of countries, again excluding the United States, for which output statistics are available.

It is also clear that these high averages are not simply a reflection of large public enterprise sectors in a few countries: public enterprises are now of major quantitative importance in most of the countries included in Table 1. There are also broad similarities in their shares, especially in output, in countries that are diverse in terms of geographical location and economic development. African countries generally have noticeably larger public enterprise sectors than other areas. However, average output and investment shares are very similar for developing countries in Asia, South America, and Europe. Although, in the mid-1970s, the investment share for all developing countries of 27 percent was much higher than that of 11 percent for industrial countries, the output share of both groups was close to 9 percent. The majority of countries in both groups had investment shares of between 10 percent and 25 percent and output shares of between 5 percent and 15 percent.

These similarities probably result in part from differences in the coverage of public enterprise statistics. However, more important is the fact that they reflect the variety of factors that have contributed to the development of substantial public enterprise sectors in a large number of countries.[6]

First, socialist policies have been of some significance in several countries and the dominant factor in a few, for example, Burma and

---

[5] The area averages shown in the tables are weighted averages for 1974–77 or the closest period for which data are available. The weights are GDP in U.S. dollars for all quantities except investment for which the weights are gross fixed capital formation in U.S. dollars. The period averages are simple averages of the ratios for individual years.

[6] These are discussed in more detail in, for example, Malcolm Gillis, "The Role of State Enterprises in Economic Development," *Social Research*, Vol. 47 (Summer 1980), pp. 248–89.

Table 1. Output and Investment Shares of Public Enterprises

	Years	Percentage Share in GDP at Factor Cost[1]		Percentage Share in Gross Fixed Capital Formation[2]	
"World" (average)[3]		**9.4**	**(9.4)**	**13.4**	**(17.1)**
Industrial countries (average)[3]		**9.6**	**(9.6)**	**11.1**	**(15.0)**
Australia[4]	1954–57	9.1		22.7	(. .)
	1958–62	10.4		19.9	(. .)
	1963–65	10.5		18.4	(5.3)
	1966–69	10.3		19.1	(6.0)
	1970–73	9.8		17.8	(6.1)
	1974–77	9.2		18.7	(6.5)
	1978–79	9.4		19.2	(5.9)
	1980	. . .		19.2	(5.2)
Austria[1]	1970–73	15.8		. . .	
	1974–75	15.6		. . .	
	1976–77	14.5		19.2	
	1978–79	14.5		19.2	
Belgium	1953	. . .		16.2	
	1954–57	. . .		14.2	
	1958–61	. . .		12.9	
	1962–65	. . .		10.4	
	1966–69	. . .		11.6	
	1970–73	. . .		12.4	
	1974–77	. . .		12.6	
	1978–79	. . .		13.1	
Canada[2,4]	1970–73	. . .		10.9	(. .)
	1974–77	. . .		14.7	(. .)
	1978–81	. . .		14.8	(2.8)
	1982	. . .		21.7	(. .)
Denmark	1965	6.9		10.0	
	1974	6.3		8.3	
Finland[2]	1970–73	. . .		10.1	
	1974–75	. . .		13.6	
France[5]	1959–61	12.7	(7.6)	23.0	(14.5)
	1962–65	12.8	(7.3)	20.6	(11.4)
	1966–69	12.8	(6.9)	19.0	(10.2)
	1970–73	12.2	(6.0)	15.4	(7.5)
	1974	11.9	(5.3)	14.0	(7.3)
	1975–77	. . .	(5.8)	. . .	(9.7)
	1978–81	. . .	(6.2)	. . .	(12.0)
	1982	. . .	(6.5)	. . .	(12.5)
Germany, Fed. Rep. of[1]	1962–65	. . .		10.4	
	1966–69	. . .		11.0	
	1970–73	. . .		12.3	
	1974–75	. . .		14.5	
	1976–77	10.3		12.3	
	1978–79	10.2		10.8	
Ireland	1974–77	. . .		13.1	
	1978	. . .		11.8	

Table 1 (continued). Output and Investment Shares of Public Enterprises

	Years	Percentage Share in GDP at Factor Cost[1]	Percentage Share in Gross Fixed Capital Formation[2]
Italy[1]	1967–70	7.0	14.2
	1970–73	7.1	19.4
	1974–77	7.7	17.2
	1978	7.5	16.4
	1979–80	. . .	15.2
Japan[2]	1965	. . .	13.6
	1966–69	. . .	12.7
	1970–73	. . .	9.9
	1974–77	. . .	11.6
	1978–81	. . .	11.2
Luxembourg	1970–73	. . .	7.7
	1974	. . .	9.2
Netherlands[2]	1968–70	. . .	14.8
	1971–73	3.6	13.8
	1974–77	. . .	14.1
	1978	. . .	12.6
Norway[4]	1959–61	. . .	13.4 (. . .)
	1962–65	. . .	14.6 (. . .)
	1966–69	. . .	14.1 (. . .)
	1970–73	. . .	14.8 (7.8)
	1974–77	. . .	17.7 (9.9)
	1978–80	. . .	22.2 (12.2)
Spain[1]	1974	. . .	12.3
	1977–78	. . .	14.5
	1979	4.1	16.6
	1980	. . .	15.6
Sweden[1,4]	1978–80	. . . (6.0)	15.3 (11.4)
United Kingdom	1938	. . .	4.7
	1946–49	. . .	11.0
	1950–53	. . .	21.5
	1954–57	. . .	22.4
	1958–61	. . .	21.3
	1962–65	10.3	19.8
	1966–69	10.4	20.1
	1970–73	10.0	16.3
	1974–77	11.3	18.6
	1978–81	10.9	16.8
	1982	11.2	17.1
United States[2]	1960	. . .	4.0
	1963	. . .	4.1
	1965	. . .	4.0
	1967–69	. . .	4.3
	1970–73	. . .	4.2
	1974–77	. . .	4.9
	1978	. . .	4.4

Table 1 (continued). Output and Investment Shares of Public Enterprises

	Years	Percentage Share in GDP at Factor Cost[1]		Percentage Share in Gross Fixed Capital Formation[2]	
Developing countries (average)[3]		**8.6**	**(8.6)**	**27.0**	**(25.2)**
Oil exporting countries					
Algeria	1965	. . .		5.5	
	1966–69	. . .		21.1	
	1970–73	. . .		47.5	
	1974–77	. . .		70.2	
	1978–81	. . .		67.6	
Venezuela[1,6]	1968	. . .		15.3	
	1972–73	2.9		22.0	
	1974–77	15.0	(2.5)	22.3	(20.1)
	1978–80	27.5	(3.0)	36.3	(25.7)
Africa (average)[3]		17.5		32.4	
Benin[1,7]	1976	7.6		. . .	
Botswana[1]	1974–77	7.7		16.5	
	1978–79	7.3		7.7	
Ethiopia	1976–77	. . .		17.6	
	1978–80	. . .		36.5	
Gambia, The	1978–80	. . .		37.9	
Guinea[1]	1979	25.0		. . .	
Ivory Coast[1]	1965–69	. . .		16.5	
	1970–73	. . .		27.9	
	1974–77	. . .		28.8	
	1978	. . .		38.2	
	1979	10.5		39.5	
Kenya	1964–65	7.5		9.7	
	1966–69	8.1		13.0	
	1970–73	8.7		10.6	
	1974–77	. . .		18.1	
	1978–79	. . .		17.3	
Liberia	1973	. . .		24.3	
	1974–76	. . .		14.1	
	1977	6.8		. . .	
Malawi	1969	. . .		20.2	
	1970–73	. . .		29.4	
	1974–77	. . .		28.1	
	1978	. . .		21.2	
Mali[7]	1975–77	11.2		20.9	
	1978	9.4		7.6	
Mauritania	1973	. . .		85.8	
	1974–77	. . .		31.1	
	1978–79	. . .		37.2	
Mauritius	1977–79	. . .		14.4	
Senegal[1]	1970	8.4		. . .	
	1974	19.9		17.9	
Sierra Leone	1979	7.6		19.6	
Tanzania	1964–65	. . .		9.2	

Table 1 (continued). Output and Investment Shares of Public Enterprises

	Years	Percentage Share in GDP at Factor Cost[1]	Percentage Share in Gross Fixed Capital Formation[2]
Tanzania	1966–69	9.3	22.7
	1970–73	12.7	48.2
	1974–77	12.3	30.3
	1978–79	. . .	16.3
Togo	1980	11.8	. . .
Tunisia	1967–68	. . .	30.9
	1969	25.9	25.2
	1970–73	. . .	34.1
	1974–77	. . .	39.1
	1978–79	25.4	44.6
	1980–81	. . .	35.8
Zambia	1972	37.8	49.7
	1979–80	. . .	61.2
Asia (average)[3]		8.0	27.7
Bangladesh	1974	5.7	31.0
Burma	1968–69	. . .	43.4
	1970–73	. . .	43.3
	1974–77	. . .	39.6
	1978–80	. . .	60.6
India	1960–61	5.3	34.7
	1962–65	6.1	36.8
	1966–69	6.5	29.6
	1970–73	7.3	29.0
	1974–77	9.8	33.8
	1978	10.3	33.7
Korea[2]	1963–64	5.5	31.2
	1965–69	. . .	24.2
	1970–73	7.0	21.7
	1974–77	6.4	25.1
	1978–80	. . .	22.8
Nepal	1971–73	1.1	12.9
	1974–75	1.3	. . .
Pakistan	1961	4.5	. . .
	1966	4.1	. . .
	1970–73	4.4	19.3
	1974–75	6.0	33.3
	1976–77	. . .	43.5
	1978–81	. . .	44.6
Papua New Guinea	1977	. . .	18.8
Philippines[2]	1960	. . .	2.0
	1965	. . .	1.8
	1966–69	. . .	1.8
	1970–73	. . .	0.7
	1974–77	1.7	9.5
	1978	. . .	10.9
Sri Lanka	1961	4.8	16.3

Table 1 (continued). Output and Investment Shares of Public Enterprises

	Years	Percentage Share in GDP at Factor Cost[1]		Percentage Share in Gross Fixed Capital Formation[2]	
Sri Lanka	1962–65	. . .		21.8	
	1966	6.1		29.0	
	1967–69	. . .		22.2	
	1970–73	. . .		19.4	
	1974	9.9		15.7	
	1975–77	. . .		18.4	
	1978	. . .		28.4	
Taiwan*	1951–53	11.9		31.4	
	1954–57	11.7		34.3	
	1958–61	13.5		38.1	
	1962–65	14.1		27.7	
	1966–69	13.6		28.0	
	1970–73	13.3		30.5	
	1974–77	13.6		35.0	
	1978–80	13.5		32.4	
Thailand	1969	3.5		9.8	
	1970–73	3.6		8.5	
	1974–77	. . .		8.1	
	1978–79	. . .		12.8	
Europe (average)[3]		6.6		23.4	
Greece[2]	1975	5.8		10.8	
	1976–78	. . .		9.3	
	1979	6.1		8.7	
Malta[8]	1955–57	. . .		18.3	
	1958–61	. . .		11.4	
	1962–65	3.7		10.8	
	1966–69	4.2		12.8	
	1970–73	4.2		8.9	
	1974–77	3.8		11.6	
	1978–80	4.2		6.3	
Portugal[2,9]	1962–65	. . .		6.2	
	1966–69	. . .		6.7	
	1970–73	. . .		6.9	
	1974–75	. . .		9.0	
	1976	14.3	(9.7)	31.0	(29.1)
	1978–80	. . .		33.2	
Turkey[1,10]	1952	7.0		. . .	
	1957	7.0		. . .	
	1960–61	. . .		12.6	
	1962–65	7.0		14.5	
	1966–69	7.6		17.4	
	1970–73	8.1		22.6	
	1974–77	5.8		23.5	(29.4)
	1978–81	5.2		28.7	
	1982	5.8		30.4	

Table 1 (continued). Output and Investment Shares of Public Enterprises

	Years	Percentage Share in GDP at Factor Cost[1]	Percentage Share in Gross Fixed Capital Formation[2]
Middle East			
Egypt	1976–79	. . .	47.8
Western Hemisphere (average)[3]		6.6	22.5
Argentina[7]	1968–69	. . .	15.4
	1970–73	. . .	17.5
	1974–75	. . .	18.2
	1976–77	4.8	20.7
	1978–80	4.6	19.6
Bahamas	1975–77	. . .	20.4
	1978–79	. . .	31.6
Barbados	1975–77	. . .	9.6
	1978–80	. . .	11.4
Bolivia[1]	1960	. . .	31.1
	1968	. . .	39.1
	1970	. . .	36.0
	1971–73	10.2	39.5
	1974–77	12.1	40.9
Brazil	1968	. . .	14.0
	1980	. . .	22.8
Chile[7]	1961	. . .	10.5
	1964	. . .	11.7
	1968	. . .	15.2
	1974–77	15.2	20.0
	1978–80	13.0	12.9
Colombia[4]	1974–77	. . . (1.9)	10.3 (6.6)
	1978–80	. . . (2.6)	8.9 (5.6)
Costa Rica	1960	. . .	5.0
	1968	. . .	7.3
	1977–79	. . .	19.6
Dominica	1975–77	. . .	25.5
	1978–79	. . .	7.8
Dominican Republic[7]	1971–73	. . .	12.2
	1974–77	. . .	11.1
	1978–79	. . .	8.4
Guatemala	1975–77	. . .	11.2
	1978–80	1.1	13.3
Guyana[1]	1973	12.7	26.6
	1974–77	22.8	38.3
	1978–80	37.2	35.1
Haiti[2,7]	1976–77	. . .	16.3
	1978–80	. . .	12.4
Honduras	1978–79	. . .	14.6
Jamaica[2,7]	1976–77	. . .	40.1
	1978–81	. . .	27.4
Mexico[11]	1970–74	. . . (. . .)	22.0 (. . .)

Table 1 (concluded). Output and Investment Shares of Public Enterprises

	Years	Percentage Share in GDP at Factor Cost[1]	Percentage Share in Gross Fixed Capital Formation[2]
Mexico	1975–77	... (6.1)	27.0 (21.8)
	1978	... (7.4)	29.4 (23.5)
Panama[2]	1960	...	3.7
	1965	...	7.7
	1966–69	...	7.2
	1970–73	...	12.8
	1974–77	...	32.7
	1978–79	...	27.7
Paraguay[1]	1970–73	2.9	14.5
	1974–77	2.7	10.4
	1978–80	3.1	6.5
Peru	1960	...	5.1
	1966	...	10.2
	1968–69	...	11.2
	1970–73	...	11.2
	1974–77	...	22.1
	1978–79	...	14.8
St. Lucia	1975–77	...	12.3
	1978–79	...	6.7
Uruguay	1971–73	...	13.2
	1974–77	...	16.6
	1978–80	...	18.3

Source: Appendix.

[1] Share in GDP at market prices where indicated. (For most countries for which both measures are available, the share at market prices is lower than that at factor cost because of the importance of subsidies in the factor incomes received by public enterprises.)

[2] Share in gross domestic capital formation, including change in stocks, where indicated.

[3] Weighted average for 1974–77 or closest available period using GDP at market prices and gross fixed capital formation expressed in U.S. dollars for 1974–77 as weights. Figures in parentheses are averages for countries for which both GDP and capital formation figures are available. Differences between countries in the measures of GDP and capital formation that are available were ignored in calculating averages.

[4] Figures in parentheses exclude public enterprises at the regional or local level.

[5] Figures in parentheses are for eight large enterprises only.

[6] Figures in parentheses exclude iron ore and petroleum enterprises nationalized in 1975.

[7] Major enterprises only.

[8] Excluding industrial enterprises.

[9] Figures include financial enterprises except for those in parentheses which exclude such enterprises. Figures for investment in 1976 relate to gross fixed capital formation; figures for other years relate to total gross capital formation.

[10] Figures relate to state economic enterprises; figure in parentheses includes an estimate of investment by other public enterprises. See Appendix for further discussion.

[11] Figures in parentheses include 22 major public enterprises only.

* Refers to Taiwan Province of China.

Tanzania. Also of importance is that, in this group of countries, government intervention in public enterprise operations is often particularly great, especially in pursuit of noncommercial objectives.

Second, historical and other political factors have resulted in substantial extensions in public ownership. Many public enterprises were established as a result of the political upheavals of World War II as, for example, in France and Korea. Others were set up following the financial collapse of large private companies, as, for example, in Argentina and the United Kingdom, or were established to reduce foreign ownership of industry, especially of former colonial powers, as, for example, in Egypt and Indonesia. In principle, these enterprises could eventually have been sold to the private sector. However, in practice, there have been few instances of public enterprises being returned to private ownership, at least not on a large scale.[7] This partly reflects political factors, notably a reluctance to give up the additional policy instrument provided by public ownership, and partly the large size and persistent financial problems of many public enterprises, making it difficult to find private sector buyers.

Third, the pursuit of economic objectives has been a major reason for the establishment of public enterprises.[8] Probably the most fundamental, and certainly the most widespread, objective in this respect has been the promotion of allocative efficiency. As is shown below, certain industries where economies of scale or externalities are important are almost universally operated by public enterprises because of the failure of private markets to satisfy the conditions for an optimum allocation of resources. Another notable factor in developing countries, especially with respect to enterprises in the manufacturing sector, has been the encouragement of economic growth. Public enterprises have been established to boost investment and saving because of the perceived failure of the private sector to achieve socially optimal levels as a result of such factors as excessive risk aversion, inadequate capital markets, or high rates of time preference. Improving the distribution of income and economic stabilization, especially of prices or employment, have also played a role, although, generally, these goals have been tied to other objectives and have not been the prime motive for the establishment of public enterprises.

Finally, the similarity in shares can partly be explained by structural factors. As is shown in Section II under "Sectoral Distribution of Public Enterprises," there are substantial differences between sectors in the

---

[7] One exception is the denationalization program in Chile in the mid-1970s. However, the circumstances there were rather special in that the enterprises had only recently been taken over from the private sector. A number of countries, for example, the United Kingdom, have also recently embarked on programs involving the return of major public enterprises to private ownership.

[8] These are discussed by, for example, Leroy P. Jones and Edward S. Mason in "Role of Economic Factors in Determining the Size and Structure of the Public Enterprise Sector in Less-Developed Countries with Mixed Economies," in *Public Enterprise in Less Developed Countries*, Leroy P. Jones (ed.) (Cambridge University Press, 1982), and by Armeane M. Choksi in "State Intervention in the Industrialization of Developing Countries: Selected Issues," World Bank Staff Working Paper, No. 341 (Washington: World Bank, 1979).

extent of penetration by public enterprises that are common to most countries. Also, countries with a relatively large public enterprise presence in most sectors often have relatively large shares of their total output or investment in the sectors where public enterprise penetration is generally low. These two factors operate in opposite directions and may therefore offset one another. This effect is especially important in explaining the similarity of shares between industrial and developing countries. In developing countries, public enterprises are generally more important in individual sectors, especially manufacturing, than they are in industrial countries. However, developing countries also have relatively large shares of output in agriculture, where penetration by public enterprises is low in all countries, and correspondingly small shares in manufacturing.

A further notable feature is the change over time in the shares of output and investment. In industrial countries there appears to have been no dramatic change in recent years in the relative size of the public enterprise sector, but in developing countries there has been a large increase. For industrial countries, the shares of public enterprises in output and capital formation actually fell between the early 1960s and the end of the 1970s, although by only half a percentage point in each case.[9, 10] For these countries, the major increases in the size of the sector occurred in earlier periods than those covered by available statistics. For example, there were substantial increases in the 1930s or 1940s in France, Italy, and the United Kingdom.

For developing countries, the share of public enterprises in GDP rose by 4½ percentage points between the late 1960s and the end of the 1970s and the share in investment increased by 10½ percentage points. While this partly reflected spectacular growth in a few countries, such as Venezuela, shares rose in most of the developing countries for which data are available. Moreover, there also appear to have been very large increases in the size of the public enterprise sector in many developing countries, especially African ones such as Zaïre, for which adequate runs of data could not be obtained.

Sectoral Distribution of Public Enterprises

Although public enterprises have traditionally been viewed as operating only in a limited number of natural monopoly industries, they can now be found operating in virtually all types of economic activity.

---

[9] All figures for changes in shares are adjusted for changes in country coverage. They were derived from the changes in weighted average shares between successive four-year periods, including in each case only countries for which data were available for both periods.

[10] These figures do not take account of, in particular, recent nationalizations in France.

This is evident from Tables 2 and 3. Table 2 shows the percentage shares of public enterprises in output or investment in major sectors; Table 3 provides qualitative information on the industries in which public enterprises are most frequently found.

Public enterprises are still relatively most important in the traditional industries. In most countries, the major part, and often almost the whole, of the public utilities—electricity, gas, and water—and the communications and nonroad transport industries are publicly owned. This mainly reflects the economies of scale in these industries, which would make it difficult to achieve socially optimal levels of output under private ownership.

Many countries, especially developing ones, also have a large part of their natural resource industries operated by public enterprises. Public ownership of petroleum and natural gas, coal, and other hard minerals, such as copper and tin, is especially common. This is partly because of the high risks and large-scale operations that are typically involved and partly because of the large economic rents obtainable and the desire to ensure that these accrue to the nation or the government.

The quantitative importance of public enterprises in manufacturing is generally less than in the previous two sectors. However, it is the public manufacturing sector that has grown most rapidly in recent years. There are also notable differences between countries. A few countries, mainly industrial ones, such as the United States, have virtually no public sector involvement in manufacturing. Then, a group of countries, including industrial countries, such as Italy, and developing ones, such as Korea, have 10–25 percent of manufacturing output or investment accounted for by public enterprises. Finally, many developing countries, especially in Africa, Asia, and the Middle East, have more, and often considerably more, than 25 percent of their manufacturing sectors under public ownership. In several of these, public enterprises dominate the modern manufacturing sector, while the private sector largely consists of small cottage industries.

Within manufacturing, public enterprises are most prominent in heavy industry, particularly petroleum refining, chemicals, iron and steel, transport equipment, and textiles. In industrial countries, public manufacturing activities are largely confined to these industries, and most developing countries have public enterprises operating in at least some of them. Such industries generally require large-scale production and are often regarded as of key economic importance because of their forward links with other parts of the economy or because of their links with international trade. Public enterprises can be found in most other manufacturing activities, but are much less widespread. Probably most common are enterprises in agro-based industries, such as sugar refining, and fiscal monopolies for beverages and tobacco.

Table 2. Percentage Shares of Public Enterprises in the Output or Investment of Major Sectors

	Years	Agriculture, Hunting, Forestry, and Fishing	Mining and Quarrying	Manufacturing	Electricity, Gas, and Water	Construction	Wholesale and Retail Trade, Restaurants, and Hotels	Transport, Storage, and Communications
Industrial countries								
Australia (GDPF)[1]	1967–69	0.3	8.9	3.4	95.6	14.8	0.2	50.2
	1970–73	0.3	5.1	3.3	95.0	13.8	0.1	50.0
	1974–77	0.2	3.5	3.9	94.9	15.1	−0.1	48.0
	1978–79	0.1	3.9	4.0	95.3	15.8	0.1	48.8
Austria (GDPM)	1970–75	3.0	23.0		78.0[2]	2.0	1.0	78.0[2]
Belgium (GFCF)	1962–65	—	—	0.2	21.8	—	—	79.2
	1966–69	—	—	0.1	21.8	—	—	84.2
	1970–73	—	—	0.3	19.7	—	—	83.8
	1974–77	—	—	0.4	21.1	—	—	82.3
	1978–79	—	—	0.4	19.8	—	—	77.6
Finland (GFCF)	1971–73	...	32.3		...	...	...	...
	1974–77	...	31.9		...	...	...	...
	1978–80	...	27.1		...	...	...	...
France (GFCF)	1971	—	11.4		96.9	—	...	68.3
Ireland (GFCF)	1974–77	...	63.2³	9.4	63.2³	—	—	55.6
Italy (GFCF)	1967–69	...	17.9		67.7	8.2	4.6	63.3
	1970–73	...	31.3		69.7	11.9	3.8	69.5
	1974–77	...	20.4		62.6	16.5	3.2	68.3
	1978	...	18.6		61.2	20.3	2.3	63.7

	Year							
Netherlands (GFCF)	1970–73	—		37.0		—	—	46.2
United Kingdom (GFCF)	1962–65	—		1.2		—	—	58.7
	1966–69	—		2.5		—	—	58.0
	1970–73	—	34.8	8.2	83.5	—	—	55.5
	1974–77	—	16.1	11.8	95.4	—	—	59.7
	1978–81	—	27.2	5.3	97.4	—	—	57.6
Developing countries								
Oil exporting countries								
Iraq (GFCF)	1960	..	..	15.2	..	..	..	..
	1970	..	..	48.3	..	..	..	..
	1975	..	..	96.7	..	..	..	..
Nigeria (GFCF)	1970–74	..	..	..	17.7	..	..	..
Africa								
Benin (GFCF)	1975–77	..		57.9		..		
	1978–79	3.1[4]		57.4		..		
Congo (GO)	1976	..		15.7	92.6	12.9		52.3
Ethiopia (GDPF)	1979–80	..		60.9		..		
Ghana (GO)	1962	..		18.9		..		
	1966	..		32.2		..		
	1970	..		32.9		..		
Ivory Coast (GDPF)	1979	0.1	25.2	13.1	87.6	12.8		35.2
Kenya (GDPF)	1970–73	0.4	4.2		69.0	8.4	2.6	68.7
Morocco (GFCF)	1973	..		9.3				
	1974–76	..	99.2	26.2				
Senegal (GDPM)	1974	0.9		19.0	100.0	5.7	23.7	37.8
Sierra Leone (GDPF)	1979	5.3	26.1	14.2	91.6	—	0.1	8.8
Somalia (GDPF)	1974–77	..		59.1	..	..		..

Table 2 (concluded). Percentage Shares of Public Enterprises in the Output or Investment of Major Sectors

	Years	Agriculture, Hunting, Forestry, and Fishing	Mining and Quarrying	Manu-facturing	Electricity, Gas, and Water	Construction	Wholesale and Retail Trade, Restaurants, and Hotels	Transport, Storage, and Communications
Tanzania (GDPF)	1966–69	1.3	84.2	14.9	76.3	5.1	5.7	44.4
	1970–73	2.4	86.5	31.9	80.1	3.1	14.3	45.0
	1974–77	2.2	90.5	37.9	73.6	2.7	20.3	45.7
Tunisia (GFCF)	1978–81	18.3	47.3	58.8	89.4	...	...	60.4
Asia								
Bangladesh (GDPF)	1974	—	62.0	...	78.1	2.8	7.5	18.8
	1975–77	...	69.2		...	...	...	...
	1978	...	70.6					
Burma (GDPM)[5]	1980	0.5	85.8	56.2	100.0	...	...	45.4
India (GDPF)	1970–73	1.5	45.7	13.1	80.7	13.1	2.9	56.2
	1974–77	1.9	80.8	16.2	83.5	16.2	4.7	54.2
	1978	2.3	79.7	15.7	84.0	15.7	5.2	53.6
Korea (GDPF)	1963–64	0.3	30.5	14.8	92.4	2.9	1.8	46.0
	1970–73	0.4	20.3	17.3	78.6	4.2	1.0	24.2
	1974–77	—	14.8	14.9	74.9	5.3	0.6	18.2
Nepal (GDPF)	1971–73	0.1	—	4.0	40.5	20.8	...	10.4
	1974–75	0.1	—	4.4	47.4	36.7	...	13.0
Pakistan (GDPF)	1970–73	—	19.9	4.1	75.0	—	0.5	34.8
	1974–75	—	10.6	7.8	82.7	...	6.8	34.1
Singapore (GDPF)	1972	...	...	14.2	...	...	...	...

Country	Year							
Sri Lanka (GDPF)	1966	0.1	—	7.6	90.9	4.2	4.1	39.0
Taiwan* (GFCF)	1974	0.5	0.5	33.5	93.5	6.8	10.6	45.6
	1980	13.4	85.5	31.9	95.9	25.8	11.0	49.5
Thailand (GDPF)	1970–73	0.2	0.3	5.2	73.1	—	0.3	17.2
Europe								
Greece (GDPF)	1975	—	69.0³	1.7	69.0³	...	...	39.8
	1979	—	71.4³	1.3	71.4³	...	...	42.7
Portugal (GDPF)	1976	0.9	4.9	12.0	78.2	—	1.0	43.5
Turkey (GFCF)	1974–77	15.4		42.1 ⎱		—	—	23.3
Middle East				54.8 ⎰				
Egypt (GFCF)	1975	...	90.6	...	...	...	...	...
	1979	...	80.4	...	...	...	...	...
Syrian Arab Republic (GFCF)	1970	...	...	70.5	...	...	...	...
	1975	...	...	95.9	...	...	...	...
Yemen Arab Republic (GFCF)	1975–76	...	...	59.5	...	...	...	...
Western Hemisphere								
Bolivia (GDPF)	1973–75	0.1	85.4	5.9	9.9	0.6	—	9.0

Source: Appendix.
[1] GDPF = gross domestic product at factor cost; GFCF = gross domestic fixed capital formation; GDPM = gross domestic product at market prices; GO = gross value of output.
[2] Share in electricity, gas, and water, plus transport, storage, and communications.
[3] Share in electricity, gas, and water, plus mining and quarrying.
[4] Share in agriculture only.
[5] Share in GDPM at 1970 prices.
* See note to Table 1, page 122.

Table 3. Industry Coverage of Public Enterprises[1]

Part A

	Agriculture, Forestry, and Fishery[2]	Mining and Quarrying[3]	Food, Drink, and Tobacco[4]	Textiles and Clothing[5]	Leather and Footwear[6]	Wood Products and Furniture[7]	Paper and Printing[8]	Petroleum Refining and Distribution[9]
Industrial countries								
Australia								
Austria	FO	C,P,M	D,T				PR	P
Belgium			F					P
Canada		P						P
Denmark	FO	P		C				
Finland	A	C,P	F	T			PA	P
France		C	T					P
Germany, Fed. Rep. of		C	D					P
Ireland	FI	M	S,F					
Italy		C	F,T	T,C			PR	P
Japan			D,T					P
Luxembourg								
Netherlands	FO,FI	C,P						
Norway	FO	C,P	F,D					
Sweden		P,M	T	T		W	PR	
United Kingdom		C,P					PR	
United States								
Developing countries								
Oil exporting countries								
Indonesia	A,FI	C,P,M	S,T	T			PA	P

Nigeria	A,FI	C,P	S,F,D	T			PA	P
Venezuela		P,M	S					P
Africa								
Benin	FO,AD		F,D	T			PR	
Botswana	AD							
Congo	A,FI	M	F,D,T	T		W,F	PR	P
Ethiopia	AD		S,D	T,C	L,F	W	PA,PR	
Gambia, The	FI							
Ghana	AD	M	F,D				PA	
Ivory Coast	AD,FI	P,M	S,F	T	F		PR	P
Kenya	A,FI	M	S,F	T,C	F			P
Liberia	AD		S,F					P
Mali		M	F	T				
Mauritania	A,FI	M		C				
Mauritius	AD		F					
Morocco	AD	P,M	S,F,D,T					P
Niger	AD	M					PR	P
Senegal	AD	P,M		T		W,F		P
Sierra Leone	FI	M	D		L	W		P
Somalia	FI		D,T	T			PA,PR	
Tanzania	AD,FI	M	S,F,D,T	T		W		P
Togo	AD,FI	M	F	T				P
Tunisia	FI	P,M	S,D,T		F		PR	P
Upper Volta	A		S	T		W	PR	P
Zambia	A	M	S,F,T	T			PR	P
Asia								
Bangladesh	AD,FI	M	S,F,T	T	L	W	PA	P
Burma	A,FO,FI	M	F,D	T		W	PA	P
India	A,FI	C,M	F	T	L		PA	P

Table 3 (continued). Industry Coverage of Public Enterprises[1]

	Agriculture, Forestry, and Fishery[2]	Mining and Quarrying[3]	Food, Drink, and Tobacco[4]	Textiles and Clothing[5]	Leather and Footwear[6]	Wood Products and Furniture[7]	Paper and Printing[8]	Petroleum Refining and Distribution[9]
Korea	AD,FI	C,M	F,D,T				PR	P
Nepal	A,FO	M	S,T	T	L			P
Pakistan	AD	C,P,M	F				PR	P
Papua New Guinea	A		S					P
Philippines	AD		T	T				P
Sri Lanka	AD,FI	M	S,F,D,T	T		W	PR	P
Thailand	FO,FI	M	S,F,T	T		W	PA	P
Europe								
Greece	FI		S,T					P
Malta	FI		F	C	F			
Portugal	A,FO,FI	C,M	S,F,D,T	T		F	PA,PR	P
Turkey		C,M	S,F	T			PA	P
Middle East								
Syrian Arab Republic			F,T	T			PR	P
Western Hemisphere								
Argentina	FO	C,P,M	S					P
Bahamas	AD							
Barbados	AD	P,M						
Bolivia	AD,FO	C,M	F					P
Brazil		C,M	S				PR	P
Chile	AD	C,M	F		L			P
Colombia		C,M	S,F				PR	P
Costa Rica		M						P
Dominica	FO							P

	Chemicals[10]	Pottery, Glass, and Cement[11]	Basic Metal Industries[12]	Transport Equipment[13]	Other Engineering (E)	Electricity, Gas, and Water[14]	Construction (C)	Wholesale and Retail Trade[15]
Dominican Republic	A,FI	M	S,F	T	L,F		PA	P
Ecuador	A,FO	M	D				PA,PR	P
Guyana			S,F,D	T	L,F		PR	
Haiti			F,T		F			
Honduras	FO		S					
Jamaica	AD	M	F	T,C				P
Mexico	A,FO	P,M	S,F	T				P
Panama	A	M	S					
Paraguay							PA	P
Peru		P,M	F					P
St. Lucia								
Uruguay								

Part B

Industrial countries

	Chemicals[10]	Pottery, Glass, and Cement[11]	Basic Metal Industries[12]	Transport Equipment[13]	Other Engineering (E)	Electricity, Gas, and Water[14]	Construction (C)	Wholesale and Retail Trade[15]
Australia	PH, C	P			E	E		T
Austria				A	E	E	C	
Belgium						E		
Canada						E	C	A
Denmark						E		T
Finland	C			M		E		
France	C			A		E	C	T
Germany, Fed. Rep. of	C	P	I,B	M,S	E	E		T
Ireland	FE,C		I			E	C	
Italy	PH,C	C	I	M,A,S	E	E	C	A,T
Japan						E	C	A
Luxembourg	C					E		
Netherlands	C		I			E		A
Norway	PH,C		I,B			E		T

Table 3 (continued). Industry Coverage of Public Enterprises[1]

	Chemicals[10]	Pottery, Glass, and Cement[11]	Basic Metal Industries[12]	Transport Equipment[13]	Other Engineering (E)	Electricity, Gas, and Water[14]	Construction (C)	Wholesale and Retail Trade[15]
Sweden	PH,C		I	M,S		E	C	A
United Kingdom			I	M,A,S		E		T
United States				M,A,S		E		T
Developing countries								
Oil exporting countries								
Indonesia	PH,FE	P,C	I	M,A,S	E	E	C	T
Nigeria	FE	C	I	M,S	E	E		T
Venezuela	FE,C		I,B			E	C	A,T
Africa								
Benin		P				E		A,T
Botswana					E	E	C	A
Congo	PH,C	P,C		S		E	C	A,T
Ethiopia	PH	P				E	C	A,T
Gambia, The				S		E		A,T
Ghana	PH	P			E	E	C	A,T
Ivory Coast	FE	P,C,B				E	C	A,T
Kenya	FE,C			M	E	E	C	A
Liberia						E		
Mali	PH	C,B				E		A,T
Mauritania	PH					E		A
Mauritius						E		A,T
Morocco					E	E		A

Niger		P,C				E	C	A
Senegal	FE					E	C	T
Sierra Leone		B				E	C	A,T
Somalia	PH,FE	C				E		A,T
Tanzania	PH					E		A,T
Togo		P,C	I	M	E	E		T
Tunisia	PH,FE	B	I,B			E		
Upper Volta						E	C	A,T
Zambia	C	P,C		M	E	E	C	A,T
Asia								
Bangladesh	PH,FE,C	C	I	M	E	E		T
Burma	C				E	E		A,T
India	PH,FE,C	P	I	M,S	E	E	C	A,T
Korea	FE,C	C	I,B	M	E	E	C	A
Nepal		P,C			E	E	C	A,T
Pakistan	FE,C	C	I	M,S	E	E		A,T
Papua New Guinea						E		A
Philippines	FE,C					E	C	A
Sri Lanka	PH,FE	P,C		M	E	E	C	A,T
Thailand	PH	P				E		A,T
Europe								
Greece				A	E	E		A,T
Malta				S	E	E		A
Portugal	PH,C	P,C	I	S	E	E	C	A,T
Turkey	C	C	I		E	E		A
Middle East								
Syrian Arab Republic	PH					E		A

Table 3 (continued). Industry Coverage of Public Enterprises[1]

	Chemicals[10]	Pottery, Glass, and Cement[11]	Basic Metal Industries[12]	Transport Equipment[13]	Other Engineering (E)	Electricity, Gas, and Water[14]	Construction (C)	Wholesale and Retail Trade[15]
Western Hemisphere								
Argentina	C		I	S		E		
Bahamas						E		
Barbados						E		A,T
Bolivia	C	C	I			E		A,T
Brazil	FE,C		I	A,S		E		A
Chile	C				E	E		A
Colombia	FE	C		M,A,S		E		T
Costa Rica		C				E		A,T
Dominica						E		A
Dominican Republic	C	P,C		M		E		A,T
Ecuador	FE		I			E		A
Guyana	PH	P,C				E		T
Haiti						E		A,T
Honduras						E		A,T
Jamaica						E		T
Mexico	C		I			E	C	A
Panama		C				E		
Paraguay			I	S		E		
Peru	C		I			E		A
St. Lucia						E		A
Uruguay		C				E		T

Part C

	Hotels (H)	Land Transport[16]	Air and Water Transport[17]	Posts and Telecommunications[18]	Housing (H)
Industrial countries					
Australia	H	R	A,W	P	
Austria	H	R,B	A,AP,W	P	H
Belgium		R,B	A,P	P	H
Canada		R,B	W,P	P	
Denmark		R,B	A,AP,W,P	P	H
Finland		R,B	A	P	
France		R,B	A,AP,W	P	
Germany, Fed. Rep. of		R	A	P	H
Ireland		R,B	A,AP,W,P	P	
Italy		R,B	A	P	
Japan		R	AP	P	H
Luxembourg		R	AP	P	
Netherlands		R,B	A,AP,W,P	P	
Norway		R	A	P	H
Sweden		R	A	P	H
United Kingdom		R,B	A,AP,W,P	P	
United States		R	AP	P	
Developing countries					
Oil exporting countries					
Indonesia	H	R,B	A,W	P	
Nigeria	H	R	A,AP,W,P	P	
Venezuela	H	R,B	A,AP,W,P	P	

Table 3 (continued). Industry Coverage of Public Enterprises[1]

	Hotels (H)	Land Transport[16]	Air and Water Transport[17]	Posts and Telecommunications[18]	Housing (H)
Africa					
Benin	H	R	W,P	P	
Botswana	H			P	H
Congo	H	R,B	A,W,P	P	H
Ethiopia	H	R,B	A,W	P	H
Gambia, The	H		A,P	P	
Ghana	H	R,B	A,P	P	H
Ivory Coast	H	R,B	A,P	P	H
Kenya	H	R,B	A,W,P	P	
Liberia			A,AP,W,P	P	H
Mali	H	R,B	A,W	P	
Mauritania	H	B	A	P	H
Mauritius		B	AP,P	P	H
Morocco	H	R	A,AP,P	P	
Niger	H	B	A	P	H
Senegal	H	R	A,W,P	P	
Sierra Leone		B	A,AP,W,P	P	
Somalia	H		A,W	P	
Tanzania	H	R	A,W,P	P	
Togo	H	R	A,W,P	P	
Tunisia	H	R,B	A,AP,W,P	P	H
Upper Volta		R	A	P	H
Zambia	H	R,B	A,W	P	H

Country					
Asia					
Bangladesh		P	W	R,B	
Burma		P	A,W	R,B	
India		P	A,AP,W	R,B	
Korea	H	P	A,W,P	R	H
Nepal		P	A	B	H
Pakistan		P	A,W	R,B	
Papua New Guinea		P	P		
Philippines	H	P	W,P	R	H
Sri Lanka	H	P	A,W,P	R	
Thailand	H	P	A,AP,W,P	R,B	H
Europe					
Greece	H	P	A,P	R,B	
Malta		P	A,AP,W,P		
Portugal		P	A,W,P	R,B	
Turkey		P	A,AP,W	R	
Middle East					
Syrian Arab Republic	H	P	A,AP,P		
Western Hemisphere					
Argentina	H	P	A,W,P	R	H
Bahamas		P	A,P		H
Barbados	H	P	AP,P	B	H
Bolivia		P	A,AP	R	H
Brazil		P	A,W,P	R,B	
Chile		P	A,P	R,B	H
Colombia		P	W,P	R,B	
Costa Rica		P	W,P	R,B	
Dominica	H	P	P		

Table 3 (concluded). Industry Coverage of Public Enterprises[1]

	Hotels (H)	Land Transport[16]	Air and Water Transport[17]	Posts and Telecommunications[18]	Housing (H)
Dominican Republic			A,AP,P	P	H
Ecuador		R	AP,W,P	P	
Guyana			A,W,P	P	
Haiti		B	A,AP,P	P	
Honduras		R	P	P	
Jamaica	H	R,B	A,AP,P	P	H
Mexico		R,B	AP	P	H
Panama		R,B		P	
Paraguay		R	A,AP,W,P	P	
Peru		R,B	A,AP,W,P	P	H
St. Lucia	H		P	P	
Uruguay		R	A,P	P	

Sources: International Monetary Fund, *Government Finance Statistics Yearbook* (Washington, 1982); Appendix.

[1] Industries in which at least one public enterprise is operating. Coverage of sector-wide and subsidiary enterprises and of enterprises owned by local governments is incomplete.

[2] A = agricultural production; FO = forestry; FI = fishing; AD = agricultural development (enterprises mainly engaged in the promotion of private sector production, for example, through the provision of inputs, rather than directly in production).

[3] C = coal; P = petroleum and natural gas; M = other and general mining and quarrying.

[4] S = sugar; F = other food and agricultural processing; D = drink; T = tobacco.

[5] T = textiles; C = clothing.

[6] L = leather; F = footwear.

[7] W = wood products; F = furniture.

[8] PA = paper; PR = printing.

[9] P = petroleum refining and/or distribution.

[10] PH = pharmaceuticals; FE = fertilizer; C = other and general chemicals.

[11] B = bricks; C = cement; P = pottery and glass.

[12] I = iron and steel; B = other basic metals.

[13] M = motor vehicles; A = aircraft; S = shipbuilding.

[14] E = electricity, gas, and/or water.

[15] A = agricultural marketing; T = other wholesale or retail trade.

[16] R = railways; B = bus and other land transport.

[17] A = airlines; AP = airports; W = water transport; P = ports.

[18] P = posts and/or telecommunications.

Public enterprises in the remaining nonagricultural sectors—construction, trade, and services—are generally less significant in quantitative terms, although there are again differences between countries. In these sectors, the economic arguments for public ownership are less powerful. Public enterprises engaged in the provision of housing and in construction, especially public works, are common in both industrial and developing countries, and government hotels are found in a large number of developing countries. However, the most important enterprises in these sectors are government marketing agencies. Public enterprises engaged in wholesale or retail distribution, especially of basic commodities, are found in many developing countries, but especially common are marketing boards for agricultural products. Although these enterprises are usually small in terms of, for example, capital formation, they can have a substantial economic impact through their pricing policies, especially as they are generally statutory monopolies.

Finally, in most countries, public enterprises are of minor importance in quantitative terms in agriculture, forestry, and fishing. Some countries have public enterprises engaged in forestry and fishing, but few have much direct public sector involvement in the production side of agriculture. This mainly reflects the dominance of small-scale operations in agriculture in developing countries. This is not to say that public enterprises do not have a major impact on the agricultural sector. Apart from government marketing boards, a large number of developing countries have publicly owned agricultural development corporations. These are generally partly financial institutions, but they are also often engaged in other activities, such as the provision of agricultural inputs.

Other Important Characteristics

Two other characteristics of public enterprises are noteworthy. First, the public enterprise sector is invariably highly capital-intensive. In the mid-1970s, for those countries for which both output and investment figures are available, the average share of public enterprises in capital formation was 17 percent, almost twice the average share in GDP of 9½ percent.[11] In none of the countries in Table 1 has the share in output been consistently higher than that in investment.

This mainly reflects the industrial distribution of public enterprises, particularly their prominence in industries that are by their nature capital-intensive, for example, electricity, telecommunications, and steel.

---

[11] A complete treatment of capital intensity would also require an analysis of public enterprise shares in employment and employment income. Information on these is

It may also reflect differences in the relative factor prices faced by public and private enterprises, although the influences here are not all in the same direction. In many countries, the cost of capital to public enterprises is lower than that to private enterprises: government finance is often provided in the form of transfers or low-interest loans; especially in developing countries, public enterprises obtain finance at subsidized rates from domestic monetary institutions or aid agencies. As a result, the use of relatively capital-intensive techniques will be encouraged.[12] On the other hand, public enterprises are often under political pressure to employ labor, which could work in the opposite direction. In some countries, for example, Egypt, public enterprises are expected to act as employers of last resort, while, in most countries, it is difficult politically for public enterprises to shed labor.

Second, although there are countries with a substantial number of small public enterprises, many individual public enterprises are very large in absolute terms. For example, measured by sales value, 18 of the largest 100 companies outside the United States in 1980, and 54 of the largest 500 companies, were public enterprises.[13] A public enterprise is the largest enterprise in, for example, Argentina, Chile, India, Italy, Turkey, and the Philippines, and Zambia. Moreover, the importance of large public enterprises has increased substantially. In 1960, only 6 of the largest 100 companies outside the United States were public enterprises. The sales and assets of large public enterprises have also generally grown much faster than their private sector counterparts.[14]

---

limited. However, for those countries for which data are available, the share of public enterprises in employment is generally less than that in GDP. Some examples are:

	Percentage Share in GDP	Percentage Share in Employment
United Kingdom (1974–77)	11.3	8.1
Sierra Leone (1979)	7.6	1.3
Pakistan (1975)	5.8	2.1
Turkey (1978–80)	5.0	3.9
Source: Appendix.		

At least in developing countries, average wages in public enterprises are likely to be higher than those in private enterprises because of the concentration of public enterprises in the more advanced sectors of the economy. As a result, the share of public enterprises in employment income is probably higher than that in employment.

[12] A low cost of capital need not inevitably work in this way. For example, in the United Kingdom, public enterprises are expected to use a discount rate for decisions on the choice of technique that is higher than the rate they pay on their borrowing—see, for example, David Heald, "The Economic and Financial Control of U.K. Nationalized Industries," *Economic Journal*, Vol. 90 (June 1980), pp. 243–65.

[13] See "The Foreign 500," *Fortune* (August 10, 1981), pp. 206–18.

[14] See Douglas F. Lamont, *Foreign State Enterprises, A Threat to American Business* (New York: Basic Books, 1979).

This large size again partly reflects the high incidence of public enterprises in industries requiring large-scale production. It also reflects the practice in many countries of combining public enterprises into large conglomerates. It is significant because it can make government control easier, and also because such enterprises can exert considerable economic power in both domestic and international markets.[15]

III. MEASURES OF MACROECONOMIC IMPACT OF PUBLIC ENTERPRISES

Overall Deficits of Public Enterprises

The principal summary indicator of the macroeconomic impact of public enterprises is their overall deficit or financing requirement. This provides a measure of the effect of public enterprise operations on the balance between demand and supply in the economy and is thus of particular relevance for analyzing economic stabilization.

Figures for the overall deficits of public enterprise sectors, expressed as percentages of GDP, are given in Table 4. The overall deficit is defined here as the difference between (1) current plus capital expenditure; and (2) revenue plus receipts of current transfers and of nongovernment capital transfers. Government capital transfers are also conventionally included in receipts in defining the overall deficit.[16] However, although the distinction between capital transfers and other forms of financing is significant for the financial position of the enterprise, especially in formal legal terms, it is much less useful for economic analysis as both represent a financial and a resource burden that has to be met by other sectors of the economy.

An additional reason for excluding such transfers, especially when making intercountry comparisons, is that there are differences between countries in the extent to which government finance is provided in the form of transfers or equity and loans. As there is often little expectation that dividends will be paid on equity, and loans are frequently on very soft terms, these differences may be of little practical significance, but they will affect the deficit as conventionally defined.

There is a case for also excluding government current transfers from receipts. These do not correspond to any market flow of com-

---

[15] The effects of this are discussed in Lamont (op. cit.).

[16] For example, the definition suggested by the International Monetary Fund includes such transfers as receipts for the purpose of calculating the overall deficit. See International Monetary Fund, *A Manual on Government Finance Statistics* (Draft) (Washington, June 1974), pp. 295–311.

modities and also represent a burden to be met by other sectors.[17] Accordingly, the overall deficit, before crediting receipts of government current transfers, is also shown in Table 4.

The large size of the overall deficits of public enterprise sectors is striking. In the mid-1970s, these averaged 2 percent of GDP. By way of comparison, central government overall deficits averaged 3¼ percent of GDP for the same group of countries. The exclusion of government current transfers increased public enterprise overall deficits by an average of 1¼ percent of GDP for the more limited group of countries for which this information is available.

Overall deficits are also generally much larger in developing than in industrial countries. In the mid-1970s, they averaged 1¾ percent of GDP in industrial countries, but almost 4 percent of GDP in developing countries. They were particularly large in Asia, where they averaged over 5½ percent of GDP, and in developing countries in Europe. Over this period, public enterprise deficits in developing countries were, in fact, slightly higher than central government deficits. Large deficits are of particular significance in developing countries in that, with low incomes and underdeveloped capital markets, such countries are likely to experience considerable difficulty in generating offsetting surpluses in other domestic sectors of the economy.

A further key feature is that public enterprise overall deficits have increased in recent years, especially in developing countries. In industrial countries, overall deficits increased by an average of ¼ of 1 percent of GDP between the late 1960s and the mid-1970s, but this rise has largely been reversed in the period since then.[18] In developing countries, overall deficits rose by 2½ percent of GDP between the late 1960s and the mid-1970s, with much of the increase taking place in the later part of this period, and the resulting high levels of deficits were maintained to the end of the 1970s. Particularly notable were large increases in overall deficits in a number of countries, such as Korea, where, at least according to the measures shown in Table 1, the size of the public enterprise sector did not increase significantly.

While the overall deficit is a valuable indicator, it cannot by itself be used to assess the performance or impact of public enterprises. In particular, overall deficits for public enterprises are not undesirable

---

[17] Some of the issues in defining the overall deficit are discussed by Walter Eltis in "The True Deficits of the Public Corporations," *Lloyds Bank Review*, No. 131 (January 1979), pp. 1–20.

[18] Some of the changes in overall deficits and in other quantities shown in the tables may reflect cyclical, as well as trend factors. While the periods used for averaging took some account of cycles in world economic activity, and hence should have partly removed cyclical effects, they were mainly determined by the periods for which data could be obtained.

Table 4. Overall Balances of Public Enterprises
(As percentages of GDP at market prices)

	Years	Overall Surplus/ Deficit (−)[1]		Overall Surplus/ Deficit (−) Less Government Current Transfers	
"World" (average)[2]		**−2.0**	**(−3.0)**	**(−4.2)**	
Industrial countries (average)[2]		**−1.7**	**(−2.1)**	**(−3.5)**	
Australia	1966	−4.0		...	
	1968–69	−3.7		...	
	1970–73	−3.3		...	
	1974–77	−3.5		...	
Belgium	1964–65	−0.4		...	
	1966–69	−0.7		...	
	1970–73	−0.9		...	
	1974–77	−0.9		...	
	1978–79	−0.5		...	
Canada	1970–73	−1.5		...	
	1974–77	−2.8		...	
	1978–81	−2.3		...	
	1982	−3.1		...	
Finland	1970–73	−1.5		...	
	1974–75	−2.6		...	
France[3]	1959–61	−2.5	(−1.1)	3.9	(−1.6)
	1962–65	−2.7	(−1.0)	4.5	(−1.8)
	1966–69	−2.8	(−0.9)	4.9	(−1.8)
	1970–73	−2.0	(−0.6)	3.9	(−1.2)
	1974	−1.8	(−1.0)	3.5	(−1.6)
	1975–77	...	(−1.3)	...	(−2.0)
	1978–81	...	(−1.5)	...	(−2.2)
	1982	...	(−1.8)	...	(−2.6)
Italy	1969	−2.1		...	
	1970–73	−3.6		...	
	1974–77	−3.5		...	
	1978–80	−3.0		...	
Japan	1970–73	−2.5		...	
	1974–77	−3.4		...	
	1978–81	−2.7		...	
Netherlands	1968–69	−2.5		...	
	1970–73	−1.9		...	
	1974–77	−0.5		...	
	1978	−0.5		...	
Norway[4]	1968–69	−0.9		...	
	1970–73	−1.2		...	
	1974–77	−2.7		...	
	1978	−2.6		...	
Spain	1979–80	−3.1		−4.4	
United Kingdom	1946–49	−0.7		−0.8	
	1950–53	−1.7		−1.7	
	1954–57	−2.2		−2.2	
	1958–61	−2.2		−2.5	
	1962–65	−1.7		−2.2	

Table 4 (continued). Overall Balances of Public Enterprises
(As percentages of GDP at market prices)

	Years	Overall Surplus/ Deficit (−)[1]	Overall Surplus/ Deficit (−) Less Government Current Transfers
United Kingdom	1966–69	−1.9	−2.3
	1970–73	−1.7	−2.1
	1974–77	−1.9	−3.0
	1978–81	−1.0	−1.8
	1982	−0.8	−1.7
United States	1960	−0.6	. . .
	1963	−0.6	. . .
	1965	−0.6	. . .
	1967–69	−0.6	. . .
	1970–73	−0.6	. . .
	1974–77	−0.7	. . .
	1978	−0.6	. . .
Developing countries (average)[2]		**−3.9 (−4.6)**	**−5.5**
Oil exporting countries			
Venezuela[5]	1972–73	−5.4	−5.4
	1974–77	−5.2 (−6.3)	−6.3 (−7.4)
	1978–80	−5.1 (−9.6)	−5.9 (−10.4)
Africa (average)[2]		−3.1	. . .
Botswana	1974–77	−4.7	. . .
	1978–80	−0.6	. . .
Gambia, The	1979	−4.9	. . .
Guinea	1976–77	−8.0	. . .
	1978–79	−23.4	. . .
Ivory Coast	1965–69	−0.9	. . .
	1970–73	−3.6	. . .
	1974–77	−3.5	. . .
	1978–79	−8.4	. . .
Malawi	1970–73	−2.7	−2.8
	1974–77	−2.5	−2.5
	1978	−3.5	−3.5
Mali[6]	1975–77	−5.9	. . .
	1978	−2.7	. . .
Senegal[7]	1974	2.2 (−2.6)	. . .
Tanzania[8]	1966–69	−1.5	−1.5
	1970–73	−2.6	−2.7
	1974–75	−2.8	−3.9
Zambia	1972	−3.4	. . .
Asia (average)[2]		−5.6	. . .
Burma	1968–69	−1.4	. . .
	1970–73	−1.5	. . .
	1974–77	−1.2	. . .
	1978–80	−10.6	. . .
India	1966–69	−4.2	−4.2
	1970–73	−4.3	−4.4
	1974–77	−6.3	−6.9
	1978	−6.2 ·	−6.8

Table 4 (continued). Overall Balances of Public Enterprises
(As percentages of GDP at market prices)

	Years	Overall Surplus/ Deficit (−)[1]	Overall Surplus/ Deficit (−) Less Government Current Transfers
Korea	1963–65	− 2.8	. . .
	1966–69	− 3.3	. . .
	1970–73	− 3.8	. . .
	1974–77	− 5.4	. . .
	1978–80	− 5.2	. . .
Nepal	1971–73	− 0.5	. . .
	1974–75	− 2.1	. . .
Taiwan*	1951–53	− 3.7	. . .
	1954–57	− 2.6	. . .
	1958–61	− 3.5	. . .
	1962–65	− 1.3	. . .
	1966–69	− 2.4	. . .
	1970–73	− 3.7	. . .
	1974–77	− 7.3	. . .
	1978–80	− 5.5	. . .
Thailand	1969	− 0.8	. . .
	1970–73	− 0.8	. . .
	1974–77	− 1.1	. . .
	1978–79	− 2.0	− 2.1
Europe			
Greece	1975	− 1.6	. . .
	1979	− 1.6	. . .
Portugal	1978–80	− 8.1	− 12.6
Turkey	1964–65	− 1.4	− 1.8
	1966–69	− 2.2	− 2.6
	1970–73	− 4.0	− 4.1
	1974–77	− 7.0	− 8.3
	1978–81	− 7.6	− 9.7
	1982	− 5.2	− 6.4
Western Hemisphere (average)[2]		− 2.5	. . .
Argentina[6]	1968–69	. . .	− 1.8
	1970–73	. . .	− 2.9
	1974–75	. . .	− 4.3
	1976–77	− 3.1	− 4.1
	1978–80	. . .	− 3.4
Bahamas	1975–77	− 1.9	− 2.7
	1978–79	− 1.7	− 2.1
Barbados	1975–77	− 1.8	− 2.8
	1978–80	− 2.1	− 3.4
Bolivia	1971–73	− 3.4	− 3.6
	1974–77	− 4.4	− 4.5
Brazil	1980	− 1.7	. . .
Chile[6]	1974–77	− 0.2	− 1.2
	1978–80	− 0.4	− 0.7
Colombia[9]	1974–77	− 0.9 (− 0.6)	− 1.2 (− 0.9)
	1978–80	− 0.1 (− 0.1)	− 0.5 (− 0.4)

Table 4 (concluded). Overall Balances of Public Enterprises
(As percentages of GDP at market prices)

	Years	Overall Surplus/ Deficit (−)[1]	Overall Surplus/ Deficit (−) Less Government Current Transfers
Costa Rica	1977–79	−4.4	−4.4
Dominica	1975–77	−4.4	−5.0
	1978–79	−1.2	−4.1
Dominican Republic[6]	1972–73	0.1	—
	1974–77	−0.2	−0.8
	1978–79	−1.6	−2.3
Guatemala	1975–77	−1.8	−1.9
	1978–80	−2.1	−2.1
Guyana	1973	−3.7	−4.4
	1974–77	−6.6	−7.7
	1978–80	−1.4	−2.5
Haiti[6]	1976–77	−2.0	. . .
	1978–80	−0.9	. . .
Honduras	1978–79	−2.3	−2.3
Jamaica[6]	1976–77	−4.3	−4.5
	1978–81	−3.0	−4.0
Mexico[6]	1975–77	−3.9	−4.9
	1978	−3.7	−4.6
Panama	1960	−0.2	. . .
	1965	−0.9	. . .
	1966–69	−1.1	. . .
	1970–73	−2.7	. . .
	1974–77	−7.1	. . .
	1978–79	−7.1	. . .
Paraguay	1970–73	−1.2	−1.3
	1974–77	−1.6	−1.7
	1978–80	−0.9	−1.0
Peru	1968–69	−1.3	−1.4
	1970–73	−1.3	−1.5
	1974–77	−4.8	−5.2
	1978–79	−1.7	−1.8
St. Lucia	1975–77	−4.6	−5.0
	1978	−2.8	−3.2
Uruguay	1976–77	—	−0.3
	1978–80	−0.8	−1.1

Source: Appendix.

[1] Excluding government capital transfers. The definition of the overall balance is discussed on page 144.

[2] Weighted average for 1974–77 or closest available period using GDP at market prices in U.S. dollars as weights. Figures in parentheses are averages for countries for which figures for the overall balance less government current transfers are available.

[3] Figures in parentheses are for eight large enterprises only.

[4] Central government enterprises only.

[5] Figures in parentheses exclude iron ore and petroleum enterprises nationalized in 1975.

[6] Major enterprises only.

[7] Figures in parentheses exclude phosphate company.

[8] Figures include parastatal enterprises only; former East African Community enterprises are excluded.

[9] Figures in parentheses exclude public enterprises at the regional or local level.

* See note to Table 1, page 122.

per se and even a low deficit is not necessarily an appropriate aim. Public enterprises produce marketable outputs and, just like private enterprises, it may well be desirable for them to run deficits to finance the investment needed to expand output.[19] It is therefore necessary to examine the factors contributing to these deficits and the ways in which they are financed. Information on these is provided in the next two subsections.

Components of Overall Deficits of Public Enterprises

Table 5 provides a breakdown of overall deficits of public enterprises into the contributions of the current and capital accounts. More disaggregated information on the components of the current account is also given.

The capital account balance broadly equates to gross capital formation by public enterprises—the only difference is that nongovernment capital receipts, which are generally small, are also included as an offsetting factor. The current account includes the operating balance, which is the difference between sales revenue and expenditure on goods and services, other than capital assets, and thus shows the gross (commercial) return on investment. The current balance is then obtained by adding on (net) receipts of current transfers and deducting (net) expenditure on interest, dividends, and direct taxes. The current balance is also shown after deducting depreciation.

Care needs to be taken in using current balance figures, especially in interpreting them as absolute or comparative measures of performance. First, the current balance is affected by the type and terms of finance and by the tax system applied to public enterprises.[20] These vary substantially between countries and are frequently determined more by administrative and institutional factors than by economic considerations.[21] Of particular importance is that public enterprises

---

[19] Indeed, a deficit somewhere in the economy is needed to absorb the overall surplus in the household sector that arises in industrial countries and in many developing countries.

[20] These effects will also be reflected in the figures for the overall deficit which, therefore, also need to be treated with caution.

[21] For example, public enterprises are generally not expected to pay a substantial dividend on their profits. However, in some countries, such as Guinea, they are required to transfer all or most of their profits, including depreciation allowances, to the government. Also, in many countries, for example, the United Kingdom, public enterprises obtain a high proportion of finance in the form of loans at fixed nominal interest rates. Under inflationary conditions, interest payments on such loans will implicitly contain an element of capital repayment compensating for the effects of inflation. In such cases, the current balance shown net of replacement cost depreciation will involve some double counting of capital costs.

Table 5. Components of Overall Balances of Public Enterprises[1]
(As percentages of GDP at market prices)

Years	Operating Surplus/Deficit (−) Before Depreciation and Subsidies	Subsidies	Current Account Surplus/Deficit (−)		Capital Account Surplus/Deficit (−)	Overall Surplus/Deficit (−)
			Before depreciation	After depreciation[2]		
"World" (average)[3]	**1.0**	**1.2**	**0.8 (0.8)**	**−0.4**	**−2.8 (−2.8)**	**−2.0 (−2.0)**
Industrial countries (average)[3]	**0.5**	**1.4**	**0.7 (0.7)**	**−0.4**	**−2.4 (−2.4)**	**−1.7 (−1.7)**
Australia[4]						
1966	3.4	...	1.4	—	−5.4	−4.0
1968–69	3.6	...	1.4	—	−5.1	−3.7
1970–73	3.3	...	1.3	—	−4.6	−3.3
1974–77	2.2	...	1.0	—	−4.5	−3.5
Belgium						
1964–65	...	...	...	...	...	−0.4
1966–69	...	...	...	...	...	−0.7
1970–73	...	...	...	...	...	−0.9
1974–77	...	...	...	...	...	−0.9
1978–79	...	...	...	...	...	−0.5
Canada						
1960	...	...	1.0	0.2	...	...
1963	...	...	1.1	0.2	...	...
1965	...	...	1.1	0.3	...	...
1966–69	...	...	1.0	0.3	−2.4	−1.5
1970–73	...	...	0.9	0.2	−3.6	−2.8
1974–77	...	...	0.8	0.1	−3.5	−2.3
1978–81	...	...	1.2	...	−4.1	−3.1
1982	...	...	1.0	...	...	−1.5
Finland						
1970–73	...	...	1.4	...	−2.9	−1.5
1974–75	...	...	2.0	...	−4.6	−2.6

Table 5 (continued). Components of Overall Balances of Public Enterprises[1]
(As percentages of GDP at market prices)

Years	Operating Surplus/Deficit (−) Before Depreciation and Subsidies	Subsidies	Current Account Surplus/Deficit (−) Before depreciation	Current Account Surplus/Deficit (−) After depreciation[2]	Capital Account Surplus/Deficit (−)	Overall Surplus/Deficit (−)
France[5]						
1959–61	... (2.0)	1.4 (0.5)	3.0 (1.9)	... (...)	−5.5 (−3.0)	−2.5 (−1.1)
1962–65	... (1.4)	1.8 (0.8)	2.8 (1.7)	... (...)	−5.5 (−2.7)	−2.7 (−1.0)
1966–69	... (1.0)	2.1 (0.9)	2.9 (1.5)	... (...)	−5.7 (−2.4)	−2.8 (−0.9)
1970–73	... (1.1)	1.9 (0.6)	2.7 (1.3)	... (...)	−4.7 (−1.9)	−2.0 (−0.6)
1974	... (0.6)	1.7 (0.6)	2.9 (0.9)	... (...)	−4.7 (−1.9)	−1.8 (−1.0)
1975–77	... (0.8)	... (0.7)	... (1.0)	... (...)	... (−2.3)	... (−1.3)
1978–81	... (1.2)	... (0.7)	... (1.2)	... (...)	... (−2.7)	... (−1.5)
1982	... (1.2)	... (0.8)	... (1.1)	... (...)	... (−2.9)	... (−1.8)
Italy						
1969	...	...	0.6	−0.9	−2.7	−2.1
1970–73	...	...	−0.1	−1.5	−3.5	−3.6
1974–77	...	...	−0.4	−2.2	−3.1	−3.5
1978–80	...	...	−0.3	−2.0	−2.7	−3.0
Japan						
1970–73	...	...	1.1	0.1	−3.6	−2.5
1974–77	...	...	0.4	−0.6	−3.8	−3.4
1978–81	...	...	0.9	−0.1	−3.6	−2.7
Netherlands						
1968–69	...	...	1.7	0.3	−4.2	−2.5
1970–73	...	...	1.7	0.1	−3.6	−1.9
1974–77	...	...	2.6	0.9	−3.1	−0.5
1978	...	...	2.3	0.6	−2.8	−0.5
Norway[6]						
1968–69	2.7	0.7	1.2	...	−2.1	−0.9
1970–73	2.0	0.6	1.0	...	−2.2	−1.2

Country	Year						
Spain	1974–76	1.9	0.7	0.9	:	−3.6	−2.7
	1977–80	:	:	0.8	:	−3.4	−2.6
United Kingdom	1979–80	:	1.3	:	:	:	−3.1
	1946–49	0.9	0.1	0.6	:	−1.3	−0.7
	1950–53	1.8	—	1.2	:	−2.9	−1.7
	1954–57	2.0	—	1.2	:	−3.4	−2.2
	1958–61	2.1	0.3	1.3	:	−3.5	−2.2
	1962–65	2.4	0.5	1.7	−0.2	−3.4	−1.7
	1966–69	2.6	0.4	1.8	−0.3	−3.7	−1.9
	1970–73	2.2	0.4	1.3	−1.1	−3.0	−1.7
	1974–77	2.1	1.1	1.7	−1.1	−3.6	−1.9
	1978–81	2.2	0.8	1.8	−0.9	−2.8	−1.0
	1982	2.4	0.9	2.0	−0.7	−2.8	−0.8
United States	1960	0.1	:	0.1	−0.2	−0.7	−0.6
	1963	0.2	:	0.2	−0.2	−0.8	−0.6
	1965	0.2	:	0.2	−0.2	−0.8	−0.6
	1967–69	0.3	:	0.2	−0.1	−0.8	−0.6
	1970–73	0.2	:	0.2	−0.2	−0.8	−0.6
	1974–77	0.2	:	0.2	−0.2	−0.9	−0.7
	1978	0.2	:	0.2	−0.2	−0.8	−0.6
Developing countries (average)[3]		**3.8**	**0.9**	**1.6 (1.5)**	**0.4**	**−6.0 (−6.0)**	**−3.9 (−4.5)**
Oil exporting countries			—	0.5	:	−5.9	−5.4
Venezuela[7]	1972–73	0.8 (0.6)	1.1 (1.1)	2.4 (0.5)	:	−7.6 (−6.8)	−5.2 (−6.3)
	1974–77	12.4 (0.6)	0.8 (0.8)	6.9 (−0.8)	:	−12.0 (−8.8)	−5.1 (−9.6)
	1978–80	23.1 (0.1)	:	4.6	:	−7.7	−3.1
Africa (average)[3]		2.8	:	1.5	:	:	:
Benin[8]	1977	4.1	:	2.0	0.5	−6.7	−4.7
Botswana[4]	1974–77	5.4	:	1.7	1.2	−2.3	−0.6
	1978–79	4.9	:	:	0.9	:	:
Congo	1976	−1.5	:	7.1	:	:	:
Gambia, The	1979	:	:	:	:	−12.0	−4.9
Guinea	1976–77	:	:	:	:	:	−8.0

Table 5 (continued). Components of Overall Balances of Public Enterprises[1]
(As percentages of GDP at market prices)

	Years	Operating Surplus/Deficit (−) Before Depreciation and Subsidies	Subsidies	Current Account Surplus/Deficit (−)		Capital Account Surplus/Deficit (−)	Overall Surplus/Deficit (−)
				Before depreciation	After depreciation[2]		
Guinea	1978–79	...	...	...	...	...	−23.4
Ivory Coast	1965–69	...	...	1.9	...	−2.8	−0.9
	1970–73	...	...	2.2	...	−5.8	−3.6
	1974–77	...	...	3.0	...	−6.5	−3.6
	1978–79	...	...	2.8	...	−11.2	−8.4
Malawi	1970–73	...	0.1	3.1	1.9	−5.8	−2.7
	1974–77	...	—	3.9	2.6	−6.4	−2.5
	1978	...	—	2.9	1.5	−6.4	−3.5
Mali[8]	1975–77	0.8	...	−1.3	−2.5	−4.6	−5.9
	1978	−0.9	...	−2.0	−3.0	−0.7	−2.7
Senegal[9]	1974	...	...	4.9 (−)	3.2 (−1.4)	−2.7 (−2.6)	2.2 (−2.6)
Tanzania[10]	1966–69	3.0	—	1.1	0.5	−2.6	−1.5
	1970–73	4.0	0.1	2.6	1.4	−5.2	−2.6
	1974–75	4.1	1.1	2.8	1.7	−5.6	−2.8
	1976–78	4.1	0.3	...	...		
Tunisia	1976–77	...	...	3.1	0.3	...	...
	1978–80	...	...	3.4	0.6	...	...
Zambia	1972	...	...	12.7	5.7	−16.1	−3.4
Asia (average)[3]		3.5	...	1.7	...	−7.3	−5.6
Burma	1968–69	...	...	3.4	...	−4.8	−1.4

Country	Period	(1)	(2)	(3)	(4)	(5)	(6)
India	1970–73	-1.5	-4.5	…	3.0	…	…
	1974–77	-1.2	-3.7	…	2.5	…	…
	1978–80	-10.6	-12.3	0.2	1.7	—	2.7
Korea	1966–69	-4.2	-5.4	0.1	1.2	0.1	2.9
	1970–73	-4.3	-5.6	0.3	1.3	0.6	3.0
	1974–77	-6.3	-7.8	0.4	1.5	0.6	3.6
	1978	-6.2	-7.9	1.4	1.7	…	…
Nepal	1963–65	-2.8	-5.1	1.2	2.3	…	…
	1966–69	-3.3	-5.3	0.8	2.0	…	…
	1970–73	-3.8	-5.3	0.8	1.5	…	…
	1974–77	-5.4	-7.0	…	1.6	…	…
	1978–80	-5.2	-7.3	…	2.1	…	…
	1971–73	-0.5	-0.9	0.5	0.4	…	…
	1974–75	-2.1	-2.4	0.9	0.3	…	…
Taiwan*4	1951–53	-3.7	-5.8	1.5	2.1	…	4.9
	1954–57	-2.6	-5.2	1.5	2.6	…	5.1
	1958–61	-3.5	-7.1	2.3	3.6	…	7.3
	1962–65	-1.3	-5.0	2.0	3.7	…	8.0
	1966–69	-2.4	-6.6	2.1	4.2	…	7.3
	1970–73	-3.7	-7.7	2.4	4.0	…	7.2
	1974–77	-7.3	-11.4	…	4.1	…	6.3
	1978–80	-5.5	-10.2	…	4.7	…	6.3
Thailand	1969	-0.8	-2.4	…	1.6	…	…
	1970–73	-0.8	-1.9	…	1.1	…	…
	1974–77	-1.1	-1.8	…	0.7	…	…
	1978–79	-2.0	-3.2	…	1.2	0.1	…
Europe							
Greece	1975	-1.6	…	…	…	…	…
	1979	-1.6	…	…	…	…	…
Portugal	1978–80	-8.1	…	…	…	4.5	…

Table 5 (continued). Components of Overall Balances of Public Enterprises[1]
(As percentages of GDP at market prices)

Years	Operating Surplus/Deficit (−) Before Depreciation and Subsidies	Subsidies	Current Account Surplus/Deficit (−) Before depreciation	Current Account Surplus/Deficit (−) After depreciation[2]	Capital Account Surplus/Deficit (−)	Overall Surplus/Deficit (−)
Turkey						
1964–65	...	0.4	1.0	—	−2.4	−1.4
1966–69	...	0.4	1.1	0.2	−3.3	−2.2
1970–73	2.9	0.1	1.1	—	−5.1	−4.0
1974–77	−0.1	1.3	0.2	−0.8	−7.2	−7.0
1978–81	−0.8	2.1	1.0	0.2	−8.6	−7.6
1982	1.4	1.2	1.7	1.1	−6.9	−5.2
Western Hemisphere (average)[2]	3.3	...	1.2	...	−4.4	−2.5
Argentina[8,11]						
1968–69	...	...	(1.2)	...	−3.0	(−1.8)
1970–73	...	...	(0.6)	...	−3.5	(−2.9)
1974–75	...	...	(−0.4)	...	−3.9	(−4.3)
1976–77	1.7	1.0	2.1 (1.1)	...	−5.2	−3.1 (−4.1)
1978–80	...	...	(0.6)	...	−4.0	... (−3.4)
Bahamas						
1975–77	...	0.8	0.4	...	−2.3	−1.9
1978–79	...	0.4	2.1	...	−3.8	−1.7
Barbados						
1975–77	...	1.0	0.3	...	−2.1	−1.8
1978–80	...	1.3	0.3	...	−2.4	−2.1
Bolivia						
1971–73	5.4	0.2	2.6	...	−6.0	−3.4
1974–77	8.0	0.1	2.4	...	−6.8	−4.4
Brazil						
1980	...	...	...	...	...	−1.7

Country	Period						
Chile[8]	1974–77	9.3	1.0	2.9	...	−3.1	−0.2
	1978–80	8.2	0.3	1.5	...	−1.9	−0.4
Colombia[12]	1974–77	(0.8)	0.3 (0.3)	0.8 (0.4)	...	−1.7 (−1.0)	−0.9 (−0.6)
	1978–80	(1.5)	0.4 (0.3)	1.3 (1.0)	...	−1.4 (−0.9)	−0.1 (−0.1)
Costa Rica	1977–79	...	—	0.6	...	−5.0	−4.4
Dominica	1975–77	...	0.6	1.6	...	−6.0	−4.4
	1978–79	...	2.9	2.4	...	−3.6	−1.2
Dominican Republic[8]	1972–73	...	0.1	1.9	...	−1.8	0.1
	1974–77	...	0.6	2.1	...	−2.3	−0.2
	1978–79	...	0.7	0.3	...	−1.9	−1.6
Guatemala	1975–77	0.4	0.1	0.3	...	−2.1	−1.8
	1978–80	0.5	—	0.3	...	−2.4	−2.1
Guyana	1973	5.6	0.7	2.7	...	−6.4	−3.7
	1974–77	10.7	1.1	3.8	...	−10.4	−6.6
	1978–80	13.5	1.1	6.5	...	−7.9	−1.4
Haiti[8]	1976–77	...	...	0.6	...	−2.6	−2.0
	1978–80	...	...	1.0	...	−1.9	−0.9
Honduras	1978–79	...	—	1.4	...	−3.7	−2.3
Jamaica[8]	1976–77	...	0.2	1.2	...	−5.5	−4.3
	1978–81	...	1.1	1.8	...	−4.8	−3.0
Mexico[8]	1975–77	3.4	1.0	0.8	...	−4.7	−3.9
	1978	4.9	0.9	1.5	...	−5.2	−3.7
Panama	1960	...	...	0.4	0.3	−0.6	−0.2
	1965	...	...	0.5	0.3	−1.4	−0.9
	1966–69	...	0.1	0.5	0.3	−1.6	−1.1
	1970–73	...	0.1	1.1	0.7	−3.8	−2.7
	1974–77	...	0.4	1.9	1.1	−9.0	−7.1
	1978–79	...	0.1	0.6	−1.8	−7.7	−7.1
Paraguay	1970–73	1.7	0.1	1.1	...	−2.3	−1.2
	1974–77	1.8	0.1	1.2	...	−2.8	−1.6
	1978–80	2.2	0.1	1.4	...	−2.3	−0.9

Table 5 (concluded). Components of Overall Balances of Public Enterprises[1]
(As percentages of GDP at market prices)

	Years	Operating Surplus/ Deficit (−) Before Depreciation and Subsidies	Subsidies	Current Account Surplus/Deficit (−)		Capital Account Surplus/Deficit (−)	Overall Surplus/ Deficit (−)
				Before depreciation	After depreciation[2]		
Peru	1968–69	...	0.1	0.4	...	−1.7	−1.3
	1970–73	...	0.2	0.5	...	−1.8	−1.3
	1974–77	...	0.4	−0.7	...	−4.1	−4.8
	1978–79	...	0.1	0.6	...	−2.3	−1.7
St. Lucia	1975–77	...	0.4	0.5	...	−5.1	−4.6
	1978	...	0.4	0.8	...	−3.6	−2.8
Uruguay	1976–77	4.9	0.3	3.4	...	−3.4	—
	1978–80	3.8	0.3	2.3	...	−3.1	−0.8

Source: Appendix.
[1] The definitions of the components of the overall balance are discussed on page 150.
[2] Depreciation is measured at replacement cost for most countries. It is measured at historic cost for Turkey. The basis of measurement in several African countries is not known.
[3] Weighted average for 1974–77 or closest available period using GDP at market prices in U.S. dollars as weights. Figures in parentheses are averages for countries for which both current and capital account surplus figures are available.
[4] Operating surplus after crediting receipts of subsidies.
[5] Figures in parentheses are for eight large enterprises only.
[6] Central government enterprises only.
[7] Figures in parentheses exclude iron ore and petroleum enterprises nationalized in 1975.
[8] Major enterprises only.
[9] Figures in parentheses exclude phosphate company.
[10] Figures include parastatal enterprises only; former enterprises of the East African Community are excluded.
[11] Figures in parentheses relate to current account surplus before crediting subsidies and to overall surplus before crediting subsidies.
[12] Figures in parentheses exclude public enterprises at the regional or local level.
* See note to Table 1, page 122.

often obtain finance on soft terms and hence may not pay the full economic cost for the resources they use. This means that the level of economic subsidy being provided cannot be deduced directly from figures for the components of the current balance.

Second, in order to calculate the return being achieved by public enterprises, components of the current balance—particularly the operating balance net of depreciation—need to be related to a measure of the capital input into the enterprises. However, there is little information on the capital stock of public enterprises that is adequate for this purpose.[22]

Third, public enterprises are generally expected to pursue objectives, principally allocational and distributional ones, which are not reflected in the commercial return to these enterprises as shown in the current balance. Any benefits in terms of these objectives have to be taken into account separately in judging performance.

Looking at the figures, one of the most striking features is the large size of the capital account deficits. These are, of course, a reflection of the high levels of investment by public enterprises. In the mid-1970s, capital account deficits averaged over 2¾ percent of GDP. They were particularly large in developing countries, averaging 6 percent of GDP, compared with 2½ percent of GDP in industrial countries. Moreover, these deficits have risen in recent years. In industrial countries, the increase has been small, less than ¼ of 1 percent of GDP between the late 1960s and the end of the 1970s. However, in developing countries, it has been substantial, the capital account deficit rising by 1¾ percent of GDP over this period.

Also notable are the low levels of the surpluses on operating and current accounts. In the mid-1970s, predepreciation current account surpluses averaged only ¾ of 1 percent of GDP. For the more limited numbers of countries for which such information could be obtained, operating surpluses averaged 1 percent of GDP, while postdepreciation current balances were in deficit, on average, by almost ½ of 1 percent of GDP. Surpluses were generally larger in developing countries than in industrial countries. However, apart from the operating

---

[22] In the United Kingdom, figures for the capital stock of the public enterprise sector are published annually in the national accounts; see Central Statistical Office, *National Income and Expenditure* (London). However, this information does not appear to be readily available for other countries. Although there are methods for estimating the capital stock from investment figures—see, for example, Arnold C. Harberger, "Perspectives on Capital and Technology in Less Developed Countries," in *Contemporary Economic Analysis*, M. J. Artis and A. R. Nobay (eds.) (London: Croom-Helm, 1978)—they are difficult to apply to public enterprises because of the lack of information in most countries on asset lives and, in particular, on the value of the assets of enterprises entering (or leaving) the sector through nationalization, etc. Differences in accounting conventions, especially in the treatment of inflation, make it difficult to use asset values in enterprise accounts for this purpose.

balance, where the surplus averaged over 3¾ percent of GDP in developing countries compared with ½ of 1 percent of GDP in industrial ones, the differences were not substantial. Also, the higher surpluses in developing countries were partly the result of very large surpluses in a few countries, such as Venezuela, where high-rent natural resource industries are under public ownership.

Even allowing for the problems of interpretation, it is clear from these figures that the return on investment in public enterprises, at least in commercial terms, has been low, particularly given the substantial investment effort over recent years. The size of these surpluses is also noteworthy because the promotion of saving has been a major motive for establishing public enterprises in many developing countries.[23]

An alternative way of looking at saving performance is in terms of the self-financing ratios of the enterprises. The current account surpluses imply that, in both industrial and developing countries, only about 25 percent of investment requirements were self-financed in the mid-1970s. The exclusion of receipts of government current transfers, which arguably provides a better measure of saving performance, reduced the self-financing ratio from 25 percent to 10 percent for those developing countries for which this information is available. It is difficult to judge what is an appropriate level for this ratio, but it is relevant to note that the degree of self-financing in the private sector appears generally to be much higher.[24]

Current surpluses have also not changed substantially in recent years, despite the growth in the output and investment of public enterprises. In fact, between the late 1960s and the mid-1970s, pre-depreciation current account surpluses fell marginally relative to GDP in industrial countries, although they have recovered since then. In developing countries, these surpluses showed negligible growth between the late 1960s and the mid-1970s, and, although there was an

---

[23] Public enterprises could increase aggregate saving by boosting saving in other sectors of the economy, rather than directly through their own saving. This might happen if savers were more willing to lend money to public rather than private enterprises because of the government guarantee, implicit or explicit, that is normally attached to such loans. However, while some such effect is possible, the beneficial effect on saving has generally been viewed as arising mainly through public enterprises' own saving efforts.

[24] For the limited number of countries, mainly industrial ones, for which data on self-financing for both sectors could be obtained, the self-financing ratio for private enterprises averaged 76 percent in the mid-1970s, and that for public enterprises, after crediting current transfers, averaged 48 percent. Although differences in tax systems and distribution policies between the two sectors mean that such comparisons need to be treated with some caution, they are unlikely to distort the qualitative conclusion that self-financing is much higher for private enterprises.

increase in the late 1970s, this was only about ½ of 1 percent of GDP. As a result, a decreasing proportion of investment has been financed out of saving. Between the late 1960s and the mid-1970s, the self-financing ratio fell by 12 percentage points for those countries for which this ratio can be calculated, although almost half of this fall appears to have been recovered since then.

Financing of Public Enterprise Deficits

Major Sources of Finance

Table 6 provides a breakdown of public enterprise overall deficits by source of finance. Comprehensive information is only available for a limited number of countries, mainly developing ones; however, it is clear that the three specific sources of finance distinguished—the central government, the banking system, and foreign borrowing—are all of major quantitative importance. In the mid-1970s, for those countries for which a complete breakdown of sources of finance is available, financing from the central government and the banking system both averaged 1¼ percent of GDP, foreign borrowing averaged 1 percent of GDP,[25] and other domestic borrowing averaged ¾ of 1 percent of GDP.[26]

These three sources are also important because of their effects on, in particular, the money supply and the balance of payments. No attempt will be made here to provide a rigorous analysis of these effects; however, further information on the individual sources is given below.

Government Financing of Public Enterprises— "Burden" on the Budget

Public enterprises do not only affect government finances through government financing of their deficits. They also contribute revenue to the government and make other demands on the budget in the form of current transfers.

In one sense, all these flows constitute the impact of the public enterprise sector on government finances. However, even if the ac-

---

[25] Some foreign borrowing by public enterprises in developing countries is channeled through government accounts and, as a result, is likely to be shown in the statistics as borrowing from the government rather than from abroad.

[26] This figure also includes the residual of unidentified financing.

Table 6. Financing of Public Enterprise Deficits
(As percentages of GDP at market prices)

	Years	Foreign Borrowing	Domestic Borrowing	Of Which: Central Government	Of Which: Banking system	Of Which: Other domestic borrowing	Total Financing[1]
"World" (average)[2]		**1.0 (0.7)**	**2.9 (2.9)**	...	...	...	**3.6 (3.6)**
Industrial countries							
Finland	1964–65	:	:	0.4	:	:	:
	1966–69	:	:	0.2	:	:	:
	1970–73	:	:	0.3	:	:	:
	1974–77	:	:	0.3	:	:	:
	1978	:	:	0.2	:	:	:
Norway[3]	1969	—	0.8	0.5	−0.4	0.7	0.8
	1970–73	0.3	0.9	1.1	0.1	−0.3	1.2
	1974–76	1.8	0.9	1.8	−0.4	−0.5	2.7
	1977–80	:	:	2.0	:	:	2.6
Spain	1979–80	0.5	2.6	1.2	1.2	0.2	3.1
Developing countries							
Oil exporting countries							
Algeria	1970–73	4.2	:	:	:	:	:
	1974–77	10.2	:	:	:	:	:
	1978–80	9.9	:	:	:	:	:
Africa							
Botswana	1978–79	0.4	0.2	:	:	:	0.6

	Year						
Gambia, The	1979	1.7	3.2	1.7	..	..	4.9
Guinea⁴	1976–77	0.9	7.1	5.7	1.4	—	8.0
	1978–79	-0.5	23.9	13.6	10.3	—	23.4
Ivory Coast	1975–77	2.6	..	..	..	..	..
	1978–80	1.7	..	..	..	..	..
Mali⁵	1975–77	..	..	..	4.1	..	5.9
	1978	..	..	..	3.8	..	2.7
Tanzania⁶	1966–69	0.4	1.1	0.3	..	..	1.5
	1970–73	1.4	1.2	0.7	..	..	2.6
	1974–75	0.7	2.1	0.8	..	..	2.8
Tunisia	1976–77	4.5	..	7.0	..	..	..
Asia							
India	1966–69	—	4.2	3.7	..	..	4.2
	1970–73	—	4.3	3.3	..	..	4.3
	1974–77	—	6.3	5.0	..	..	6.3
	1978	—	6.2	5.3	..	..	6.2
Korea	1963–65	0.7	2.1	—	0.9	1.2	2.8
	1966–69	1.5	1.8	—	1.7	0.1	3.3
	1970–73	2.2	1.6	0.1	0.5	1.0	3.8
	1974–77	1.1	4.3	—	2.0	2.3	5.4
	1978–80	1.7	3.5	0.1	1.4	2.0	5.2
Thailand	1969	0.3	0.5	0.5	..	..	0.8
	1970–73	0.4	0.4	0.4	..	..	0.8
	1974–77	0.7	0.4	0.3	..	..	1.1
	1978–79	1.6	0.4	0.4	..	..	2.0
Europe							
Portugal	1978–80	2.9	5.2	3.8	1.4	—	8.1
Turkey	1964–65	-0.1	1.5	0.5	0.6	0.4	1.4
	1966–69	0.2	2.0	0.4	0.9	0.7	2.2

Table 6. (concluded). Financing of Public Enterprise Deficits
(As percentages of GDP at market prices)

	Years	Foreign Borrowing	Domestic Borrowing	Of Which: Central Government	Of Which: Banking system	Of Which: Other domestic borrowing	Total Financing[1]
Turkey	1970–73	1.0	3.0	1.9	0.5	0.6	4.0
	1974–77	0.4	6.6	1.1	2.2	3.3	7.0
	1978–80	1.4	6.1	0.7	0.2	5.2	7.5
Western Hemisphere							
Argentina[5,7]	1976–77	0.7	2.4 (3.4)	1.7 (2.7)	...	...	3.1 (4.1)
	1978–80	1.5	... (1.9)	... (0.8)	...	...	... (3.4)
Bahamas	1975–77	–0.9	2.8	2.2	...	...	1.9
	1978–79	0.5	1.2	1.6	...	...	1.7
Bolivia	1971–73	...	...	0.7	...	...	3.4
	1974–77	3.2	1.2	0.5	0.9	–0.2	4.4
Brazil[8]	1980	0.8	0.9	...	...	...	1.7
Chile[5]	1974–77	–0.2	0.4	0.8	...	...	0.2
	1978–80	1.3	–0.9	—	...	...	0.4
Colombia[9]	1974–76	1.1 (0.9)	–0.2 (–0.3)	...	...	...	0.9 (0.6)
Dominica	1975–77	5.9	–1.5	...	...	...	4.4
	1978–79	0.8	0.4	...	...	...	1.2
Dominican Republic[5]	1975–77	0.7	–0.4	...	...	...	0.3
	1978–79	0.8	0.8	...	...	...	1.6
Guatemala	1975–77	0.1	1.7	1.3	...	...	1.8
	1978–79	—	2.1	1.9	...	...	0.9

Country	Period						
Haiti[5,8]	1976–77	1.2	0.8	...	...	...	2.0
	1978–80	0.7	0.2	...	...	...	0.9
Honduras	1978–79	1.3	1.0	1.2	0.1	...	2.3
Jamaica[5]	1976–77	−0.4	4.7	1.8	0.3	2.8	4.3
	1978–81	−0.3	3.3	2.8	...	0.2	3.0
Paraguay	1970–71	0.5	0.5	0.3	...	...	1.0
	1972–73	1.2	0.3	0.3	0.2	−0.2	1.5
	1974–77	2.0	−0.4	0.3	—	−0.7	1.6
	1978–80	1.0	−0.1	0.2	—	−0.3	0.9
Peru	1968–69	0.6	0.7	0.4	0.1	0.3	1.3
	1970–73	0.8	0.5	0.8	1.1	−0.4	1.3
	1974–77	2.3	2.5	0.8	−1.8	0.6	4.8
	1978–79	3.4	−1.7	0.5	1.3	−0.4	1.7
St. Lucia	1975–77	1.7	2.9	0.9	−0.7	0.7	4.6
	1978–79	0.9	1.9	1.4	...	1.2	2.8
Uruguay	1976–77	0.8	−0.8	0.2	...	...	—
	1978–80	1.0	−0.2	0.3	...	...	0.8

Source: Appendix.
[1] Equal to overall deficit.
[2] Weighted average for 1974–77 or closest available period using GDP at market prices as weights. Figures in parentheses are averages for countries for which both domestic and foreign borrowing figures are available.
[3] Figures relate to central government enterprises only.
[4] Figures for central government and total financing include subsidies.
[5] Major enterprises only.
[6] Figures include parastatal enterprises only; former East African Community enterprises are excluded.
[7] Figures in parentheses include subsidies.
[8] Figures exclude government capital transfers.
[9] Figures in parentheses exclude public enterprises at the regional or local level.

tivities operated by public enterprises were in the private sector, they would still affect the budget, especially through tax payments. It is only the difference between these effects and those under public ownership that represents the "burden"—or "benefit"—of public enterprises for government finances. Although this burden raises problems of measurement, both conceptual and practical, it is the most appropriate focus for analysis.

There are three components of the budgetary burden. First, and most important, public enterprises affect the budget through government transfers, both current and capital, and loan-related flows, that is, net loans and equity injections on the one hand, and dividend and interest payments on the other.[27] Second, public ownership may affect tax revenue. In several countries, there are differences between the tax systems applied to public and private enterprises, most of which involve lower tax rates for public enterprises.[28, 29] Even if the same tax system is applied, public enterprises may generate less revenue if they charge lower prices, for example, for distributional reasons, or are relatively inefficient in their use of factors. Third, there may be indirect effects on the budget because, for example, government purchases from public enterprises are subject to special conditions[30] or because public enterprises receive subsidized credit from government-owned financial institutions.

Without detailed study of the public enterprises in each country, it is only possible to quantify the first of these components. The net balance of transfers and loan-related flows was therefore adopted as the measure of the budgetary burden for use in this paper.[31] Because

---

[27] Private enterprises also receive government transfers and loans, and these are substantial in some countries; however, it seems reasonable to treat all transfers and loans to public enterprises as constituting part of the burden.

[28] Differences in income tax systems are discussed by Robert H. Floyd in "Some Aspects of Income Taxation of Public Enterprises," *Staff Papers*, International Monetary Fund (Washington), Vol. 25 (June 1978), pp. 310–42.

[29] A lower tax rate does not necessarily imply a burden since, for given prices, it will be offset by higher post-tax profits. However, in practice, it seems likely that a lower tax rate will be reflected, at least in part, in a lower level of prices. See, for example, Ralph E. Beals, "Mining Taxation and Public Enterprises," in *Tax and Investment Policies for Hard Minerals: Public and Multinational Enterprises in Indonesia*, Malcolm Gillis and Ralph E. Beals (eds.) (Cambridge: Ballinger, 1980), pp. 75–112, for a discussion of the issues here.

[30] An important example is that, in several countries, such as Liberia and the Congo, the government has at times accumulated large arrears of payments for goods purchased from public enterprises. In such cases, public enterprises are effectively providing a benefit to the budget—assuming that such arrears are not financed by government transfers.

[31] This measure shows the burden that has to be financed by the government in the short term. To the extent that loans are on commercial terms and are fully serviced, they will not represent a burden in the long term.

these are likely to constitute the bulk of the burden in most cases, the omission of the other two components is probably not a serious one. Figures for the burden defined in this way expressed as percentages of GDP are given in Table 7. Also shown are figures for direct taxes paid by public enterprises for the limited number of countries for which this information could be obtained.[32]

The notable feature of the table is the large size of the budgetary burdens in many countries. In the mid-1970s, they averaged 2¼ percent of GDP, with current transfers and investment-related flows each accounting for over 1 percent of GDP. By comparison, the overall deficits of the central government[33] averaged 4¼ percent of GDP for the same group of countries. Budgetary burdens were much higher in developing than in industrial countries. In developing countries, they averaged 3¼ percent of GDP, being particularly high in Africa and Asia, whereas, in industrial countries, they averaged 1½ percent of GDP. This difference was mainly the result of much larger investment-related flows in developing countries; current transfers were close to 1 percent of GDP in both groups of countries.

Also of importance is the fact that budgetary burdens have increased in recent years. In industrial countries, they rose by ½ of 1 percent of GDP between the early 1970s and the end of that decade, while in developing countries, they increased by 1½ percent of GDP over this period. In a number of the developing countries for which long runs of data are available, there have been some extremely large increases. For example, between the mid-1960s and the end of the 1970s, the budgetary burden rose by over 9 percent of GDP in Zambia, by 7½ percent of GDP in Sri Lanka, and by over 4½ percent of GDP in Tanzania.

The budgetary burdens imposed by public enterprises may be met by measures that increase government revenue or reduce other expenditure, or they may be passed forward into higher government deficits and hence be financed by borrowing or money creation. The interactions between all parts of the budget make it impossible to establish which particular elements adjust to accommodate these burdens. However, the relationship between the sizes of budgetary bur-

---

[32] The figures for tax payments and, in particular, the average of 2 percent of GDP for the countries included, give a misleading impression. In most of the countries for which data could not be obtained, tax payments by public enterprises appear to be very small. If figures had been included for these countries, the average would have been much lower.

[33] The overall deficit of the central government is the difference between (1) total expenditure and net lending; and (2) total revenue and grants. For a discussion of this definition see International Monetary Fund, *A Manual on Government Finance Statistics* (Draft) (Washington: IMF, 1974).

Table 7. Budgetary Burden of Public Enterprises
(As percentages of GDP at market prices)

	Years	Central Government Overall Surplus/Deficit (−)	Budgetary Burden of Public Enterprises[1]	Of Which: Subsidies and Other Current Transfers	Central Government Overall Surplus/Deficit Excluding Public Enterprise Burden	Direct Taxes Paid By Public Enterprises
"World" (average)[2]		**−3.8 (−4.2)**	**2.2 (2.2)**	**1.3**	**−2.0 (−2.0)**	**2.0**
Industrial countries (average)[2]		**−3.2 (−4.1)**	**1.6 (1.6)**	**1.4**	**−2.5 (−2.5)**	...
Australia	1973	−1.7	0.3	...	−1.4	:
	1974–77	−3.2	0.4	...	−2.8	:
	1978–80	−3.0	−0.5	...	−3.5	:
Belgium	1970–73	−3.1	2.3	2.0	−0.8	:
	1974–77	−4.6	2.9	2.6	−1.7	:
	1978–79	−7.7	3.2	2.8	−4.5	:
Denmark[3]	1970–73	3.6	0.6	0.6	4.2	:
	1974–77	−1.1	0.8	0.7	−0.3	:
	1978–80	−4.1	1.1	0.7	−3.0	:
France[4]	1959–61	...	...	1.4 (0.5)	...	(—)
	1962–65	...	...	1.8 (0.8)	...	(—)
	1966–69	...	...	2.1 (0.9)	...	(—)
	1970–73	...	...	1.9 (0.6)	...	2.0 (—)
	1974	0.5	...	1.7 (0.6)	...	2.6 (—)
	1975–77	−1.6	...	... (0.7)	...	(—)
	1978–81	−1.4	...	... (0.7)	...	(—)
Italy	1966–69	−1.5	2.2	0.9	0.7	:
	1970–73	−5.4	3.3	1.5	−2.1	:
	1974–77	−5.9	3.2	1.4	−2.7	:
	1978–80	−12.3	3.7	1.2	−8.6	:

Netherlands	1974–77	−2.2	—	1.0	−2.2	:
Norway[5]	1969	0.2	1.1	0.8	1.3	0.1
	1970–73	−1.7	1.7	0.6	—	0.1
	1974–76	−3.4	2.4	0.7	−1.0	0.1
Spain	1970–73	−0.8	1.1	0.7	0.3	:
	1974–77	−1.5	1.0	0.8	−0.5	:
	1978–79	−2.9	1.7	1.3	−1.2	:
United Kingdom[6]	1946–49	−1.1	0.5	0.1	−0.6	—
	1950–53	—	0.3	—	0.3	0.1
	1954–57	−0.3	1.4	—	1.1	0.2
	1958–61	−0.7	2.0	0.3	1.3	0.1
	1962–65	−0.9	1.3	0.5	0.4	—
	1966–69	−1.3	1.7	0.4	0.4	—
	1970–73	−1.2	0.8	0.4	−0.4	—
	1974–77	−5.2	1.3	1.1	−3.9	—
	1978–81	−4.9	1.2	0.8	−3.7	—
	1982	−3.4	1.0	0.9	−2.4	0.2
Developing countries (average)[2]		**−4.9 (−4.4)**	**3.3 (3.3)**	**1.3**	**−1.1 (−1.1)**	**…**
Oil exporting countries						
Algeria[7]	1970–73	−6.7	10.2	0.6	3.5	:
	1974–77	−7.9	22.0	3.5	14.1	23.2
	1978–80	−11.1	22.2	1.1	11.1	20.5
Indonesia	1972–73	−2.1	:	—	:	:
	1974–77	−2.6	:	0.6	:	:
	1978–80	−2.4	:	1.9	:	:
Venezuela[8]	1972–73	0.3	1.4	—	1.7	0.3
	1974–77	−1.5	2.3 (4.5)	1.1 (1.1)	0.8 (3.0)	7.8 (0.4)
	1978–80	−1.4	−0.6 (3.0)	0.8 (0.8)	−2.0 (1.6)	12.5 (0.1)

Table 7 (continued). Budgetary Burden of Public Enterprises
(As percentages of GDP at market prices)

	Years	Central Government Overall Surplus/Deficit (—)	Budgetary Burden of Public Enterprises[1]	Of Which: Subsidies and Other Current Transfers	Central Government Overall Surplus/Deficit Excluding Public Enterprise Burden	Direct Taxes Paid By Public Enterprises
Africa (average)[2]	1978–80	-5.3	3.8	1.2	-1.6	...
Ethiopia	1976–77	-4.5	...	0.5	...	...
Guinea	1976–77	9.5	-8.2	...	1.3	9.7
	1978–79	-2.4	3.3	...	0.9	11.0
Kenya[9]	1962–65	-1.6	—	—	-1.6	...
	1966–69	-2.7	0.2	—	-2.5	...
	1970–73	-4.0	0.8	—	-3.2	...
	1974	-3.0	0.6	—	-2.4	...
	1975–76	-5.8	2.2 (0.8)	0.2 (—)	-3.6 (-5.0)	...
	1977–79	-5.0	... (2.0)	... (0.2)	... (-3.0)	...
Liberia	1977	-3.0	2.6	...	-0.4	...
	1978–80	-9.4	3.0	...	-6.4	...
Malawi	1967–69	-4.9	0.5	0.1	-4.4	...
	1970–73	-7.1	2.3	0.1	-4.8	...
	1974–77	-6.2	2.2	—	-4.0	...
	1978	-8.0	1.8	0.1	-6.2	...
Sierra Leone	1979	-7.3	0.7	0.1	-6.6	1.9
Tanzania	1963–65	-1.7	0.3	0.1	-1.4	...
	1966–69	-3.7	0.5	0.1	-3.2	...
	1970–73	-6.2	3.1	0.3	-3.1	1.4
	1974–77	-7.9	5.0	0.7	-2.9	1.5
Togo	1978–80	-3.6	...	...	...	6.7

Country	Year					
Tunisia	1968–69	−6.4	1.7	1.0	−4.7	...
	1970–73	−1.8	1.4	1.1	−0.4	...
	1974–77	−4.4	4.6	1.6	0.2	...
	1978–81	−2.8	4.0	2.9	1.2	...
Zambia	1965	3.5	1.0	0.2	4.5	...
	1966–69	−0.8	5.1	0.7	4.3	...
	1970–73	−10.9	10.0	2.3	−0.9	...
	1974–77	−11.3	10.1	3.4	−1.2	...
	1978–80	−14.5	10.1	4.2	−4.4	...
Asia (average)[2]		−5.0	3.6	0.5	−1.3	...
Bangladesh	1979–81	−11.0	6.0	1.1	−5.0	...
India[3]	1966–69	−4.2	3.2	—	−1.0	0.1
	1970–73	−3.3	3.0	0.1	−0.3	0.1
	1974–77	−5.4	5.2	0.6	−0.2	0.2
	1978	−3.5	5.5	0.6	2.0	0.2
Korea[10]	1972–73	−0.8	−0.1	—	−0.9	...
	1974–77	−1.8	0.3	0.3	−1.5	...
	1978–80	−2.3	0.5	0.5	−1.8	...
Pakistan	1973	−6.7	0.7	—	−6.0	...
	1974–77	−8.5	3.2	0.3	−5.3	...
	1978–81	−7.0	3.2	0.3	−3.8	...
Papua New Guinea	1974–77	−3.1	1.5	0.1	−1.6	...
Sri Lanka	1962–65	−5.1	3.8	0.7	−1.3	...
	1966–69	−6.2	4.0	0.7	−2.2	...
	1970–73	−6.4	3.0	0.8	−3.4	...
	1974–77	−5.6	3.8	1.0	−1.8	...
	1978–80	−14.0	11.3	2.8	−2.7	...
Thailand	1969	−2.3	0.4	...	−1.9	...
	1970–73	−3.9	0.4	...	−3.5	...
	1974–77	−2.0	—	...	−2.0	...

Table 7 (continued). Budgetary Burden of Public Enterprises
(As percentages of GDP at market prices)

	Years	Central Government Overall Surplus/Deficit (−)	Budgetary Burden of Public Enterprises[1]	Of Which: Subsidies and Other Current Transfers	Central Government Overall Surplus/Deficit Excluding Public Enterprise Burden	Direct Taxes Paid By Public Enterprises
Thailand	1978–79	−3.4	0.2	0.1	−3.2	...
Europe						
Portugal	1978–80	−10.8	...	4.5	...	...
Turkey	1964–65	−1.8	0.9	0.4	−0.9	...
	1966–69	−1.6	0.8	0.4	−0.8	...
	1970–73	−2.3	1.8	0.1	−0.5	...
	1974–77	−2.6	2.3	1.3	−0.3	...
	1978–80	−4.6	3.5	2.4	−1.1	...
Middle East						
Egypt	1975–77	−18.2	...	10.5	...	...
	1978–79	−14.2	...	10.4	...	...
Western Hemisphere (average)[2]		−4.5	1.7	0.9	−2.8	...
Argentina[11]	1970–73	−3.1	1.4	...	−1.7	...
	1974–75	−8.5	2.2	...	−6.3	...
	1976–77	−5.2	2.7	1.0	−2.5	...
	1978–80	−3.1	0.9	...	−2.2	...
Bahamas	1975–77	−1.0	3.0	0.8	2.0	...
	1978–79	−0.6	2.0	0.4	1.4	...
Barbados	1975–77	−5.8	3.8	1.0	−2.0	...

Country	Period					
Bolivia	1978–80	−3.7	3.8	1.3	0.1	...
Chile[11]	1972–73	−0.7	0.5	0.2	−0.2	2.2
Chile[11]	1974–77	−0.1	−0.4	0.1	−0.5	3.7
Colombia	1974–77	−1.3	0.2	1.0	−1.1	4.7
Colombia	1978–80	3.4	−2.5	0.3	0.9	3.9
Dominican Republic[11]	1974–77	—	0.1	0.3	0.1	...
Dominican Republic[11]	1978–80	−0.5	0.3	0.3	0.3	...
Guatemala	1972–73	—	0.3	0.1	−0.2	...
Guatemala	1974–77	−3.7	1.4	0.6	1.4	...
Guatemala	1978–79	−1.4	2.1	0.7	−1.6	...
Guyana	1970–73	−1.4	0.3	—	−1.1	...
Guyana	1974–77	−2.6	1.5	0.1	0.1	...
Guyana	1978–79	−12.5	1.9	—	−0.7	...
Jamaica[11]	1971–73	−15.0	1.4	0.6	−11.1	...
Jamaica[11]	1974–77	−23.4	1.5	1.1	−13.5	...
Jamaica[11]	1978–80	−17.5	3.8	1.1	−19.6	...
Mexico[11]	1976–77	−14.2	1.9	0.2	−15.6	...
Mexico[11]	1978–81	−4.8	3.9	1.1	−10.3	4.0
Panama	1975–77	−3.0	2.1	1.0	−2.7	4.1
Panama	1978	−4.9	1.7	0.9	−1.3	...
Paraguay	1970–73	−7.5	0.8	0.1	−4.1	...
Paraguay	1974–77	−9.7	1.6	0.1	−5.9	1.1
Paraguay	1978–79	−0.7	2.5	0.4	−7.2	1.5
Peru	1970–73	0.1	0.4	0.1	−0.3	...
Peru	1974–77	0.3	0.4	0.1	0.5	...
Peru	1978–80	−2.1	0.3	0.1	0.6	...
Peru	1972–73	−2.9	0.9	0.2	−1.2	—
Peru	1974–77	0.7	1.0	0.4	−1.9	—
Peru	1978–79	−4.2	0.4	0.1	1.1	...
St. Lucia	1975–77	−1.4	1.3	0.4	−2.9	...
St. Lucia	1978–79		1.7	0.4	0.3	...

Table 7 (concluded). Budgetary Burden of Public Enterprises
(As percentages of GDP at market prices)

Years	Central Government Overall Surplus/Deficit (−)	Budgetary Burden of Public Enterprises[1]	Of Which: Subsidies and Other Current Transfers	Central Government Overall Surplus/ Deficit Excluding Public Enterprise Burden	Direct Taxes Paid By Public Enterprises
Uruguay					
1976–77	− 1.7	0.5	0.3	− 1.2	1.4
1978–79	− 0.4	0.6	0.3	0.2	1.5

Sources: Appendix; and International Monetary Fund, *Government Finance Statistics Yearbook* (various issues).
[1] Defined as central government subsidies, transfers, and net lending to public enterprises less dividends and interest payments to central government.
[2] Weighted average for 1974–77 or closest available period using GDP at market prices in U.S. dollars as weights. Figures in parentheses are averages for countries for which both government deficit and budgetary burden figures are available.
[3] General government.
[4] Figures in parentheses are for eight large enterprises only.
[5] Central government enterprises only.
[6] Figures for subsidies also include subsidies from local government.
[7] Figures for taxes include taxes on petroleum companies only.
[8] Figures in parentheses exclude iron ore and petroleum enterprises nationalized in 1975.
[9] Figures relate to all public corporations; figures in parentheses relate to all nonfinancial enterprises.
[10] Figures relate only to five nonfinancial enterprises organized as departmental enterprises.
[11] Major enterprises only.

dens and government deficits shown in Table 7 suggests that these burdens are passed forward to a substantial extent and hence can be viewed as one explanation of high and rising government deficits.

To begin with, there is a clear tendency for large government deficits to be associated with large budgetary burdens. For example, the two industrial countries with the largest budgetary burdens in recent years, Belgium and Italy, also had the largest government deficits. The four developing countries with the largest burdens, Algeria, Bangladesh, Sri Lanka, and Zambia, were among those with the highest government deficits. In addition, there is some tendency for large increases in government deficits to be associated with large increases in the budgetary burden of public enterprises. This is not very strong in industrial countries: increases in burdens can explain only a small part of the substantial increases in government deficits that have occurred in Belgium, Italy, and the United Kingdom. However, many of the developing countries that have had large increases in government deficits, such as Sri Lanka, Tanzania, Turkey, and Zambia, have also experienced substantial growth in the budgetary burdens of their public enterprises.

Financing from the Banking System

Finance from the banking system is important because of its implications for money supply growth. Of special significance from this point of view is the fact that in several countries, for example, Ghana, Korea, Peru, and Turkey, public enterprises have direct access to borrowing from the central bank. Such borrowing will have a direct impact on credit and the money supply. Borrowing from commercial banks is different in this respect in that public enterprise liabilities generally cannot be used as reserve assets by banks. Consequently, the effect may merely be to replace credit that would otherwise have been extended to the private sector. Whether this is so will depend on the extent to which additional reserve assets are made available by the authorities to match the demand for credit by public enterprises.

The available information on the growth in credit to public enterprises and on the share of this credit in total credit is shown in Table 8. It should be noted that the country coverage is limited and probably unrepresentative, being mainly confined to small, developing countries. Excluded countries, especially industrial ones, seem likely to have substantially lower shares of public enterprise credit in total credit.

It is clear that in the countries included, credit to public enterprises has generally risen markedly in recent years, although there have been substantial variations both between countries and over time. Credit to public enterprises has also increased much faster than that to other sectors of the economy. For example, in the mid-1970s, it increased at an average rate of 46 percent a year, almost twice the rate of growth of other domestic credit of 27 percent. As a result, the share of public enterprise credit in total domestic credit has increased substantially. For the countries for which an adequate run of data is available, the average share rose by 20 percentage points between the early 1970s and the end of the 1970s to stand at a level of almost 30 percent.

Of particular interest is the extent to which additional public enterprise credit leads to overall credit creation rather than just credit diversion. The large shares of public enterprise credit in total credit in many of the countries in Table 8 make it likely that a substantial proportion of any growth in public enterprise credit will be reflected in net credit creation. However, a proper analysis of this issue requires a complete modeling of the monetary system, which is beyond the scope of this paper.

Foreign Borrowing and Other Sources of Domestic Finance

Foreign borrowing by public enterprises is important particularly because of its implications for the balance of payments. Such borrowing generally has less of an impact on economic stabilization in the short term than government or bank finance. In developing countries, it is often used to purchase imported capital equipment and may therefore have little immediate effect on the overall balance of payments or domestic liquidity. Much more critical is the resulting debt burden, which can be a major source of problems in the longer term, especially as repayments will have to be made in foreign exchange.

One measure of the quantitative importance of foreign borrowing has already been given in Table 6. A further indication of its large size can be obtained from the fact that, over the period 1976–78, public enterprises accounted for 23 percent of all borrowing on international capital markets identified by the World Bank, and for 33 percent of such borrowing by developing countries.[34]

Very little information is available on the residual category of other domestic borrowing. In many cases, this probably includes a substantial element of unidentified financing from the other three sources.

---

[34] See World Bank, *Borrowing in International Capital Markets: Third Quarter, 1979* (Washington: World Bank, January 1980).

Table 8. Contribution of Public Enterprises to Growth in Domestic Credit

	Years	Total Growth in Domestic Credit (in percent a year)	Growth in Credit to Public Enterprises (in percent a year)	Public Enterprise Share in Total Domestic Credit at End-Period (in percent)
"World" (average)[1]		**29.1**	**46.1**	**24.5**
Industrial countries				
Norway	1976	. . .	. . .	4.5
	1977	21.4	21.6	4.5
	1978–81	12.4	12.7	4.5
Developing countries				
Oil exporting countries				
Indonesia	1973	. . .	. . .	17.4
	1974–77	27.9	77.9	65.3
	1978–80	11.3	24.5	91.5
Africa				
Benin	1973	. . .	. . .	15.8
	1974–77	28.4	73.7	52.8
	1978–80	30.4	31.6	54.2
Gambia, The	1973	. . .	. . .	40.2
	1974–77	29.0	2.9	16.2
	1978–81	29.3	62.4	40.5
Ghana	1963	. . .	. . .	17.6
	1964–65	45.0	24.0	12.8
	1966–69	13.5	13.5	12.8
	1970–72	12.8	31.4	20.2
	1974–77	46.2	16.3	11.0
	1978–80	35.1	66.8	20.7
Guinea	1977	. . .	. . .	73.8
	1978–80	6.0	12.0	87.1
Ivory Coast	1973	. . .	. . .	18.4
	1974–77	36.9	54.6	29.9
	1978–79	18.2	16.4	29.0
Malawi	1965	. . .	. . .	1.6
	1966–69	36.2	65.3	3.6
	1970–73	12.3	−7.5	1.6
	1974–77	40.8	186.7	28.1
	1978–81	25.4	6.7	14.7
Mali	1968	. . .	. . .	18.7
	1969	24.6	33.5	20.0
	1970–73	11.5	23.1	29.8
	1974–77	20.5	22.7	31.9
	1978	11.0	17.6	37.9
Mauritania	1975	. . .	. . .	18.3
	1976–77	36.9	−8.8	8.1
	1978–80	7.4	6.5	7.9
Niger	1975	. . .	. . .	44.9
	1976–77	−2.4	−23.8	27.4

Table 8 (continued). Contribution of Public Enterprises to Growth in Domestic Credit

	Years	Total Growth in Domestic Credit (in percent a year)	Growth in Credit to Public Enterprises (in percent a year)	Public Enterprise Share in Total Domestic Credit at End-Period (in percent)
Niger	1978–80	71.7	81.5	32.4
Senegal	1973	. . .	. . .	32.8
	1974–77	25.5	29.9	37.7
	1978	31.1	34.4	38.7
Somalia	1975	. . .	. . .	65.5
	1976–77	21.3	31.1	76.6
	1978–81	40.0	17.4	37.9
Sudan	1965	. . .	. . .	5.3
	1966–69	17.2	15.8	5.1
	1970–73	17.8	61.1	17.8
	1974–77	36.5	38.6	18.9
	1978–81	25.5	31.1	22.5
Togo	1975	. . .	. . .	29.3
	1976–77	33.5	20.4	23.9
	1978–79	22.4	18.5	22.4
Upper Volta	1973	. . .	. . .	59.7
	1974–77	90.4	64.6	33.3
	1978	35.5	13.2	27.8
Asia				
Bangladesh	1976	. . .	. . .	39.1
	1977	11.7	4.8	36.7
	1978–81	27.0	29.2	39.3
Burma	1977	. . .	. . .	21.7
	1978–80	16.4	77.0	76.4
Nepal	1975	. . .	. . .	23.0
	1976–77	14.9	−13.7	13.0
	1978–80	28.8	24.6	11.7
Pakistan	1974	. . .	. . .	7.9
	1975–77	22.2	40.1	11.9
	1978–81	17.7	24.6	15.0
Europe				
Greece	1969	. . .	. . .	5.8
	1970–73	20.9	27.2	7.1
	1974–77	25.4	22.5	6.5
	1978–79	22.2	25.5	6.8
Portugal	1976	. . .	. . .	23.3
	1977–80	18.6	20.0	24.1
Turkey	1961	. . .	. . .	1.2
	1962–65	15.0	41.9	2.9
	1966–67	16.7	18.9	4.2
	1969	18.2	7.4	6.7
	1970–73	18.2	25.6	8.6
	1974–77	43.6	67.6	15.9
	1978	26.1	32.5	16.8

Table 8 (concluded). Contribution of Public Enterprises to Growth in Domestic Credit

	Years	Total Growth in Domestic Credit (in percent a year)	Growth in Credit to Public Enterprises (in percent a year)	Public Enterprise Share in Total Domestic Credit at End-Period (in percent)
Middle East				
Egypt	1973	. . .	. . .	15.8
	1974–77	26.9	37.6	21.8
	1978–81	33.6	19.4	13.9
Yemen Arab	1971	. . .	. . .	10.5
Republic	1972–73	17.3	66.5	21.1
	1974–77	18.6	8.1	14.6
	1978–80	96.0	112.1	18.5
Western Hemisphere				
Bolivia	1973	. . .	. . .	11.7
	1974–77	27.6	74.0	40.3
Guyana	1965	. . .	. . .	21.8
	1966–69	21.5	−3.6	8.7
	1970–73	24.5	19.1	7.2
	1974–77	28.6	55.5	15.5
	1978–81	23.9	33.4	20.7
Haiti	1961	. . .	. . .	0.7
	1962–65	8.0	43.8	2.2
	1966–69	5.8	25.9	4.3
	1970–73	17.1	40.5	9.0
	1974–77	31.5	59.6	19.5
	1978–81	16.6	10.2	15.6
Peru	1961	. . .	. . .	1.3
	1962–65	18.4	53.6	3.6
	1966–69	11.9	21.2	5.0
	1970–73	24.7	50.9	10.7
	1974–77	38.6	70.0	24.3
	1978–81	55.5	30.0	11.8

Sources: International Monetary Fund, *International Financial Statistics,* various issues; and Appendix.

[1] Weighted average for 1974–77 or closest available period using GDP at market prices in U.S. dollars as weights.

The one type of such borrowing that is worth mentioning is domestic bond issues by public enterprises. These are of some quantitative importance in industrial countries. For example, the share of public enterprises in total gross domestic bond issues was 7 percent in the Federal Republic of Germany (1970–75); 6 percent in Italy (1976–79); 10 percent in Japan (1976–79); and 9 percent in Spain

(1979).[35]Many of these were taken up by the government or the banking system. However, outside holdings appear to have reached moderately high levels in some countries, for example, Belgium.

IV. CONCLUSIONS

This paper has brought together a large amount of statistical information on public enterprises in many countries. Although this has provided important insights, the comprehensiveness and comparability of some of the data is less than is desirable for cross-country analysis. A basic, albeit mundane, conclusion is therefore that there is a need to improve both the quantity and quality of statistics on public enterprises.

However, despite some statistical shortcomings, it is clear from the data presented that public enterprises are of considerable economic significance. In most countries, they now contribute substantial proportions of aggregate output and investment. They are operating in virtually all kinds of economic activity and are prominent in key sectors of the economy. It is therefore essential that governments should examine carefully the role and performance of public enterprises.

It is also clear that the overall deficits of public enterprises are extremely large in many countries. As a result, public enterprises make sizable demands on government budgets, bank credit, and foreign borrowing. The precise effects of these demands will vary from country to country depending on economic circumstances. However, their large size strongly suggests that, in many countries, public enterprises have been a major cause of stabilization problems and, as a result, have contributed significantly to inflation and balance of payments difficulties.

Of course, public enterprises may also bring economic benefits. They are widely regarded as important means of furthering allocative, distributional, and growth objectives. These issues have not been examined here. Nevertheless, it appears from the data presented that the commercial return and saving of public enterprises is generally low, which is at least of some relevance to their effect on growth. Also, the work that has been done on these aspects suggests that the benefits

[35] These figures were obtained from OECD, *Financial Statistics*.

of public ownership in terms of the three above-mentioned objectives are often not particularly great.[36] As a consequence, measures to reduce the overall deficits of public enterprises may often be particularly appropriate for countries facing stabilization problems.

---

[36] See, for example, Malcolm Gillis, "The Role of State Enterprises in Economic Development," *Social Research*, Vol. 47 (Summer 1980), pp. 248–89.

APPENDIX

Sources of Statistics

This Appendix provides details of the sources for the data shown in Tables 1–8 and some comments on the coverage of the figures for individual countries.

Five types of sources were used. First, international organizations publish statistics on certain aspects of public enterprise operations. Data on their investment and saving are published by the United Nations in the *Yearbook of National Accounts Statistics (UNNA)* and by the Organization for Economic Cooperation and Development in *National Accounts Statistics (OECDNA)* and *Financial Statistics (OECDFS)*; data on credit to public enterprises are given in the IMF's *International Financial Statistics (IFS)*; data on flows from public enterprises to central governments are provided in the IMF's *Government Finance Statistics Yearbook*.[1] In principle, each of these organizations uses a common definition for all countries. However, these definitions differ among the organizations. More important, it appears that, in practice, corrections are often not made for differences among countries in their definitions of the public enterprise sector. There is, therefore, a problem of a lack of comparability of many of the public enterprise figures in these sources.[2] Also, the country coverage of the data is generally limited—for example, public enterprise statistics are only given for 13 of the 150 countries included in the *Yearbook of National Accounts Statistics*.

Second, a number of countries separately identify public enterprises in their published statistics for national accounting, budgetary, and monetary aggregates. Some countries, including India and the United Kingdom, include public enterprise sectors in their national accounts and provide information

---

[1] These sources were generally used for aggregate national accounting, budgetary, and monetary data.

[2] Part of the problem is that the common definitions are imprecise and open to different interpretations—see Leroy P. Jones, *Public Enterprise and Economic Development: The Korean Case*, p. 39, for a discussion of this in the case of the United Nations definition. However, adjustments are also not always made to ensure that the figures conform even to these broad definitions.

on the income and capital account operations of these enterprises; some, including Denmark and Sri Lanka, show flows to and from public enterprises in published economic classifications of their budgets; and some countries, including Bangladesh and Greece, separately identify credit to public enterprises in their monetary statistics. These sources are again subject to the problem that there are significant differences among countries—and sometimes even among different sets of statistics for the same country—in the definitions of the public enterprise sector. It is usually difficult to correct for these.

Third, several countries publish information on public enterprise operations outside of an aggregate statistics framework. An example is statistics on public enterprise investment included in development plans, as in Burma and Algeria. An additional difficulty in such cases is that the definition of, say, "investment" may differ from that used for national accounting purposes.

Fourth, there have been several academic studies of public enterprises in particular countries or regions. Important examples are comparative studies of EEC countries—see Keyser and Windle (1978), Centre Européen de l'Entreprise Publique (CEEP) (1978, 1981); one of South and Southeast Asian countries undertaken by the International Development Research Centre in Ottawa, Canada—see SaKong (1979)—and one of Latin American countries—see Economic Commission for Latin America (ECLA) (1971).

Fifth, information on individual enterprises is available in their published accounts. The problem with this is the computational effort involved in obtaining aggregate statistics. Individual enterprise data were mainly used for countries with small public enterprise sectors and for improving the comparability of the statistics.

Details of the coverage and sources of the figures for individual countries are set out below. Where a source providing aggregate public enterprise data was used, the definition given is generally the heading shown in the publication from which the statistics were taken. Where possible, a more precise description of the coverage is also given. However, in many cases, no information on the exact criteria used to define the public enterprise sector could be obtained. For brevity, enterprise accounts and the other sources on individual enterprises that were used are generally not included.

Industrial Countries
Australia

Coverage: Public trading enterprises as defined in the national accounts.

Sources: Australian Bureau of Statistics, *Australian National Accounts* (Canberra) (various issues); Department of the Treasury, *Budget Speech, Budget Statements* (Canberra) (various issues); *UNNA* (various issues).

Remarks: Because of data limitations, it is assumed in the national accounts that public enterprises distribute the whole of their net operating surplus. To the extent that part of this surplus is retained, the figures shown for the current account surplus will be understated and those for the overall deficit overstated.

Austria
Coverage: Nationalized enterprises, state and municipal undertakings, excluding banks and insurance companies.
Sources: CEEP (1978, 1981).

Belgium
Coverage: Public enterprises as defined in official Belgian statistics.
Sources: Ministry of Finance, *Bulletin de Documentation* (Brussels) (various issues); National Institute of Statistics, *Annuaire Statistique de la Belgique* (Brussels) (various issues); *OECDFS* (various issues). Public enterprises in Belgium are also discussed in Keyser and Windle (1978) and CEEP (1978, 1981).
Remarks: Belgian statistics for public enterprise investment include financial enterprises, public hospitals, and agricultural research institutes. The figures were adjusted to exclude these bodies.

Canada
Coverage: Nonfinancial government enterprises at the federal, provincial, and local government levels as defined in the national accounts.
Sources: Statistics Canada, *Financial Flow Accounts* (Ottawa) (various issues); *OECDFS* (various issues); *UNNA* (various issues).

Denmark
Coverage: GDP and investment figures are for public utilities, transport, and communications enterprises included in Keyser and Windle (1978).
Sources: Danmarks Statistik, *Statistical Yearbook* (Copenhagen) (various issues). Keyser and Windle (1978). Public enterprises in Denmark are also discussed in CEEP (1978, 1981).

Finland
Coverage: Nonfinancial joint stock companies in which the majority of the share capital is owned by central government bodies or companies.
Sources: Advisory Board on State-Owned Companies, *State-Owned Companies in Finland* (Helsinki) (various issues); *OECDFS* (various issues).

France
Coverage: Public enterprises as defined in the national accounts.
Sources: National Institute of Statistics and Economic Studies (INSEE), *Les Enterprises Publiques de 1959 à 1969* (Paris, 1972); INSEE, *Les Grandes Enterprises Nationales de 1959 à 1976* (Paris, 1978); INSEE, *Rapport sur les Comptes de la Nation* (Paris) (various issues). Public enterprises in France are also discussed in Keyser and Windle (1978) and CEEP (1978, 1981).
Remarks: Since 1974, the statistics for public enterprises in the national accounts have only included eight large public enterprises engaged in energy, transport, and communications. They have excluded important public enterprises, particularly in manufacturing. Before 1974, the national accounts figures covered over 40 enterprises, including public enterprises in manufacturing. They also included public hospitals. It was not possible to exclude these from the figures.

Federal Republic of Germany
Coverage: Enterprises in which at least 50 percent of the equity or voting rights are publicly owned.
Sources: CEEP (1978, 1981), Keyser and Windle (1978).
Remarks: Housing enterprises were omitted because of lack of data.

Ireland
Coverage: State-sponsored bodies operating in energy, transport, and communications, and industry plus the Post Office.

Source: CEEP (1978, 1981). Public enterprises in Ireland are also discussed in Keyser and Windle (1978).

Italy
Coverage: GDP and investment figures are for the public enterprises included in the annual survey conducted by the Central Statistics Office; figures for components of overall deficits are for railways, posts and telephones, electricity, and 203 large public enterprises included in Mediobanca (1981).

Sources: CEEP (1978, 1981); Keyser and Windle (1978); Mediobanca, *Dati Cumulativa di 1078 Società Italiane (1968-1980)* (Milan, 1981); Ministry of Budget and Treasury, *Relazione Generale Sulla Situazione del Paese* (Rome) (various issues).

Japan
Coverage: Public enterprises as defined for United Nations national accounting purposes.

Sources: OECDNA (various issues). Public enterprises in Japan are also discussed in Chalmers Johnson, *Japan's Public Policy Companies* (American Enterprise Institute for Public Policy Research, Washington, D.C., 1978).

Remarks: The United Nations definition of a public enterprise is an incorporated or large unincorporated enterprise in which public authorities hold a majority of the shares and/or can exercise control over management decisions. See Jones (1975), p. 39, for a discussion of this definition.

Luxembourg
Coverage: Public utilities, transport, and communications enterprises included in Keyser and Windle (1978).

Source: Keyser and Windle (1978).

Netherlands
Coverage: Capital account figures are for public enterprises as defined for United Nations national accounting purposes; GDP figures are for enterprises included in Keyser and Windle (1978).

Sources: Keyser and Windle (1978); OECDFS (various issues); UNNA (various issues). Public enterprises in the Netherlands are also discussed in CEEP (1978, 1981).

Remarks: See "Remarks" under Japan.

Norway
Coverage: Enterprises in which public authorities hold 50 percent or more of the share capital.

Sources: Bank of Norway, *Economic Bulletin* (Oslo) (various issues); Central Bureau of Statistics, *Public Sector Finances* (Oslo) (various issues); IFS (various issues); OECDFS (various issues).

Spain
Coverage: Public enterprises included in CEEP (1981).

Sources: CEEP (1978, 1981).

Sweden
Coverage: Central government and municipal enterprises as defined in the national accounts.

Sources: Ministry for Economic Affairs, *The Swedish Economy*: *Prospects and Policies* (Stockholm) (various issues).

United Kingdom
Coverage: Public corporations.

Sources: Central Statistical Office, *National Income and Expenditure* (London) (various issues). Public enterprises in the United Kingdom are also discussed in Keyser and Windle (1978), CEEP (1978, 1981), and Richard Pryke, *The Nationalised Industries: Policies and Performance Since 1968* (Oxford: Martin Robertson, 1981).

Remarks: Public corporations include a number of financial enterprises and other entities, for example, the Bank of England and the National Dock Labour Board, which are not public enterprises according to the definition used in this paper; they exclude a number of enterprises, for example, British Leyland and Rolls Royce, which should be counted as public enterprises according to this definition. It was not feasible to correct for these differences in coverage. The figures for the period before 1961 were, however, adjusted to include the Post Office which, prior to that date, was a government department and not a public corporation.

United States
Coverage: Public nonfinancial enterprises as defined for United Nations national accounting purposes.

Sources: *UNNA* (various issues).

Remarks: See "Remarks" under Japan.

Developing Countries
Oil exporting countries
  Algeria
Coverage: Public enterprises as defined in the public sector investment budget.

Source: Public enterprises in Algeria are discussed in Christian Palloix, "Industrialisation et Financement lors des Deux Plans Quadriennaux (1970–77)," *Revue Tiers-Monde*, Vol. 21 (July–September, 1980), pp. 531–55.

Remarks: Figures for public enterprise investment include some expenditure that is not treated as capital expenditure in the national accounts, for example, spending on training. It was not feasible to correct for this.

  Indonesia
Coverage: Public enterprises and official entities as defined in banking statistics.

Source: Public enterprises in the mining sector are discussed in Beals (1980).

  Venezuela
Coverage: Iron ore and petroleum industries nationalized in 1975 plus about 40 enterprises, the most important of which are bus company; CADAFE (electricity); CANTV (telecommunications); CANV (shipping); CMA (agricultural marketing); IAAFE (railway); IAAM (airport); IADAN-DIANCA (docks); INOS (water); INP (ports); IVP-PEQUIVEN (petrochemicals); LAV (airline); MINERVEN (minerals); Post Office; public works company; sub-

way; tourism corporation; VENALUM and INTERALUMINA (aluminum); VENFERCA (fertilizers); VTV (television).

Africa

Benin

Coverage: Output figures are for ten enterprises: La Béninoise (brewery); OCBN (railway); SBEE (electricity); SOBEPALH (palm oil); SOBETEX (textiles); SODERA (agriculture); SONAFEL (fruit and vegetables); SONA-PECHE (fish marketing); SONIAH (irrigation); SONICOG (oilseed processing). Credit figures are for public and semipublic enterprises as defined in Banque Centrale des Etats de l'Afrique de l'Ouest (BCEAO) statistics. (Some of the above-mentioned enterprises have discontinued functioning as public enterprises.)

Sources: BCEAO, *Notes d'Information et Statistiques* (Dakar) (various issues) for credit figures.

Botswana

Coverage: Nonfinancial parastatal bodies as defined in the national accounts.

Source: Central Statistics Office, *National Accounts of Botswana*, 1978–79 (Gaborone).

Remarks: Included are statutory bodies, corporations, and companies in which public authorities have an ownership stake of at least 50 percent.

Congo

Coverage: Fifty-four major public enterprises.

Gambia, The

Coverage: Investment figures are for nine enterprises: two agricultural marketing boards; two airlines; a hotel; National Trading Corporation; Port Authority; Public Transport Corporation; Utilities Corporation.

Remarks: Credit figures include a relatively small amount of credit to local authorities.

Ghana

Coverage: Output figures are for state and mixed enterprises as defined in industrial statistics.

Sources: Tony Killick, *Development Economics in Action: A Study of Economic Policies in Ghana* (New York: St. Martin's Press, 1978); *IFS* (various issues).

Ivory Coast

Coverage: Public and mixed enterprises as defined in official statistics.

Sources: BCEAO, *Notes d'Information et Statistiques* (Dakar) (various issues); Den Tuinder, Bastiaan A., *Ivory Coast: The Challenge of Success* (Baltimore: Johns Hopkins, 1978); Direction de la Comptabilité Publique et du Tresor. Banque des données financières, *Centrale de Bilans*, 1979 (Abidjan).

Remarks: Included are most enterprises with a majority government shareholding plus some with a minority government shareholding. Exact coverage varies between different statistical series.

Kenya

Coverage: Nonfinancial parastatal bodies plus former East African Community enterprises for output and investment.

Sources: Central Bureau of Statistics, *Statistical Abstract* (Nairobi) (various issues).

Remarks: Figures for budgetary burden up to 1976 include all public corporations, financial as well as nonfinancial; those for the period after 1976 include all nonfinancial enterprises, private as well as public.

Liberia

Coverage: Nonfinancial public corporations.

Remarks: Included are 18 enterprises that are wholly government owned plus two enterprises with mixed ownership, in one of which the Government has a minority shareholding.

Malawi

Coverage: The Post Office, which is organized as a government department, plus 11 enterprises: ADMARC (agricultural marketing); airline; Book Service; two development corporations; Housing Corporation; railway; tobacco and tea authorities; water and electricity enterprises.

Sources: Ministry of Finance, *Public Sector Financial Statistics* (various issues); National Statistical Office, *Malawi Statistical Yearbook* (various issues).

Remarks: Credit figures also include credit to local authorities. Investment figures include investment in railway infrastructure counted as central government expenditure in the Malawi Government accounts.

Mali

Coverage: Twelve enterprises: Air Mali; COMATEX (textiles); EDM (energy); ITEMA (textiles); OPAM (agricultural marketing); PPM (pharmaceuticals); SCAER (agricultural inputs); SEPAMA (groundnuts); SEPOM (oilseed); SMECMA (agricultural machinery); SOMIEX (trading); SONATAM (tobacco).

Remarks: The enterprises included account for over 85 percent of the sales of the public enterprise sector.

Mauritania

Coverage: Investment figures are for 11 enterprises: airline; PHARMARIM (pharmaceuticals distribution); SAIM (metal industries); SNIM (mining); SOCOGIM (housing); SOMACAT (freight); SOMIP (fish processing); SONADER (rural development); SONELEC (public utilities); SONIMEX (agricultural marketing); STPN (bus transport).

Sources: *IFS* (various issues) for credit figures.

Mauritius

Coverage: Nonfinancial public enterprises, as defined in the national accounts, plus posts and telephones, which are organized as government departments.

Sources: Central Statistical Office, *Digest of Statistics* (Rose Hill) (various issues).

Niger

Coverage: Public and semipublic enterprises as defined in BCEAO statistics.

Source: BCEAO, *Notes d'Information et Statistiques* (Dakar) (various issues).

Senegal

Coverage: Public enterprises and mixed companies as defined in official statistics.

Sources: BCEAO, *Notes d'Information et Statistiques* (Dakar) (various issues) for credit figures; SONED, *Les activités du secteur économique moderne au Sénégal en 1974 d'apres les résultats du Recensement Général des Enterprises* (Dakar, 1976).

Remarks: Included are all enterprises in which the Government has a shareholding.

Sierra Leone

Coverage: The Post Office, which is a government department, plus 16 public corporations and companies in which the Government has a shareholding.

Sudan

Coverage: Public entities as defined in monetary statistics.

Source: Bank of Sudan, *Annual Report* (various issues).

Tanzania

Coverage: Nonfinancial parastatal enterprises and former East African Community enterprises.

Sources: Bureau of Statistics, *National Accounts of Tanzania* (Dar es Salaam) (various issues); Bureau of Statistics, *Analysis of Accounts of Parastatals* (Dar es Salaam) (various issues); Government of Tanzania, *Economic Survey* (Dar es Salaam) (various issues).

Remarks: Figures for components of overall deficits and financing are for nonfinancial parastatal enterprises only.

Togo

Coverage: Output figures are for ten enterprises: a hotel; OPAT (agricultural marketing); OTP (phosphates); SALINTO (salt); SNS (steel); SONAPH (palm oil); SOTEXMA and TOGOROUTE (agricultural machinery supply); SOTOMA (quarrying); STH (oil refinery). Credit figures are for public and semipublic enterprises as defined in BCEAO statistics. (Some of the above-mentioned enterprises discontinued functioning as public enterprises in the early 1980s.)

Sources: BCEAO, *Notes d'Information et Statistiques* (Dakar) (various issues).

Tunisia

Coverage: Government agencies, offices, and enterprises in which the Government holds more than 10 percent of the equity.

Sources: National Institute of Statistics, *Annuaire Statistique de la Tunisie* (*Statistical Abstract*) (Tunis) (various issues).

Upper Volta

Coverage: Public and semipublic enterprises as defined in BCEAO statistics.

Sources: BCEAO, *Notes d'Information et Statistiques* (Dakar) (various issues).

Zambia

Coverage: Public enterprises as defined in the national accounts.

Source: Central Statistical Office, *National Accounts 1972* (Lusaka, 1978) for output and capital account figures.

Asia

Bangladesh

Coverage: Nonfinancial public enterprises included in Bangladesh Institute of Development Studies (BIDS) (1977), plus Post Office and Telephone and Telegraph Department.

Sources: BIDS, *Public Enterprise in an Intermediate Regime: A Study in the Political Economy of Bangladesh* (Dacca, 1977); Bureau of Statistics, *Statistical Yearbook* (Dacca) (various issues).

Burma
Coverage: State economic enterprises.
India
Coverage: Departmental enterprises and public nondepartmental nonfinancial enterprises as defined in the national accounts.
Sources: Central Statistical Organization, *National Accounts Statistics* (New Delhi) (various issues). Public enterprises in India are also discussed in Indian Institute of Management, *Performance of Indian Public Enterprise Sector* (Bangalore, 1977).
Remarks: Net borrowing by the general government, as given in the national accounts, was used as a measure of the overall deficit of the general government.
Korea
Coverage: Government-invested corporations plus government enterprises, as defined in flow-of-funds accounts, for capital operations; nonfinancial enterprises included in the public enterprise sector by Jones (1975) and SaKong (1978) for output.
Sources: Bank of Korea, *Flow-of-Funds Accounts in Korea* (1978); Bank of Korea, *Economic Statistics Yearbook* (Seoul) (various issues); Jones (1975); Il SaKong, "Macro-economic Aspects of the Korean Public Enterprise Sector," *Korea Development Institute Working Paper No. 7906* (1978).
Remarks: Flow-of-funds figures include five enterprises organized as government departments and nonfinancial enterprises in which the Government has a direct majority shareholding. Jones (1975) and SaKong (1978) also include indirect shareholdings. The figures for investment and output are therefore not strictly comparable.
Nepal
Coverage: Nonfinancial public enterprises included in Office of the Corporation Coordination Council (1977) plus the Post Office.
Source: Office of the Corporation Coordination Council and Industrial Services Centre, *Performance of Public Enterprises in Nepal* (Kathmandu, 1977).
Pakistan
Coverage: One hundred and fifty nonfinancial enterprises included in Investment Advisory Centre of Pakistan (1977) for output; government enterprises plus autonomous and semiautonomous organizations engaged in mining and quarrying, manufacturing, electricity and gas, as defined in the national accounts, for investment.
Sources: Investment Advisory Centre of Pakistan, *Role and Performance of Public Enterprises in the Economic Growth of Pakistan* (1976); Statistics Division, Government of Pakistan, *Pakistan Statistical Yearbook* (Karachi) (various issues).
Remarks: Because of differences in coverage, the figures for investment and output are not strictly comparable.
Papua New Guinea
Coverage: Airline; Electricity Commission; Food Marketing Corporation; Harbours Board; palm oil joint ventures; Post Office; shipping company.
Philippines
Coverage: Public enterprises as defined for United Nations national accounting purposes.

Sources: *UNNA* (various issues).

Remarks: See "Remarks" under Japan.

Singapore

Coverage: Thirty-eight major public enterprises in manufacturing.

Sources: Sheng-Yi Lee, *Public Finance and Public Investment in Singapore* (Institute of Banking and Finance, Singapore, 1978).

Sri Lanka

Coverage: Output figures are for nonfinancial enterprises included in National Institute of Business Management (1977); other figures are for public enterprises and public corporations as defined in the national accounts.

Sources: Central Bank of Ceylon, *Review of the Economy* (various issues); National Institute of Business Management, *Public Enterprises in Economic Development of Sri Lanka* (1979).

Remarks: National accounts figures include financial enterprises and are not strictly comparable with those for output.

Taiwan*

Coverage: Public corporations and government enterprises as defined in the national accounts.

Source: Directorate-General of Budget, Accounting, and Statistics, *National Income of the Republic of China: National Accounts in Taiwan** (1981).

Thailand

Coverage: Nonfinancial public enterprises included in National Institute of Development Administration (NIDA) (1979).

Source: NIDA, *Management and Performance of Public Enterprises in Thailand* (Bangkok, 1979).

Remarks: Included are enterprises in which the Government has a majority shareholding.

Europe

Greece

Coverage: Output and investment figures are for nonfinancial public enterprises included in CEEP (1981); credit figures are for public enterprises as defined in monetary statistics.

Sources: CEEP (1981), National Statistical Service, *Statistical Yearbook of Greece* (Athens) (various issues).

Malta

Coverage: Government enterprises as defined in the national accounts.

Sources: Office of Statistics, *National Accounts of the Maltese Islands* (Auberge de Castille, Valletta) (various issues).

Remarks: Figures exclude industrial enterprises controlled by the Malta Development Corporation, which is wholly owned by the Government.

Portugal

Coverage: Public enterprises as defined for United Nations accounting purposes for the period up to 1975; public enterprises as defined in the Portuguese national accounts for the period since 1976.

Sources: Bank of Portugal, *Report of the Board of Directors* (Lisbon) (various

*See note to Table 1, page 122.

issues); OECD, *Economic Survey of Portugal 1979* (Paris, 1979); *OECDNA* (various issues).

Remarks: Figures include financial as well an nonfinancial enterprises. As a result of a change in classification, figures for the period before 1975 are not strictly comparable with those for later years. See also "Remarks" under Japan.

Turkey
Coverage: Nonfinancial state economic enterprises as defined for legal purposes.

Sources: *IFS* (various issues); OECD, *Economic Survey of Turkey* (Paris) (various issues); World Bank, *Turkey: Prospects and Problems of an Expanding Economy* (Washington, 1975); World Bank, *Turkey: Policies and Prospects for Growth* (Washington, 1980). Public enterprises in Turkey are also discussed in Bertil Walstedt, *State Manufacturing Enterprise in a Mixed Economy: The Turkish Case* (Baltimore: Johns Hopkins, 1980).

Remarks: State economic enterprises exclude some public enterprises at the national level operating mainly in manufacturing as well as enterprises operated by provincial and local governments—see Walstedt (1980). An estimate of total public enterprise investment at the national level was obtained by adding total government fixed investment in industry as given in World Bank (1980) to investment by state economic enterprises in other sectors. Allocation of government transfers to public enterprises between subsidies and capital transfers was estimated. As a result of a change in classification, output figures for the period before 1970 are not stricly comparable with those for later years.

Middle East
Egypt
Coverage: Public sector companies and public economic authorities.

Sources: Central Bank of Egypt, *Annual Report* (Cairo) (various issues) for credit figures.

Remarks: Credit figures are for public sector companies only.

Yemen Arab Republic
Coverage: Public and mixed enterprises as defined in monetary statistics.

Sources: Central Bank of Yemen, *Financial Statistical Bulletin* (various issues).

Western Hemisphere
Argentina
Coverage: Twenty enterprises: AEE, CIAE, GE, HIDRONOR, SEGBA, YCF, YPF (energy); AA, AGP, ELMA, FA (transport); ENCOTEL, ENTEL (communications); COMIF, Salte Grande, Yacireta (binational energy enterprises); AFNE, PBB (defense); ATC, YMAD.

Bahamas
Coverage: Public corporations plus the Post Office and airport, port, and water undertakings which are organized as government departments.

Barbados
Coverage: Ten enterprises: Agricultural Development Corporation; Civil Aviation Department; Housing Corporation; Industrial Development Corporation; Marketing Corporation; National Gas Corporation; Port Authority; Post Office; Transport Board; Waterworks Department.

Bolivia

Coverage: Government corporations.

Sources: Richard A. Musgrave, *Fiscal Reform in Bolivia* (Cambridge: Harvard University Law School, 1981); ECLA (1971).

Remarks: Figures for years after 1970 are for nine enterprises operating in mining, industry, transport, and communications. Figures for years prior to 1970 were taken from ECLA (1971) and their precise coverage is not known.

Brazil

Coverage: One hundred forty-five government-owned holding companies and their subsidiaries for 1980 figures.

Source: ECLA (1971).

Remarks: The figure for 1968 was taken from ECLA (1971) and its precise coverage is not known.

Chile

Sources: ECLA (1971); World Bank, *Chile: An Economy in Transition* (Washington, 1980).

Remarks: Figures for years prior to 1970 were taken from ECLA (1971) and their precise coverage is not known.

Colombia

Coverage: National nonfinancial public enterprises plus three major municipal public utilities.

Costa Rica

Coverage: Twelve enterprises mainly operating in public utilities, marketing, transport, and industrial projects.

Source: ECLA (1971).

Remarks: See "Remarks" under Chile.

Dominica

Coverage: The Post Office, which is organized as a government department, plus six enterprises: two agricultural marketing boards; Central Water Authority; External Trade Bureau; Forest Industries Development Corporation; Port Authority.

Dominican Republic

Coverage: Ten enterprises: airport and port authorities; Cotton Institute; Electricity Corporation (CDE); Price Stabilization Institute (INESPRE); State Sugar Council (CEA); three water authorities; radio and television service.

Guatemala

Coverage: Nine enterprises: AVIATECA (airline); FEGUA (railways); GUATEL (telecommunications); INDE and EEG (electricity); INFOM (municipal development); two ports; PROLAC (milk).

Guyana

Coverage: Income and capital account figures are for BIDCO (bauxite); the Guyana Rice Board (GRB); GUYSUCO (sugar); and enterprises in the GUYSTAC (Guyana State Trading Corporation) group.

Sources: *IFS* (various issues) for credit figures.

Haiti

Coverage: Capital account figures are for five enterprises: electricity company; flour mill; Port Authority; Telecommunications Company; Water Authority.

Sources: *IFS* (various issues) for credit figures.
Honduras
Coverage: Ten enterprises: BANASUPRO, COHBANA, IHMA (agricultural marketing); COHDEFOR (forestry); ENEE (electricity); ENP (harbors); FNH (railway); HONDUTEL (telecommunications); lottery; SANAA (water).
Jamaica
Coverage: Eighteen enterprises: Airline; Airport Authority; Broadcasting Corporation; bus company; food company; hotel company; Housing Corporation; Port Authority; property company; Public Service Company; shipping company; two sugar companies; two telephone companies; Urban Development Corporation; two water authorities.
Remarks: Figures exclude a number of public enterprises, particularly in mining and industry, for which no information was available.
Mexico
Coverage: Nineteen enterprises subject to budgetary control plus the Altos Hornos steel mill; the Metro Underground System of Mexico City; and the Telephone Company.
Remarks: An estimate of investment for the whole public enterprise sector, including enterprises not subject to budgetary control, was obtained as the difference between total public sector investment, as given in the national accounts, and general government investment.
Panama
Coverage: Public enterprises as defined for United Nations national accounting purposes.
Sources: *UNNA* (various issues) for capital account figures.
Remarks: Figures for budgetary burden exclude financial enterprises; other figures include financial enterprises. See also "Remarks" under Japan.
Paraguay
Coverage: Public enterprises included in World Bank (1979).
Source: World Bank, *Paraguay, Economic Memorandum* (Washington, 1979).
Remarks: Included are 13 enterprises: ANAC (airports); ANDE (electricity); ANNP (ports); ANTELCO (telecommunications); APAL (beverages); COPACAR (meat); CORPOSANA (water); FCAL (railway); FME (shipping); INC (cement); LAP and LATN (airlines); SIDEPAR (iron and steel).
Peru
Sources: ECLA (1971); *IFS* (various issues); World Bank, *Current Economic Position and Prospects of Peru* (Washington, 1972). Public enterprises in Peru are also discussed in E. V. K. Fitzgerald, *The State and Economic Development: Peru Since 1968* (Cambridge University Press, 1976).
St. Lucia
Coverage: Seven enterprises: electricity company; two marketing boards; National Development Corporation; Port Authority; Urban Development Corporation; Water Authority.
Uruguay
Coverage: Public enterprises included in World Bank (1979).
Source: World Bank, *Uruguay, Economic Memorandum* (Washington, 1979).
Remarks: Included are eight enterprises: AFE (railway); ANCAP (fuels, alcohol, and cement); ANP (ports); ANTEL (telecommunications); ILPE (fishing); OSE (water); PLUNA (airline); UTE (electricity).

REFERENCES

Beals, Ralph E., "Mining Taxation and Public Enterprise," in *Tax and Investment Policies for Hard Minerals: Public and Multinational Enterprises in Indonesia*, Malcolm Gillis and Ralph E. Beals (eds.) (Cambridge: Ballinger, 1980), pp. 75–112.

Beveridge, W. A., and Margaret R. Kelly, "Fiscal Content of Financial Programs Supported by Stand-By Arrangements in the Upper Credit Tranches, 1969–78," *Staff Papers*, International Monetary Fund (Washington), Vol. 27 (June 1980), pp. 205–49.

Böhm, Andreja, "The Concept, Definition and Classification of Public Enterprises," *Public Enterprise*, Vol. 1, No. 4 (1981), pp. 72–78.

Centre Européen de l'Entreprise Publique (CEEP), *Public Enterprise in the European Economic Community: C.E.E.P. Review 1978* (1978); *C.E.E.P. Review 1981* (1981).

Choksi, Armeane M., "State Intervention in the Industrialization of Developing Countries: Selected Issues," World Bank Staff Working Paper, No. 341 (Washington: World Bank, 1979).

Eltis, Walter, "The True Deficits of the Public Corporations," *Lloyds Bank Review*, No. 131 (January 1979), pp. 1–20.

Economic Commission for Latin America, "Public Enterprises: Their Present Significance and Their Potential in Development," United Nations, *Economic Bulletin for Latin America*, Vol. 26, No. 1 (1971), pp. 1–70.

Floyd, Robert H., "Some Aspects of Income Taxation of Public Enterprises," *Staff Papers*, International Monetary Fund (Washington), Vol. 25 (June 1978), pp. 310–42.

Gillis, Malcolm, "The Role of State Enterprises in Economic Development," *Social Research*, Vol. 47 (Summer 1980), pp. 248–89.

Harberger, Arnold C., "Perspectives on Capital and Technology in Less Developed Countries," in *Contemporary Economic Analysis*, M. J. Artis and A. R. Nobay (eds.) (London: Croom-Helm, 1978).

Heald, David, "The Economic and Financial Control of U.K. Nationalised Industries," *Economic Journal*, Vol. 90 (June 1980), pp. 243–65.

International Monetary Fund, *A Manual on Government Finance Statistics* (Draft) (Washington: IMF, June 1974).

———, *Government Finance Statistics Yearbook* (Washington: IMF), various issues.

Jones, Leroy P., *Public Enterprise and Economic Development: The Korean Case* (Seoul: Korea Development Institute, 1975).

———, and Edward S. Mason, "Role of Economic Factors in Determining the Size and Structure of the Public-Enterprise Sector in Less-Developed

Countries with Mixed Economies," in *Public Enterprise in Less Developed Countries*, Leroy P. Jones (ed.) (Cambridge University Press, 1982), pp. 17–47.

Keyser, William and Ralph Windle, *Public Enterprise in the EEC* (Sijthoff and Noordhoff, 1978).

Lamont, Douglas F., *Foreign State Enterprises, A Threat to American Business* (New York: Basic Books, 1979).

Organization for Economic Cooperation and Development, *National Accounts* (Paris), various issues.

SaKong, Il, "Macro-Economic Aspects of Public Enterprise in Asia: A Comparative Study," Korea Development Institute, Working Paper No. 7902 (January 1979).

"The Foreign 500," *Fortune* (August 10, 1981), pp. 206–18.

United Kingdom, Central Statistical Office, *National Income and Expenditure* (London: H. M. Stationery Office), various issues.

United Nations, Statistical Office, *Yearbook of National Accounts Statistics* (New York), various issues.

World Bank, *Borrowing in International Capital Markets: Third Quarter, 1979* (Washington: World Bank, January 1980).